P9-CRS-062

ARNULFO L. OLIVEIRA MEMORIAL LIBRARY
1825 MAY STREET
BROWNSVILLE, TEXAS 78520

International Strategic Management

International Strategic Management

Anant R. Negandhi
University of Illinois

Arun Savara
Purdue University

Lexington Books
D.C. Heath and Company/Lexington, Massachusetts/Toronto

Library of Congress Cataloging-in-Publication Data

Negandhi, Anant R.
    International strategic management / Anant R. Negandhi, Arun
Savara.
        p.   cm.
    Includes index.
    ISBN 0–669–20108–1
    1. International business enterprises—Management. 2.   Strategic
planning. I. Savara, Arun. II. Title.
HD62.4N439   1989
658'.049—dc19   88–31664

Copyright © 1989 by Lexington Books

All rights reserved. No part of this publication may be reproduced
or transmitted in any form or by any means, electronic or mechanical,
including photocopy, recording, or any information storage or retrieval
system, without permission in writing from the publisher.

Published simultaneously in Canada
Printed in the United States of America
International Standard Book Number: 0–669–20108–1
Library of Congress Catalog Card Number: 88–31664

The paper used in this publication meets the minimum requirements of
American National Standard for Information Sciences—Permanence of
Paper for Printed Library Materials, ANSI Z39.48–1984.
                                                            ∞™

Year and number of this printing.
88 89 90 91 92 8 7 6 5 4 3 2 1

Contents

Preface

Business policy and international business are among the most recent areas of research in management schools. Articles dealing with international competitiveness get dispersed into the many journals serving these two areas, as international competitiveness lies at the intersection of business policy and international business.

With the growing importance of international trade for all countries, and the concerns about the declining competitiveness of U.S. firms in the international arena, a need was felt for presenting the latest research on international competitiveness in a single volume. This book was thus designed to share the most recent original work of scholars of international competitiveness with other scholars, executives, and makers of public policy around the world.

The editors thank the contributors who sent in articles for inclusion in this volume, and the anonymous scholars who helped to screen them.

We hope this volume will improve the understanding and encourage the further study of international competitiveness, which is of critical importance to all businesses and nations.

Introduction

T his volume about strategic management in the international arena focuses on economic efficiency and competitiveness. One may question whether an economic efficiency/competitiveness paradigm is an appropriate lens for organizational problems, as well as human problems. If a firm is a profit-oriented *organization,* like all organizations it must satisfy all of its constituents and stakeholders, such as stockholders, suppliers, community members, and employees in all of the countries in which it does business. Organizations, after all, are only social instruments, designed by society for its benefit and use. Let us consider, however, the economic efficiency aspects of international business, and return later to this question.

The international competitiveness of U.S. firms has become the focus of attention due to the chronic and increasing trade deficits experienced by the country. The balance-of-trade deficit increased from $9 billion in 1974 to $124 billion in 1985 causing the United States—the largest creditor nation in the world in 1982 with a surplus of $136 billion—to become the largest debtor nation in the world with a foreign debt of $107 billion in 1985. The deficit is an indication of the reduction in market share of U.S. businesses around the world, as well as in the United States. In the steel industry, for instance, the U.S. share has fallen from 95 percent in 1962 to 74 percent in 1985. Since 1974 almost a quarter of a million jobs have been lost in the steel industry. Overall, U.S. imports increased from 10.3 percent of domestic demand in 1982 to 13.5 percent in 1986. On the other hand, U.S. exports in 1985 were around 14 percent of the world export market, unchanged from 1981. Both Japan and Germany have overtaken the United States, increasing their shares of the world export market to 15 percent. The increase in U.S. imports, together with the fact that Japan and Germany have surpassed the United States in exports, are signs of the inability of U.S. goods to compete as successfully with foreign goods as they did in the past.

Thus, U.S. firms have, over the past decade or two, lost their competitiveness in the international arena. This makes the study of international strategies attractive not only for academicians, but also for businessmen, managers, and policy makers.

Much has been written, and more can be, about the need for the study of international aspects of business due to the increasing importance of world trade, the increasing U.S. trade deficit, and the decline in competitiveness of U.S. firms. We shall spare our knowledgeable readers the repetition of the same. The malady is known, let us get on to the diagnosis and the cure.

When this volume was conceived, it was the editors' intention that it be suitable for both researchers in academia and practicing managers. All the contributions have relevant implications for practicing managers. To preserve academic rigor, however, the chapters do contain many references with which the practitioners may be unfamiliar and some mathematical modeling that may make the practitioner uncomfortable. We advise managers to read the introductions and conclusions to the contributions, and delve deeper into those which interest them most.

A Marriage of Strategic Management and International Business

Strategic management and international business disciplines have a lot in common, due to the nature of their turf. As a discipline, strategic management is concerned with the content of strategy that a firm has, the process by which the strategy is arrived at, and the strategy's impact on the firm's performance. The strategy of a firm may be defined as the pattern observed in a stream of decisions. These are typically decisions that impact the very business the firm is in, by impacting the product it sells or the markets it sells to. More often than not, strategic decisions involve the commitment of the firm's resources for a long time. These decisions have a long-term impact on the firm.

International business is concerned with the servicing of foreign markets, either by export, direct investment, or technology transfer. In addition, international business is concerned with the problems (or opportunities) of doing business in foreign countries, problems that do not appear in the domestic context.

Studying the decisions and decision making involved in servicing foreign markets clearly lies in the domain of international business. However, these decisions also fall in the domain of strategic management because they involve not only expanding the scope of the product-market from domestic to international but also more often than not, the long-term commitment of the firm's managerial, capital, and technological resources. Thus, the study of the decisions and decision making necessary to service foreign markets is the common ground between the two areas of international business and strategic management.

Due, however, to the enormous complexity of the international environment, and the much greater variety of options available to a firm in an international setting, the research needed for international strategies is not the same as that for domestic strategies. Thus, the need for international strategy research outside the mainstream of strategy research. As some of this research is being done by strategy researchers and some by international business researchers, we felt that the twain should meet, and hence this volume.

Research Agenda for International Strategic Management

This volume includes articles that have a variety of foci. Some of them provide conceptual frameworks, while others are empirical in nature. The articles have different units of analysis. As discussed later, such a mix of research is essential for a developing discipline.

It is important for a relatively new area of research to build on the theories and knowledge of older disciplines and extend them to examine the problems in the new discipline. In this process, not only does the line at which the old and new disciplines meet become clearer but also critical variables that discriminate between these disciplines come to light. In addition, conceptual frameworks are built to guide future research. They provide basic premises and propositions that can be empirically tested. Other researchers can build on these premises and propositions to explain additional phenomena observed.

A researcher can focus on different units of analysis in the international strategic management area. The lessons learned by studying entire industries can help managers plan their firms' international strategies, taking into account relevant industry forces. Study of corporate, business, and functional level international decisions are directly relevant to all audiences. A parallel study of different units of analysis by different researchers would provide a healthy exchange of ideas and hasten the development of the field.

To have lasting value, propositions in different frameworks, and with different units of analysis, need to be subjected to empirical verification. Empirical research makes credible those propositions not obvious to all and confirms propositions that seem obvious, but nonetheless, need confirmation so that further propositions can be built on them. Due to the involvement of overseas offices, data acquisition in the international arena may sometimes be more difficult than in the domestic arena, but researchers have to overcome this barrier.

Organization of this Book

The volume has been divided into four parts: The first part contains articles providing a framework for examining international strategies. The second part considers decision making processes for an entire organization. The third part deals with international strategies at the functional level of an organization. The final part of the volume presents empirical research linking performance with different international strategies.

In the opening chapter of part I, "Ecostructures and International Competitiveness," *Davidson* views the firm and nation as a collective system, the competitiveness of which depends on both firm and nation. Without denying the role of the firm's strategy, he highlights the impact of ecostructural factors on industrial performance. This thought-provoking analysis should provide food for thought to industrial policymakers. It should also caution managers to take such ecostructural factors into account when making foreign investment/sourcing decisions and when attempting to "import" foreign management practices to emulate the success of foreign firms.

In their chapter, "International Business-Level Strategy: The Development of a Holistic Model," *Morrison* and *Roth,* suggest that the research in international business strategy focus on those variables that are often nondiscriminating in a domestic, home nation context. They suggest that such variables would be international political substrategy variables, and international integration substrategy variables. By a review of extant literature they identify such variables used in research thus far, and so provide a path for empirical research to confirm whether these variables would be discriminating in a global context.

Mascarenhas's chapter, "Transnational Linkages and Strategy," attempts to bridge the gulf between practitioners and academicians. Both academicians and practitioners acknowledge that subtle links exist across national boundaries between firms of different nations, and even between the nations themselves. These links are seldom explicitly considered in academic frameworks, though they may be the deciding factor in the manager's planning process. By classifying linkages and pointing out the difference in focus for strategic decision making between different linkages, Mascarenhas has provided a framework on which a stream of research could be built.

In his chapter, "Foreign Market Servicing Strategies and Competitiveness: A Theoretical Framework," *Buckley* lays the framework for building a theoretic model and verifying empirically the relationship between competitiveness and the mode of servicing foreign markets. After examining the extant literature, he concludes that the extant models need consolidation and more careful specification. He emphasizes to managers that the decision on how to service a foreign market should be a dynamic one, subject to change as circumstances change.

In his chapter, "Five Organizational Typologies for Developed and Developing Nations: A Stage of Development Contingency Framework," *Rodrigues* builds on earlier theories from other disciplines, something we need to see more often in all business research. He proposes that technology changes the sociocultural, economic, and cultural systems of nations. This, in turn, changes the needs of individuals in the nation, forcing changes in the type of organization. This framework provides an opportunity for empirical testing and also cautions against the use of similar organizations in both developed and underdeveloped nations.

The authors in part I provide different frameworks for examining international strategies; those in part II examine decision making processes for the organization as a whole. *Lorange's* chapter, "Challenges to Strategic Planning Processes in Multinational Corporations," provides a road map for firms wishing to improve global strategic management. Lorange suggests that firms must strengthen their strategic planning systems. He explains why this is necessary and how it may be achieved. Lorange also discusses the importance and implications of international cooperative agreements.

In his chapter, "Strategic Issues in Corporate Planning in United States- and United Kingdom-Based Multinationals," *Coates* reports on the influence of the headquarter's environment on the strategic planning process. He interviewed key actors in twelve multinationals from the United States and the United Kingdom. His chapter, therefore, echoes actual practice as it exists. Coates's study could not substantiate the hypothesis that the headquarter's environment makes a material difference to the strategic planning process, perhaps due to the similarity in the environments in the United States and United Kingdom. He does conclude that a multinational corporation has to collect much more data for the strategic planning process than a purely domestic firm. The strategic planning process also helps integrate plans across different cultures but the process is more political than analytic.

Strategic planners would do well to take intercountry cultural differences into account. Most academic models of international business, however, do not explicitly consider culture as a variable. *Snodgrass* and *Sekaran's* chapter, "The Cultural Components of Strategic Decision Making in the International Arena," uses Hofstede's (1980) four dimensions of culture to explain the role of culture in the strategic management process.

Part III deals with strategic decision making for the functional areas in the international setting. In their chapter, "International Market Entry Strategies and Level of Involvement in Marketing Activities," *Akhter* and *Friedmann* suggest that the mode of entry into foreign markets should depend on the economic opportunity and political risk in the market. They propose that a grid developed through the interaction of these two variables could be helpful to practitioners in determining entry strategies for foreign markets.

Eom and *Lee's* chapter, "A Model for Designing Global Financing Strategy under Conflicting Goals," presents a decision support model for formulating global financing strategy. The model enables managers to satisfy multiple—and often conflicting—management goals and to analyze the trade-offs between different factors, such as financing costs, foreign exchange risk, and political risk. Use of the model permits considering simultaneously a larger number of alternatives than would be possible otherwise. The model does not aim to substitute managerial judgment, but enhances it by providing quicker and more comprehensive analyses. Use of such models can increase the competitiveness of multinationals and enable them to take advantage of their presence in many countries.

Jacque and *Perlmutter's* chapter, "Global Financing for MNCs: The Search for Geocentric Advantage," considers global financing in the conceptual framework developed by Perlmutter (1969); it classifies firms into ethnocentric, polycentric, and geocentric firms. The authors illustrate how differences in capital markets and exchange rate volatility can be managed and converted into opportunities increasing firms' competitiveness.

The preceding chapters have shown that the area of international strategic management offers fertile ground for conceptualizing analytical frameworks and modeling. Data related issues make empirical research more difficult. So it is heartening to see empirical investigations attempting to verify relationships between performance and strategic variables in an international setting, as the chapters in part IV do. *Franko's* chapter, "Unrelated Diversification and Global Corporate Performance," examines 105 U.S., European, and Japanese firms for relationships between diversification and performance.

Bühner's chapter, "Technology Strategy for Global Competitiveness," examines the impact of technology level on performance for a sample of German firms. It is always interesting to compare empirical results in different countries to determine whether or not management principles validated in one country can be transferred to other countries with similar economic philosophies. It would be interesting to see a replication of Bühner's study with a similar sample of U.S. firms.

The results of both the empirical chapters have significant implications for managers in the international arena. They illustrate how academia can assist practitioners by drawing generalizations from many companies, something not possible from the practitioner's experience base.

International Integration

The benefits to be obtained from international business have overcome many social and political barriers to make the world more integrated. Mainland China has opened its doors to foreign investment and there are signs of liberalization in the U.S.S.R. The Japanese are letting down tariff and non-tariff barriers. Capital can now flow freely between many countries in the free world, reducing comparative advantage due to capital costs. By locating plants abroad in lower wage countries, multinationals are making use of the comparative advantage in labor costs. In the process of doing so, they are also raising the wages in those countries and raising the standard of living of the workers abroad. Ideally, a free world should also allow total mobility of labor; in which case, wage differences across countries would reflect mainly differences in skill levels and transaction costs. Given the forces that drive political boundaries, this is unlikely to happen, but to some extent the world is being moved in the same direction by multinationals locating their plants in low-wage countries. Thus, the drive for economic efficiency by firms engaged in international business has forced some global integration and continues to do so. The strategy of such firms is shaping the environment for the future.

To revert to the question in our opening paragraph, the firms engaged in international business must be socially responsible, not only in their own countries, but also in foreign countries. They must continue to make the world more integrated. Many firms have demonstrated social responsiveness, for instance, by moving out of South Africa, or refusing to sell defoliants which may cause unforeseen damage. There are, however, many other firms exporting chemical and pharmaceutical products banned in the developed countries to third world countries. Conversion by multinationals of food producing farmlands to coffee or other cash crop production may have contributed to the scarcity of inexpensive, staple foods in some developing nations. Thus, there is room for multinationals to be more socially responsive to the citizens of the countries they service.

Organizations are only an instrument of society. If society does not find an organization to be beneficial, society discards the organization. To ensure an environment conducive for international business in the future, firms should profit from economic efficiencies, rather than by taking advantage of populations deprived of human rights by corrupt politicians. The former strategy ensures success for the firm in the future; the latter strategy gains only a footnote in history.

Part I
Frameworks for Analyzing International Strategy

1

Ecostructures and
International Competitiveness

William H. Davidson

ny country's international competitiveness is determined by the performance of corporate enterprises. Yet, these corporations' performance depends to a great extent on the nature of the economic
system that sponsors them. The drama of global competition between corporations reflects a broader underlying rivalry between different national
economic systems. The structure of those economic systems ultimately determines the competitiveness of national industries in world markets.

That is not to discount the role that management variables play in industrial competitiveness: It only places them in perspective. A large portion of the
competitiveness literature in recent years has focused on comparative management practices, implying that American management deficiencies are primarily responsible for U.S. ineffectiveness in international competition (Ouchi
1981; Schonberger 1982; Athos and Pascale 1981; Abegglen and Stalk 1985).
Treatises on Japanese management have emphasized functional areas such as
quality control, inventory and human resources management, and cultural
aspects of management practices as critical sources of competitive advantage.
These managerial factors deserve attention, but ecostructural factors may
have played a more important role in determining the outcome of international competition in recent years.

Ecostructural variables capture those characteristics of economic systems
that influence the outcome of international competition. By definition, these
are factors beyond the control of corporate management. In particular, public
policy issues such as antitrust policy, the structure of capital and labor markets, public research funding and procurement practices, educational policies
and structures, tax systems, and trade policies all have an important impact
on the performance of a nation's industrial sector in global markets.

Ecostructural factors can outweigh managerial factors in determining
industrial performance. If the United States or any other national economy
desires to improve its international competitiveness, it is vital that programs
be developed to systematically eliminate ecostructural disadvantages, as well
as managerial inadequacies.

Ecostructural Dimensions

International competitiveness was never a primary concern of the policy-makers who established the postwar economic system in the United States. National economic policies focused first on the objective of stimulating domestic demand through management of fiscal and monetary policies. The objective of stimulating economic growth through international trade and investment came second. Despite rapid growth in international trade, the postwar U.S. economic system focused on domestic demand first and foremost. Tax and financial systems were designed to support the domestic consumer as the key force in postwar economic growth. For the most part, the U.S. economic system was self-contained: that is, national monetary and fiscal policies were focused on stimulating domestic demand to purchase goods produced by domestic industry. As late as 1980, imports and exports totaled less than 20 percent of U.S. Gross National Product (GNP).[1] The domestic demand economy created in the United States, however, exists within an open global system containing national economies with different focuses and philosophies.

While the domestic demand model was applied in most of the Western world, a very different philosophy of economics was applied in the Far East. Japan, Korea, Taiwan, and Singapore, most notably, developed new export-oriented economic systems. The Pacific philosophy of economics, as applied by these nations, differed sharply in many respects from the U.S. domestic demand model, or the import substitution version of that model adopted in other developing economies. Production capacity in these countries is geared primarily to serving foreign markets; to filling demand generated by the expansive economic policies of other countries. These export economies did little to encourage domestic consumption. In fact, in each of these countries, economic structures actively discouraged domestic consumption. In each case, consumer and housing finance was virtually unavailable; credit cards, personal checks, and other mechanisms that facilitate consumption were almost nonexistent. The primary function of the average citizen was not to consume, as in the United States, but to save. Saving rates, even well into the 1980s, have averaged more than 20 percent of personal income in Japan, Korea, and Taiwan. (See table 1–1.)

Tax and financial systems in these countries actively encourage and even force high levels of personal savings. In the export-oriented economies, citizens must first earn and save the funds necessary to complete any purchase: in the United States consumer credit is readily available to the average citizen. Consumer interest expense has been fully tax-deductible in the United States, encouraging borrowing to finance consumption activity. In Japan interest income from postal savings accounts has been tax-exempt, to encourage savings. Extensive social security and private pension systems in the United States

Table 1–1

Housing and Consumer Credit Outstanding in the United States and Japan
(dollars in billions)

	United States		Japan	
	1980	*1985*	*1980*	*1985*
Personal savings rate (percent of personal income)	6.73%	4.32%	16.2%	20.8%
Consumer credit outstanding	$371.3	$668.2	$3.8	$9.0[a]
(as a percent of disposable personal income)	19.4%	23.9%	0.6%	0.8%
Home mortgages	$1,366.3	$2,167.7	$92.775	$107.7[a]
Value of private pension funds	$584.5	$1,132.6	$117.2	NA

[a] Japan Statistical Yearbook, 1985, p. 412.

reduce the need for personal savings for retirement purposes: the average Asian citizen does not enjoy such benefits.

The tax systems in these export-oriented economies all supported high levels of personal savings. In each country a percentage of interest income is exempt from taxation, and interest expense is generally not tax deductible. This structure encourages high rates of personal saving. Just as important, the tax system in these nations actively discourages consumption. In each country there is a relatively high reliance on consumption taxes as a source of government revenue.

In Korea value-added, excise, and other consumption taxes account for more than 40 percent of government revenue. In contrast, such taxes account for less than 5 percent of U.S. federal tax revenues. In Japan although consumption taxes accounted for 24 percent of government revenue in 1980, corporate income taxes are the largest source of revenue. Corporate income taxes are widely believed to be passed on in their entirety to consumers in the form of higher prices.

Consumption taxes are viewed in U.S. policy-making forums as regressive and are thus minimized in total federal tax revenues. As table 1–2 shows, in the export-oriented economies consumption taxes are a critical source of tax revenue. These taxes represent a significant penalty on consumption. The presence of such taxes discourages consumption and encourages savings. In contrast, the American tax system actively encourages borrowing to finance consumption at the expense of savings.

The huge differentials in personal savings rates between the United States and Asian countries does not occur solely as a result of cultural conditions. These gaps exist because of different structural conditions. Between 1920 and

Table 1–2
Sources of Government Revenue
(in percentages)

Country	Income Tax		Social security	Domestic taxes on goods and services[a]
	Individual	*Corporation*		
United States				
1980	44.6	13.5	27.7	3.8
1985	42.3	7.8	32.9	4.5
Singapore				
1980	27.6		1.5[b]	16.1
1985	29.1		0.9[b]	13.7
Japan[b]				
1980	31.9	32.6	13.6	24.0
1985	30.7	23.6	15.2	13.2
Korea				
1980	13.0	12.4	1.1	43.2
1985	13.25	11.71	1.49	42.6
Taiwan				
1980	17.9		—	59.0
1985	22.1		2.4[b]	47.3

Source: *Government Finance Statistics Yearbook,* International Monetary Fund, Publications Unit, Washington, D.C. 1981 and 1986.

[a] Includes sales, excise, VAT, utility, motor vehicle, and miscellaneous domestic taxes.

[b] These numbers measure the percentage of government expenditure, not the percentage of revenue.

1940 the average rate of personal savings in the United States stood at 18 percent of income; during the same period, personal savings averaged less than 10 percent of income in Japan. The reversal of these numbers occurred primarily in response to new economic structures installed after World War II. The U.S. system was restructured to maximize personal consumption, and Japanese and other Asian systems were redesigned to maximize personal savings.

Savings levels in these countries were stimulated because of (1) tax policies that emphasized consumption taxes; (2) tax exemptions on interest income and taxation of interest expense; (3) the absence of social security, unemployment, and major medical insurance at a time of declining family support for the elderly; (4) the unavailability of housing and consumer financing mechanisms; and (5) limited corporate bonus and pension systems. In each instance, the opposite trend appears in the United States.

Capital Costs and Competitiveness

The high rates of personal savings induced in these economies created a large pool of low-cost capital. This capital has been actively channeled into export-oriented industries, often at the expense of nonexport activities. A critical characteristic of the Pacific economic model is the concentration of resources and structural support in the export sector of the economy. This pattern of concentration results in hyperefficient, competitive export industries; it also often results in extreme inefficiency in nonexport sectors.

Inefficiency in domestic industries appears not only as a by-product of resource deprivation, but it may also appear as a goal of public policy. For example, distribution, transportation, and other service sectors are highly undeveloped in Japan and other Asian countries relative to their Western counterparts. Wholesale and retail distribution provide a useful insight: 1.9 million wholesalers and retailers in the United States serve 250 million active consumers. Japan, with half the population and lower levels of consumption activity, has 2.1 million wholesalers and distributors. In the U.S. distribution system, the average product passes through two to three layers of intermediaries between the producer and the consumer. In Japan the average is closer to five layers.[2] In countries with value-added taxes, a tax is applied on top of the markup at each layer in the channel. When the product is finally sold in a small mom and pop retail outlet, it carries a very high price to the consumer.

These nations' retail systems remain fragmented and inefficient not only because of cultural preferences. In Japan national law requires that all retail establishments with floor space over a certain limit must have public parking equal to four times their retail floor space. Similar patterns and structures appear elsewhere in Asia and other parts of the world. The resulting inefficiencies in the distribution sector—shown in table 1–3—further discourage

Table 1–3
Nonexport Sector Efficiency Comparisons

	United States[a]	Japan
Postal service (items per employee)	188,306	118,156[b]
Rail transport (passenger miles per employee) JNR and Amtrak	255,230	76,352[c]
Wholesale and retail distribution (number of)	1,900,000	2,151,000[d]
Air transportation (passenger miles per employee)	558,766	77,012[c]

Sources:[a] *Statisitical Abstract of the United States, 1987,* (Washington, D.C.: U.S. Department of Commerce, 1987), pp. 591–607.
[b] *Report on the Present State of Communications in Japan, 1985* (General Planning Division, Ministry of Posts and Telecommunications Tokyo, 1986), p. 42.
[c] *Japan Statistical Yearbook* (Tokyo: Statistics Bureau, 1986), chapter 8.
[d] *Japan Statistical Yearbook,* chapter 9.

consumption due to the resulting high prices for goods and services. This structure also creates a larger employment base, a stable probusiness political constituency, larger inventory pipeline for domestic industry, and a barrier to import penetration.

Although financial and legal conditions may restrict modernization of domestic service industries in these nations, the reverse is true in their export sectors. Export-oriented industries enjoy access to relatively low-cost capital for financing investments in capacity to produce goods for export markets. In Korea so-called policy loans provide low-cost money to export industries. The Central Bank of Japan exerts "window guidance" over the loan portfolios of Japanese commercial banks, promoting low-cost loans to export industries. The resulting pattern of capital investment is biased in favor of export sector industries. In Japan, the results are apparent in the relative levels of capital intensity in the service and manufacturing sectors, although as table 1–4 shows the gap has narrowed sharply in recent years.

Low-cost capital provided the principal competitive advantage for Japanese firms in the early target sectors: steel and automobiles. These two industries received one-third of all Japanese industrial capital investments between 1945 and 1985. (See table 1–5.) These industries were targeted for preferential treatment primarily because of their high levels of capital intensity. If a nation's primary competitive advantage is low-cost capital, it is most

Table 1–4
Capital Investment Intensity in Japanese Manufacturing and Services
(sector capital investment/sector value added)

Sector	1965	1970	1973	1976	1979	1981
Manufacturing	1.691	1.568	1.659	1.897	1.7231	1.637
Services	.398	.398	.543	.760	.927	1.127

Source: Horiye, Yasuhiro, "The Service Economy in Japan." In *Monetary and Economic Studies,* Bank of Japan, vol. 2, no. 2 (December 1984): 95.

Table 1–5
Gross Capital Investment in Japan by Sector
(yen in billions)

	1960	1970	1975	1980
Total manufacturing capital investment	¥947	¥4,384	¥5,995	¥7,751
Steel	170	1,131	1,449	1,244
Automobiles	128	548	496	1,236
Total	31.5%	38.3%	32.5%	32.0%

Sources: *Japan Statistical Yearbook,* annual.
Economic Statistics Annual, Research and Statistics Department, Bank of Japan, annual.

Table 1–6
Capital-Intensity of United States and Japanese Industries
(Fixed Assets/Industry Sales, 1981)
(Return on Capital 1970–1981 average)

	United States		Japan	
Industry	*Assets/Sales*	*Return/Assets*	*Assets/Sales*	*Return/Assets*
Shipbuilding	.50	N.A.	1.98	N.A.
Automobile	.51	8.45	.57[a]	6.55
Steel	.76	4.01	1.41	0.92

Source: *Sekai Kiqyo No Keiei Bunseki,* Tokyo, annual.

[a] The automobile comparison is somewhat misleading because it includes the automotive parts manufacturers as well as the car makers themselves. If the comparison was made between Toyota and Nissan as one group and Ford and General Motors as the other, the two Japanese firms were between three and four times as capital intensive as their American counterparts in 1980 (see Doz, Y. "Automobiles Shifts in International Competitiveness," in *Revitalizing American Industries* eds. M.S. Hochmuth and W.H. Davidson (Cambridge, Mass.: Ballinger, 1985), 195.

likely to succeed in highly capital-intensive industries. Japanese firms also exhibit much higher levels of capital-intensity than their U.S. counterparts in these industries.

The export-oriented economy provides low-cost capital to export industries, permitting those industries to exhibit higher levels of capital-intensity and lower levels of return on assets than found in U.S. counterparts. These patterns emerge clearly from analysis of the U.S. and Japanese steel, auto, shipbuilding, and other industries. (See table 1–6.)

Managed Foreign Exchange Rates

In addition to a cost-of-capital advantage, each of these Asian countries has successfully separated its international trade and payments activity from the foreign exchange market. The result is a foreign exchange rate favorable to exports. Historically in Japan, Korea, and Taiwan it has been illegal for exporters or banks to freely convert foreign currencies into local currency. American importers have paid for the vast majority of their imports from these countries in U.S. dollars. Those dollars are paid directly to the exporter's bank, which cannot freely convert dollars into local currency. These banks must transmit the dollars to the central bank, which then provides local currency in exchange. There is, in fact, an exchange of currency, but not in the open foreign exchange market.

The central bank accumulates dollars in the form of foreign exchange reserves, and typically invests them in U.S. government securities. The dollars never enter the foreign exchange market. As a result, these nations have historically been able to run huge trade surpluses without any measurable appreciation in their currencies. They have successfully installed a structure that separates international trade and payment activity from foreign exchange rate movements. The resulting undervaluation of currencies provided a critical source of competitive advantage to their national industries. The primary cost of this policy is borne by domestic consumers who must pay more for all traded goods and services. In these nations, however, there is no intent to maximize consumer benefits.

Extending the Art of Competitor Analysis

In assessing any competitor, it is appropriate to examine the rival's strengths, weaknesses, strategies, and management and organizational characteristics. That exercise, in a global context, must include the ecostructural as well as the managerial dimensions of the competitor's profile.

Capital costs and foreign exchange rates are two primary ecostructural variables. A number of nations have been able to provide significant competitive advantages to their industry in these two important dimensions. Low-cost capital permits firms to make higher levels of investment than their foreign rivals, permits lower rates of return over any given time period, or permits a longer time horizon for realizing returns. The mechanics of discounted cash flow analysis dictate that a lower discount rate results in a higher net present value for any income stream, and particularly for long-term returns. Firms with access to attractive sources of capital develop competitive strategies that exhibit higher levels of investment, lower rates of return, and longer time horizons than their rivals. Undervalued currency rates tend to support the export sector of an economy while protecting domestic industry from imports. The ability to sustain an undervalued currency provides an important source of advantage to industries in competition with foreign rivals.

Even though these macroeconomic variables clearly affect the outcome of international competition, other ecostructural factors are more immediately related to the organization and management of industry.

Industrial Organization and International Competitiveness

In the postwar period, a new philosophy of economics emerged in the Pacific Basin that represented a distinct alternative to Western practice. That philosophy concentrated national resources in the export sector of the economy and minimized domestic consumption while emphasizing export-led growth. The structure and focus of the financial system in these countries differed sharply from that found in the Western economies. Further distinctions become apparent while examining the organization of industry, particularly in Japan and Korea.

Japanese and Korean industry are dominated by large industrial groups. These group structures have no counterpart in the West, even though they have some similarity to traditional Western holding companies. The Japanese Keiretsu and Korean Chaebol groups differ in several key respects from their Western counterparts. These group structures do not exhibit vertical ownership patterns as seen in Western holding companies. Share ownership is dominated by mutual shareholding patterns. For example, shares of Toshiba Corporation, an affiliate of the Mitsui Group in Japan, are held by the Mitsui City Bank, Mitsui Trust Bank, Mitsui Insurance Company, Mitsui Holding Company, and other members of the Mitsui family. Toshiba itself reports on its balance sheet, under fixed assets, a category entitled "Investments in affiliated companies." Toshiba owns interests in the same companies that own its shares. This mutual shareholding system offers several important advantages.

Mutual shareholding provides an important vehicle for financing industrial development. By way of example, it is possible to create large equity balances in a series of companies through mutual share purchase activity. In extreme form, envision three companies with initial assets of $1 million each. Each firm has $200,000 in cash. If each of these firms invests $100,000 in the shares of its two counterparts, the firms each report an asset position of $1.2 million, marketable securities of $200,000, and cash of $200,000. The stated net worth of each company increased by $200,000. This exercise can be repeated indefinitely to create any desired level of reported net worth. Of course, these equity balances are of value only to the extent that financial institutions or markets are willing to provide additional debt capital based on the company's stated equity positions. Again, the group structure prevalent in Japan and Korea is most helpful in that regard.

In Japan each of the major industrial groups contains a city bank and a trust bank, as well as a major insurance company. Twelve of the thirteen city banks in Japan control almost half of all banking assets in that country; they exist as part of a larger industrial group. The seven trust banks are affiliates of major industrial groups, and the insurance industry is dominated by affiliates of the major industrial groups. These financial institutions own shares in their affiliated industrial companies and provide the primary source of debt capital to those firms. NEC, a Sumitomo group company, provides an example. The majority of its private domestic debt is held by Sumitomo financial institutions (see table 1–7). With friendly financial institutions willing to loan two, four, or more times the stated equity value of the company, it is possible to establish large, well-financed corporations in a relatively short time. When the debt is provided at relatively low cost, the benefit is compounded.

The mutual shareholding ownership phenomenon promotes economic development in nations with limited equity markets. It has been an impor-

Table 1–7
NEC Corporation Financing
(millions of yen)

Total Private Domestic Borrowings	¥132,578 (100%)
Sumitomo Group Total	¥91,879 (69.3%)
Sumitomo Bank	47,071
Sumitomo Trust & Banking	32,625
Sumitomo Mutual Life Insurance	12,183
Sumitomo Marine & Fire Insurance	—

Source: *Industrial Groupings in Japan* (Tokyo: Dodwell, 1985).

tant source of support for Korea's rapid industrialization. A recent study by the Fair Trade Commission in Korea indicated that 509 companies in the 32 major business groups held 3,474 billion won ($4.3 billion), or 44 percent of their combined net worth, in cross-investment equity holdings.[3] The group structure is clearly beneficial in promoting economic development. However, its benefits extend beyond the development phase of the economy. The ownership pattern implicit in the group structure imparts a management orientation that differs sharply from that found in the typical Western economy.

A recent private survey of American chief executive officers concluded that the primary concern of the average American CEO was a hostile takeover. Other key concerns were share price, quarterly earnings per share, and return on capital. These concerns are clearly reflected in the behavior and focus of the typical American executive. In contrast, hostile takeovers are literally unknown in Japan and Korea. The lack of acquisition activity in these countries is not solely a reflection of unique cultural conditions in those economies. It is very difficult to execute an acquisition in these countries, in part because a significant portion of equity ownership is held in long-term, stable, friendly, mutual ownership patterns. Given this ownership structure, it is not surprising that management exhibits a different set of concerns.

Japanese CEOs do not cite share price, quarterly earnings, or return on capital in their list of critical concerns. The unique equity and debt financing structures found in Japan impart a different orientation, and motivate different management practices. The resulting differences in management style are often ascribed to cultural characteristics. It is equally important to analyze the structural foundations of these differences in comparative management practices.

The group structure exhibits another noteworthy characteristic. Group members exhibit a tendency to utilize internal suppliers for their procurement needs. Statistics suggest that in several of the major Japanese groups, as much as one-third of all purchases are made from internal vendors. Indications from Korea suggest that the ratio may be higher in that country.[4] This tendency has a significant effect on import activity. These group structures are highly impervious to imports, and in some cases, to other domestic sources of supply. The very structure of industry precludes penetration by foreign rivals. Such industrial organization patterns represent a very significant nontariff barrier to trade.

Group structures present another subtle characteristic that can influence international competitiveness. In countries such as the United States, where industries tend to be largely independent of each other, political discussions surrounding national resource allocation and policy support can become highly politicized. In countries where industry groups dominate the industrial sector, a very different process and outcome is possible. In Japan and Korea, where a handful of industrial groups dominate, the resource allocation process functions differently. The key power centers, the industrial groups, are each active in virtually all industries. They can be highly objective regarding the selection of industries for special treatment, because they know they will participate regardless of the industry chosen for preferential support. This industrial structure permits a concentration of resources in selected industries that would be politically impossible in western countries.

The group structure clearly provides important sources of support to national competitiveness. Are there also disadvantages associated with this structure? There may be incentive problems associated with the group structure due to the captive nature of ownership, financing, and transaction patterns. However, the pressures applied by affiliated equity holders and internal financial institutions offset these inertial tendencies. In addition, these groups do compete actively with each other in the local market and abroad. Pressures for efficiency and competitiveness remain high despite the relatively protected nature of these groups' internal structures. Also, a portion of each group affiliate's stock is publicly traded, providing further performance incentive.

Cooperative Structures

While these large groups compete actively with each other, they also cooperate extensively. One of the primary vehicles for cooperation in Japan is the industry association. Over three hundred and fifty industry associations are active in Japan. These associations contain governing boards made up of representatives from each of the major groups, as well as the Ministry of Industry. These associations set technical and other standards, manage joint R&D projects, manage capacity for the industry, set price levels on occasion, and represent the industry in the political arena. This association structure provides a series of useful advantages to the industry.

Cooperative associations and industrial groups are not uniquely Asian. Variations on these themes can be found in German industry associations, Mexican grupos, in Italy (IRI), Belgium (Société Générale de Belgique), Germany (Flick Group), Sweden (Wallenberg), and elsewhere. Such structures evolved in the United States in the late-nineteenth century. The Mellon group, Morgan group, and even the Standard Oil family exhibited characteristics similar to these structures. U.S. public policy has focused on dismantling such concentrations of economic power, while national policies in Asia actively permit or encourage such structures.

Industrial groups and industry association structures can exist only in environments with limited or nonexistent antitrust policies. These structures are directly related to public policy. Industrial organization represents an important dimension in examining the ecostructure of any national economy.

Some Conclusions

In comparing the economic and industrial structures of different nations, it is possible to conclude that certain countries provide a series of fundamental advantages to their industries. Firms in countries practicing the export-driven economic philosophy can enjoy a host of structural advantages. These benefits could include:

- Low-cost capital.
- Undervalued foreign exchange rates.
- Favorable debt financing relationships.
- Domestic procurement subsidies.
- Protected home markets.
- Superior tax system.
- Superior labor market.
- Supportive education system.
- Positive industry structures, including industry associations and cartels.
- Positive government relationships.

These advantages can have a major impact on the outcome of international competition. Competitiveness in the modern global economy begins with pro-competitive public policies and supportive ecostructures. Without such supports, national firms and industries find it difficult to sustain their positions in domestic and foreign markets. However, firms may partially separate their fates from that of their home economy. Individual enterprises can establish offshore production and sourcing options that reduce their vulnerability to foreign competition. Many U.S. companies have aggressively pursued these options. The concept of the "hollow corporations," or "solar system organization" (Piore and Sabel 1984) has permeated the mainstream of American management practice. Offshore sourcing provides a discrete means of survival for individual firms. National economies have few such options. It may be possible to import cheap foreign labor in the form of "gastarbeiter" or wetback, but underlying structural noncompetitiveness can only be solved by restructuring of the national economic system.

Managerial or Structural Failure?

It is painfully apparent to all observers in the mid- to late-1980s that the U.S. economic system is no longer competitive. U.S. industry cannot reestablish its position in world markets through managerial initiatives alone. The decline of American industrial competitiveness is not due to managerial failure as much as it is to ecostructural gaps. The steel industry provides a useful example.

Perhaps no industry, with the possible exception of automobiles, has been as widely maligned for the qualities of its management as the U.S. steel industry.

> The U.S. Steel industry's underlying assumptions about the steel business prevented it from making aggressive investments in modernization that were needed to match the pace of Japanese investment. From the U.S. companies' point of view, the discounted cash flow return from a new mill could not justify its construction . . . because of its high capital costs, the Bethlehem Steel plant at Burns Harbor, Indiana, was long viewed as unprofitable, even though it is the only fully integrated large-scale greenfield plant built in the U.S. since 1952. I.C. Magaziner and R.B. Reich, *Minding America's Business* (New York: Vintage Books, 1983), pp. 165–66.

The fact is that aggressive capital investment in traditional steel capacity would have been idiocy. Between 1960 and 1970, the U.S. steel industry reported an average return on capital (total assets) of about 4 percent, or half the prevailing return for U.S. industry as a whole. The Japanese steel industry, with significantly lower wages and other advantages, reported a return on capital for the decade of less than 1 percent.[5] Japanese firms invested heavily in modern capacity. As a result, they reported higher capital intensity, more automation, higher productivity, and lower costs. Yet, those investments never realized returns remotely close to prevailing market returns. If Japanese firms, with a host of other advantages, could not realize a 1 percent return on their investments, how could U.S. firms justify similar investments? Indeed, the one world class steel facility built in the postwar United States, Bethlehem's Burns Harbor plant, could not operate at a profit. There is no evidence that the American steel industry behaved irresponsibly by neglecting to modernize its capacity. In fact, management would have been negligent to make such investments.

An excerpt from U.S. Steel's 1965 *Annual Report* reads as follows: "Given current tax and depreciation laws in the United States, management does not believe it can justify further capital investment in steel smelting plants and equipment."

One finds it difficult to defend steel industry management, but the truth is they faced almost insurmountable odds. The majority of new steel capacity that has come on stream worldwide in the last fifteen years is government owned. Private investment in this industry, outside of minimill capacity, which has much lower capital requirements, has virtually come to a halt.

Yet the very characteristic that makes this industry unattractive to U.S. investors—its capital intensity—makes it most attractive to countries like Japan. Japan's, and to a larger extent Korea's, postwar industrial activities were based on three principles:

1. Create and channel low-cost capital into export industries.

2. Concentrate resources in industries with the highest probability of success in world markets.

3. Implement industrial strategies through a guided free enterprise system.

In applying the preceding principles, Japan's postwar industrial system sharply shifted its emphasis toward capital-intensive industries in which its structural advantage, low-cost capital, would be most powerful. Thus, steel and shipbuilding, the two most capital-intensive major industries, become the first target sectors in postwar Japan, and later in Korea. Steel industry management in these countries successfully converted ecostructural advantages into competitive advantages in world markets.

These managers deserve full credit. Enterprises in other nations that have received massive public support have failed to compete successfully in the world market. Yet, here again, an element of structure appears. There exists a world of difference between the Japanese steel industry and publicly owned steel companies in other countries. Nippon Steel was not owned, controlled, and managed by the Japanese government, although it enjoyed extensive public support. Rather, its administrative orientation reflected the principle of guided free enterprise so unique to the Japanese economic system.

The Japanese government is able to exert influence over private enterprise via dozens of subtle, yet powerful, mechanisms. The Ministry of International Trade and Industry (MITI) controls business licensing approval, public R&D budgets, technology licensing, export promotion incentives, and capacity management activities, for example (Johnson 1982). The Ministry of Finance can exert considerable influence over public financial institutions such as the Industrial Bank of Japan, the primary source of long-term capital for capacity investment in Japan, and over private financial institutions. The major Japanese banks are highly dependent on Central Bank loans. The average debt to equity ratio for the twelve major "city banks," the largest private industry lenders, has typically fluctuated between 40 and 70 to 1, three or four times the U.S. ratio. These banks are critically dependent on short-term loans from the Central Bank, and sensitive to window guidance, or suggestions about the composition of their loan portfolios. Such banking structures facilitate the channeling of resources into certain sectors of the economy; but it is noteworthy that the banks remain fundamentally private, market-oriented organizations.

This system stands in contrast to the recent French experience. In one of its first initiatives, to facilitate the channeling of capital into desired industries, the Mitterrand government nationalized the French banking system. It went a step further and nationalized a series of firms and whole industries to permit more direct public control over the implementation of French industrial policy. By the mid-1980s, France began to reverse that process through privatization of banks and industries.

In contrast to conventional state-owned enterprise models, the Japanese model possesses all of the benefits of public guidance and control, while retaining the market, profit, and efficiency instincts of private enterprise. So long as private institutions operate within broad bounds established in the public sector, they remain free to implement industrial strategies. That leaves room for managerial initiative. Japanese industrial activities are implemented by market-focused, performance-oriented, innovative management. The combination is a powerful one, and the Japanese steel industry was its first application.

The same story is being repeated today in the semiconductor industry. Most observers would credit the U.S. semiconductor industry with progressive, dynamic management. Yet, the recent decline of this industry was just as inevitable as the steel industry's. The semiconductor industry exhibits a level of capital intensity comparable to the steel industry. In semiconductors, however, capital-intensity is compounded by frequent recapitalization requirements. In the memory chip segment, for example, each new generation of device, from the 16K RAM through 64K, 256K, 512K, and megabit RAM requires new process technology and capital equipment.

Capital investment requirements are high and rising. (See figure 1–1). That characteristic imparts a significant advantage to Japanese enterprise, that enjoys the structural advantages of stable equity ownership, friendly debt-financing relationships, low-cost capital, and semicaptive group customers for their products (Davidson 1984).

As table 1–8 indicates, over the past decade the prevailing rates of return on sales and assets in the semiconductor industry have declined to such a level that further investments are sometimes difficult to justify.

ARNULFO L. OLIVEIRA MEMORIAL LIBRARY

1825 MAY STREET

BROWNSVILLE, TEXAS 78520

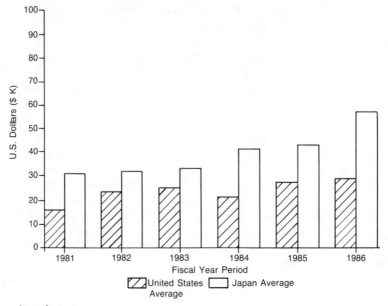

Source: Annual reports.

Figure 1–1. Semiconductor Capital Investment per Employee in the United States and Japan

The U.S semiconductor industry has been fighting a losing battle over that period, and the prospect of further competitive losses is very real. U.S. semiconductor trade with Japan turned negative in 1981 and has steadily declined since that time. Given the characteristics of this industry, it would be inappropriate to conclude that the decline of the U.S. industry's international standing was due to managerial failures. This industry presented an excellent vehicle for application of the structural advantages implicit in the Japanese economic system. The competitive results are due to ecostructural gaps, not management failure.

Restructuring of the U.S. System

The U.S. economic system is obsolete. It has been displaced by an economic model that promotes superior competitiveness in global markets. If the U.S. economy is to reestablish its competitiveness, then structural changes—adjustments in the very foundation of the U.S. economic system—must be implemented. Such adjustments will require new directions in public policy. The proposal that a return to free-market principles will solve U.S. industrial

Table 1–8
Rate of Return in Semiconductor Industry

	1981	1982	1983	1984	1985	1986
Return on Assets						
United States	7.95	5.54	5.05	8.48	4.18	1.98
Japan	4.24	3.49	4.13	4.19	4.06	1.81

Source: Compiled from annual reports, 1980–1987.

woes misses the point. International competitiveness cannot be achieved or sustained by private industry alone. It is naive to assume that a reduction in government intervention will solve the competitiveness problem. That point has been made by several observers (Phillips 1984; Vogel 1985; Mitroff 1987).

Certainly, the elimination of anticompetitive government restrictions and regulations would represent a positive step. Some aspects of public policy are anticompetitive and their reversal would be welcomed. It is more important to recognize that unencumbered private enterprise alone is at a disadvantage in modern world markets. Private firms find it difficult to compete successfully in industries like steel and semiconductors without the benefit of procompetitive public policies and structural support. Those firms that have been successful in such industries through innovation, agility, and operating excellence would benefit as well from procompetitive policies and improve their performance.

The need for procompetitive public policy does not lead to the conclusion that direct public involvement in formulating and implementing an industrial policy is necessary. Rather, the appropriate focus for the public sector is to create an environment conducive to enhanced competitiveness. That suggests creating structures supportive of private industry's efforts to innovate and improve operations. It suggests that general incentives and supports for entrepreneurship and capital investment would be desirable, not direct intervention à la the French model.

Programs that improve base conditions in labor and capital markets would provide a foundation on which industries can build or rebuild. Nothing short of a new economic system will succeed in offsetting the structural gaps now faced by U.S. industry. A systematic agenda must be developed to neutralize or eliminate each of the structural advantages enjoyed by rival economic systems.

Restructuring Activity in the United States

It is possible to identify a number of restructuring initiatives in the United States over the past decade. Some of these initiatives are very discrete and visible; others, while less visible, may have a more pervasive effect on the performance of the U.S. economy. Even though it is clear that no master plan or planner exists for these efforts, independent initiatives can be identified within virtually all areas of public policy that pertain to industrial competitiveness.

Antitrust Policy

American antitrust policy appears to have shifted dramatically in the decade of the 1980s. Antitrust policies that were appropriate in a domestic economy with few linkages to the international system can be self-destructive in an internationally competitive environment. Domestic measures of industrial concentration are extremely misleading in industries that have shifted from domestic to global competitive boundaries (Vernon 1977). Although antitrust litigation has declined sharply in the 1980s, it is always possible that a new administration could reverse this trend in a relatively short time. Nevertheless, there have been several legislative initiatives that suggest a long-term shift in antitrust enforcement.

Perhaps the most significant piece of antitrust legislation of this decade occurred in 1984. A bill initiated by Bruce Merrifield, Assistant Secretary of Commerce, passed both houses of Congress unanimously. This bill eliminated antitrust liabilities for firms engaged in joint research and development projects. Since that time government support of cooperative research activity has grown dramatically.

National Science and Technology Policy

Concern for competitiveness reaches its greatest intensity in the high technology industrial sector. This concern is motivated as much or more by military security considerations as it is by commercial concerns. Two agencies of the federal government play a particularly critical role in promoting scientific and technological programs. In the industrial sector, the National Science Foundation (NSF) has dramatically increased its activities in the past decade. The National Science Foundation has witnessed one of the highest rates of budget growth during the Reagan administration. Its budget has more than tripled since 1980 during a period of budgetary restraint in a number of other areas. NSF initiatives in the past decade include sponsorship of engineering development centers at a number of universities; a grant program to sponsor commercially oriented technology development in small business corporations; increased funding for industrial automation and engineering research, as well as basic scientific research; and sponsorship of foreign technology assessment activity.

In the defense arena, the Defense Advanced Research Projects Agency

(DARPA), plays a critical role in funding advanced technologies development activities. Some of the most important new projects funded through the Department of Defense (DOD) in the past decade include the VHSIC (Very High Speed Integrated Circuits) project, which provides more than $500 million for advanced semiconductor development by a consortium of industrial companies; more than half a billion dollars in supercomputer research over the decade; a gallium arsenide development initiative; the ICAM process technology initiative for integrated circuit manufacturing techniques; and a series of other technology development programs.

In January of 1984, the Department of Defense issued a memorandum informing its suppliers that a 50 percent surcharge would be added to all foreign bids on selected DOD advanced technology contracts. DOD procurement activities have greatly benefited a number of firms in the embattled semiconductor industry. Texas Instruments, for example, derived more than 100 percent of its profits from DOD sales during several years in the mid-1980s. Defense CCCI, Command, Control, Communication, and Intelligence, procurement levels more than tripled between 1984 and 1987 alone.

In addition, the military has placed a new emphasis on cooperative research activities. The federal government is encouraging, and even requiring, joint development activity on a series of new major defense development programs, including the advanced tactical fighter and the advanced tactical bomber.

Joint research and development efforts have become a primary thrust in a number of high technology sectors. The Microelectronics and Computer Center (MCC) in Austin, Texas, was the first and most visible of these efforts, but many others have been initiated in the last several years. In the spring of 1986, an interagency task force hosted by the National Science Foundation began to explore the possibility of providing more than $1 billion in federal funds to a cooperative program to develop the next generation of semiconductor memory technology. This federal initiative, which culminated in the SEMATECH Program, was a direct response to concern over the future health of the American semiconductor industry. Another federally sponsored joint research and development effort has also been initiated in the machine tool industry.

Trade Policy

Although the Reagan administration has remained firmly devoted to a policy of free trade, a number of trade initiatives have suggested a harder line on trade policy. Trade relations with Japan, Korea, and Taiwan, in particular have been very intense during the past several years; pressures are now appearing in a number of other areas as well. On the Japanese front, the past decade has witnessed the imposition of quotas on Japanese cars, television sets, and steel imports; countervailing duties on consumer electronic products, semiconductor devices, and mobile telephones; tariff increases on lightweight trucks and motorcycles; and federal intervention in the fiber-optic cable market. The Market Opening Sector Selective (MOSS) talks with Japan have emphasized increased access to a number of Japanese markets.

Trade liberalization discussions with Korea and Taiwan have been successful in reducing barriers to market access in those countries. Additional pressure was imposed on Korea in January of 1988 to further open selected markets to U.S. goods or face severe trade sanctions. Taiwan, Korea, Singapore, and Hong Kong were removed from preferential treatment under the General Agreement on Tariffs and Trade (GATT) in February of 1988. Intense negotiations with Brazil regarding elimination or softening of its market reserve position on domestic computer and software markets have set a new tone on trade policy in that region. A series of tough trade negotiations with the European Economic Community also indicated a stronger stance on trade issues, and the market integration initiative with Canada represents a significant trade policy direction.

Overall, it is apparent that access to the U.S. market has proved to be more difficult and costly in a number of cases for foreign suppliers. U.S. trade negotiators have also sought to increase market access for American firms in several foreign countries. In addition, the trade in services initiative, sponsored by the United States, seeks to establish a GATT agreement to liberalize international trade in services, an area of competitive advantage for U.S. industry.

Foreign Exchange Policy

Led by the Treasury Department, American policymakers have actively attempted to manage the value of the dollar over the past several years. The most important specific initiatives were the financial liberalization agreement signed with Japan and Taiwan and the Group of Seven Nations' efforts to establish a new foreign currency equilibrium, as reflected in the 1984 Plaza Accord and the 1987 Louvre Accord.

One of the most significant events in the international financial arena was the May 1984 signing of a financial liberalization agreement with Japan. This little-known but critically important agreement called for the elimination of limits on Japanese banks' ability to exchange foreign currency into yen and established a yen denominated trade-financing system. Both initiatives encouraged the flow of dollars used to purchase Japanese exports into foreign exchange markets where they would impact the value of the yen. Prior to the agreement, virtually all American imports from Japan were paid for with U.S. dollars. Those dollars were received by the exporter's bank, which was unable to convert them into yen in the open foreign exchange market and transmitted them to the Central Bank of Japan in exchange for local currency. This payment structure allowed international payments balances to be separated from supply and demand for yen in the foreign exchange market.

The liberalization agreement permitted trade patterns to be linked to supply and demand for foreign exchange in the open market. This development was one of several initiatives that supported the appreciation of the yen in the 1986 and 1987 time period. Formal agreements between the Group of Seven Nations to adjust currency values were also negotiated in New York in 1984, and in Paris in 1987. Each round of currency adjustments resulted in a significant depreciation of the dollar.

Although currency shifts have not had an immediate positive result on the U.S. trade deficit in dollar terms, there has been a shift in the volume of international imports and exports experienced by the United States. Import volumes declined in 1987, and U.S. manufacturing employment increased by more than 300,000 workers in the same year.

Labor Environment

The National Labor Relations Board (NLRB) was restaffed by the Reagan administration in 1980. NLRB rulings and regulations on labor relations matters have followed a sharply different pattern than that prevailing in the previous several decades. These new rulings and regulations provided a strong basis for renegotiation of union agreements in a number of industries. Firm federal bargaining positions in the professional air traffic controllers' strike, and in an aborted national truckers strike, helped set a pattern in the labor relations arena. In the fall of 1987, the federal government, in an unprecedented move, appointed a federal trustee to administer a local union at the Fulton Fish Market in New York City, on the grounds of union corruption and racketeering. At about the same time, a similar program was initiated to establish federal control of the Teamsters Union. Such initiatives suggest a very different federal policy on labor relations issues.

Not all federal initiatives were punitive in nature or designed to weaken the labor movement. A 1984 bill greatly strengthened the benefits associated with the use of Employee Stock Ownership Plans (ESOPs). The benefits include tax credits on funds transferred from traditional pension plans to ESOPs, and exemption from capital gains taxation for company owners who sold their shares to an ESOP. This shift in ownership provides a powerful foundation for the development of cooperative labor management efforts to improve company performance. This new ownership structure also creates a new set of incentives and a different orientation for American management and workers. By shielding corporations from the threat of a hostile takeover because a large fraction of stock is held by the ESOP, concerns for short-term share price, quarterly earnings, and return on capital diminish in favor of increased sensitivity to the long-term performance of the corporation.

Whatever the cause, in 1987 U.S. labor productivity increased at the

Table 1–9
1987 Labor Trends

	United States	Japan	Germany
Labor productivity gain	3.7%	1.2%	2.5%
Wage increase	3.3	1.7	3.6
Unit labor cost change ($)	−0.4	42.2	25.1

Source: *Monthly Labor Review*, U.S. Department of Labor.

fastest relative rate witnessed in the last several decades. As table 1–9 indicates, labor productivity gains in 1987 exceeded wage increases by a significant margin, the first such event in recent history. On a dollar cost basis, Japanese labor costs rose 45 percent relative to American labor costs in 1987. The bulk of this shift was, of course, due to foreign exchange movements, but manufacturing productivity trends have been very positive. Fundamental trends of this nature indicate a much more positive outlook for American industrial competitiveness.

Capital Markets

Several recent developments in U.S. capital markets indicate fundamental restructuring of the financial system in the United States. Stimulation for the development of the money market fund industry in the early 1980s lead to significant disintermediation of funds from traditional savings institutions. Those funds had been widely used to finance home mortgages, home construction, and real estate development activity. This shift of funds, totaling in excess of $240 billion, may have led to a different pattern of usage for that capital. Money market funds used their capital to purchase financial securities, only a small fraction of which are real estate related. This shift in capital markets may provide a stimulus for industrial investment. In addition, the creation of Individual Retirement Accounts (IRAs) and personal Keogh plans also resulted in a dramatic shift of capital from traditional institutions. More than $270 billion was invested in IRAs between 1984 and 1987. This capital again largely came from traditional institutions and uses and was redirected toward alternative uses. Individual's IRA funds may be invested only in financial securities, with the recent exception of U.S. gold and silver coins. Real estate, art, antiques, and collectibles are not allowed as IRA investments.

Tax Policy

Several significant shifts in tax policy may also influence investment patterns. A reduction of capital gains tax rates from 50 percent to 20 percent effective in 1980 stimulated a dramatic surge in venture capital activity. Venture capital investments totaled about $15 billion between 1980 and 1985, more than five times the amount of investment in the previous five-year period. These investments have supported the creation of new firms and industries in the high technology arena.

The Tax Reform Act of 1986 lowered overall tax rates, but eliminated deductions for consumer interest expense and sales taxes. These changes in tax policy suggested a basic shift in philosophy: They resulted in reduced structural support for consumption. Support for real estate investment was also reduced. Real estate depreciation schedules were lengthened, and lower tax rates reduced the value of interest and depreciation deductions for wealthy investors.

Investments in nonindustrial construction in the United States have averaged $340 billion per year in the 1980s. Such investments may not rise as fast in the future, given reduced tax incentives and benefits. Capital may be diverted to other uses. Office construction actually fell by 22 percent in 1987, while industrial construction rose by just under 5 percent in 1987. Notably, the Senate version of the 1986 Tax Reform Act contained a section that called for elimination of the Investment Tax Credit, except for investments in manufacturing, extraction, or information systems capacity. That section did not appear in the final bill, which eliminated all investment tax credits, but it indicates a desire to create incentives to encourage investment in export-oriented capacity.

Trade and Competitiveness Legislation

The U.S. Congress devoted top priority to trade and competitiveness legislation in 1987. A broad consensus exists about the importance of this issue, but not on the appropriate means for addressing it. It is notable that one clause in the Senate version of the bill read roughly as follows: "Federal statutes that inhibit the competitivenes of U.S. industry may be waived for firms in industries facing severe foreign competition." A question was raised on the Senate floor: "Does this include minimum wage legislation? EPA? OSHA? The Foreign Corrupt Practices Act?" The response by the Senate leadership suggested that an open-ended statement was appropriate in this instance. Such exchanges suggest that a new set of priorities and perspectives dominate the public policy arena in the United States. Concern for competitiveness is driving a basic reorientation and restructuring of the U.S. economic system.

Outlook

Recent shifts have appeared in virtually all areas of U.S. public policy. A significant restructuring of the U.S. economic system is in fact occurring. Many of the ecostructural gaps have already been closed. These changes may go a long way toward improving U.S. industrial competitiveness. The broad ecostructural shifts of the past decade provide an environment significantly more supportive of business performance. However, such public policy initiatives are necessary but not sufficient to ensure improved economic performance. If ecostructural disadvantages have been neutralized, the other half of the equation, managerial performance, will now determine industrial competitiveness.

Management and industry may not yet be widely aware of the fundamental shifts in the business environment that have occurred in recent years. Even though there has been a fundamental transformation in the aims of public policy, the role of government, and the basic structure of the American economic system, many U.S. corporations practice business as usual. Innovation in management practices and structures may also be necessary to complete the renovation of the industrial system. Only when public and private transformations are complete can future competitiveness be assured.

Notes

1. In 1980 U.S. imports totaled $252.9 billion, exports were $220.7 billion, and the GNP stood at $2,732 billion. Trade as a percentage of GNP totaled 17.3 percent.
2. *Industrial Goods Distribution in Japan.* (Tokyo: Dodwell and Company, 1987).
3. *Business Korea.* August 1987, p. 13.
4. S. Yoo, and S.M. Lee "Management Style and Practice of Korean Chaebols," *California Management Review,* Summer 1987, pp. 95–110; Hattori, T. "Comparison of Large Corporations in Korea and Japan" in *The Structure and Strategy of Korean Corporations,* eds. H. Lee and K. Chung (Seoul: Bupmunsa, 1986).
5. *Sekai Kigyo No Keiei Bunseki.* Industrial Financial Statistics Yearbook (Tokyo: Ministry of International Trade and Industry, annual).

References

Abegglen, J.C., and Stalk, Jr., G. 1985. *KAISHA.* New York: Basic Books.

Athos, A., and Pascale, R. 1981. *The art of Japanese management.* New York: Warner Books.

Davidson, W.H. 1984. *The amazing race.* New York: John Wiley & Sons.

Johnson, C. 1982. *MITI and the Japanese miracle.* Stanford: Stanford University Press.

Magaziner, I.C., and Reich, R.B. 1983. *Minding America's business.* New York: Vintage Books.

Mitroff, I. 1987. *Business not as usual.* San Francisco: Jossey-Bass.

Ouchi, W. 1981. *Theory Z.* Reading, Mass.: Addison-Wesley.

Phillips, K. 1984. *Staying on top: The business case for a national industrial strategy.* New York: Random House.

Piore, M.J., and Sabel, C.F. 1984. *The second industrial divide.* New York: Basic Books.

Schonberger, R. 1982. *Japanese manufacturing techniques.* New York: Free Press.

Scott, B.R., and Lodge, G.C. eds. 1985. *U.S. competitiveness in the world economy.* Boston: Harvard Business School Press.

Thurow, L. 1985. *The zero-sum solution.* New York: Simon and Schuster.

Vernon, R. 1977. *Storm over the multinationals.* Cambridge: Harvard University Press.

Vogel, E.F. 1985. *Comeback.* New York: Simon and Schuster.

2

International Business-Level Strategy: The Development of a Holistic Model

Allen J. Morrison
Kendall Roth

International trade and competitiveness are issues critically important to many firms today. Increasingly, firms are being challenged at home by foreign competitors and are themselves seeking new methods of competing outside their domestic markets. Indeed, the phenomenon of growing international trade has forced firms in many industries to fundamentally reassess both how they compete and in which markets they do business. Considerable disagreement exists, however, over the appropriateness of applying the domestically oriented strategic management paradigm in determining international business strategy (Doz 1980; Fayerweather 1982; Roth and McDougall 1986). In particular, the broad spectrum of environmental variance facing businesses competing internationally encourages an emphasis on unique patterns of the elements forming the basis of the more traditional, domestically focused conceptualization of strategy content (Daniels, Pitts and Tretter 1984; Douglas and Rhee 1987). Nevertheless, the current relationship between the domestic approach to strategic management and the approach proposed by international theorists remains strained and unbridged.

The purpose of this chapter is to synthesize the contributions of both the domestic and international business perspectives of strategic management and, in so doing, to identify the generic patterns of strategic behavior that provide a holistic understanding of the content of strategy for a multinational business unit. First, we review the domestic strategic management paradigm with particular emphasis on the dimensions or components that comprise a firm's strategy. Second, attention shifts to international business strategy. Here we argue that investment, political, and integration "substrategies" take on added importance. These substrategies, in conjunction with the domestically emphasized components of strategy, define the elements by which patterns of international competition can be derived. Third, we present a model highlighting patterns of international strategic behavior along a continuum extending from multidomestic operations to global activity.

Domestic Strategy Perspective

In a domestic context, the content of a firm's strategy has been identified along two dimensions: scope and competitive methods (Vancil and Lorange 1975; Bourgeois 1980a, 1980b). Scope is defined as the "extent of the organization's present and planned interactions with its environment" (Hofer and Schendel 1978. 25). Scope is often referred to as the domain of the organization's activity governing its product and market segments served. Competitive methods describe how an organization applies its resources and skills to differentiate its products or offerings from those of its rivals and in so doing best serves its customers (Chrisman, Hofer, and Boulton 1988). Competitive methods are based on resource and skill deployments within the functional areas of the organization.

Scope and competitive methods collectively comprise the business-level strategy of the organization. They are elements of strategy which are difficult, if not impossible, to completely separate. A business unit's scope and competitive methods are designed to accommodate concurrent appraisals made by the firm of its environmental opportunities and risks and its resources and distinctive competencies (Andrews 1986). Under this definition, we assume that scope and competitive methods are controllable by organizational participants, as efforts are made to match the organization's distinctive capabilities and competencies with its competitive environments in pursuit of organizational goals (Schendel and Hofer 1979). This "matching" is, in effect, the strategy of the firm.

The match that an individual business unit achieves with its contextual setting is specific to that organization. Recently, however, strategic management researchers have recognized that despite the specificity of this match, generalizations across multiple firms are possible. Termed "generic" strategies, these classifications serve to distinguish alternate business conduct at a broad level and are important for several reasons: Classifications facilitate our understanding of broad patterns of strategic activity (Hambrick 1980; Herbert and Deresky 1987) enabling researchers to deal in a systematic and collective manner with a cluttered, random group of variables (McKelvey 1975; Hambrick 1984). Furthermore, from a methodological perspective, classification must be completed before the laws of science can be verified. Indeed, the classification of phenomena often represents the first procedure in theory development (Wolf 1926; Hunt 1983; Punj and Stewart 1983).

Recognizing the importance of classifying business conduct, an extensive review was conducted of "taxonomic" studies that have attempted to either empirically derive or establish classification schemes of business strategy (Galbraith and Schendel 1983; Woo and Cool 1983; Dess and Davis 1984; Robinson and Pearce 1985; Davis 1986; Roth 1986; White 1986). The taxonomic approach has been viewed as the state-of-the-art approach for studying business strategy (Robinson and Pearce, forthcoming). The review indicated that several common themes run throughout the taxonomic research. However, what is identified through the review is not a commonality of conclusions but rather a commonality of methodology, definitions, and of the operationalization of business strategy in the development of strategy classifications.

The general approach in the taxonomic studies has been to operationalize the concept of business level strategy through the specification of a comprehensive set of strategy variables. Strategy variables are defined as discrete elements of functional level activities which together determine the business's specific forms of activity. Strategy variables have been typically based on a combination of variables found to be important in previous research and variables theoretically posited as capturing the nature of strategic competition at the business level (Galbraith and Schendel 1983).

In each taxonomic study, following the specification of strategy variables, surveys of businesses measured the importance of each variable to the strategic behavior of the business. The final step in the determination of strategic classifications typically involved utilizing a multivariate technique, such as principal component analysis, factor analysis, or cluster analysis that identified generalizable patterns of emphasis among the strategy variables.

The taxonomic studies were further analyzed to determine the degree of consistency of the set of strategy variables typically employed. Interestingly, a rather high degree of consistency existed. Specifically, our analysis identified seventeen variables common in multiple studies and identified as discriminating. Table 2–1 reviews the discriminating strategy variables identified in each taxonomic study.[1]

Although taxonomic research has enhanced our understanding of business strategy, it contains several limitations particularly relevant to international strategic management. Unlike the emphasis of existing taxonomic research on a single strategy dimension, it is posited that businesses competing internationally emphasize a richer array of strategy dimensions to obtain a match between their distinctive competencies and the diverse industry contexts in which they operate (Jolly 1988). Not only does competition occur within a given market context as has been posited in the research reviewed, but also as Porter (1985) suggests, international competition transcends markets and national boundaries.

Furthermore, the strategy variables in table 2–1 identified as discriminating are predominantly related to the competitive positioning of the business in a given environmental context. Competitive positioning can be defined as those policies specifying the relationship the business establishes with the market in which it competes. Yet, the competitive positioning of the business actually represents only one element or substrategy dimension of its overall strategy (Hofer and Schendel 1978). Indeed, Hofer and Schendel (1978)

Table 2–1
Competitive Position Substrategy Variables

	Studies				
Discriminating Variables	*Galbraith & Schendel* (1983)	*Robinson & Pearce* (1985)	*Dess & Davis* (1984)	*Davis* (1986)	*Roth* (1986)
Emphasize product quality	X	X	X	X	X
Promote new product development	X	X	X	X	X
Build brand identification		X	X	X	X
Emphasize specialty products		X	X	X	X
Develop innovative marketing techniques		X	X	X	X
Emphasize customer service and service quality	X	X	X	X	X
Develop an efficient manufacturing process			X	X	X
Utilize skilled labor		X	X	X	X
Influence and control channels of distribution		X	X	X	X
Price below competitors		X		X	X
Produce products in high-priced market segments		X	X	X	
Emphasize plant newness	X			X	
Tightly control overhead and variable costs				X	X
Promote an innovation in the manufacturing process	X	X	X	X	X
Build reputation in industry		X	X		
Emphasize advertising and promotion	X		X	X	
Forecast and track market opportunities constantly			X	X	

X = commonly identified discriminating variable.

suggest two additional substrategy dimensions: investment and political substrategies. A fourth substrategy dimension—integration—is implicitly suggested by Porter (1980, 1985), White and Poynter (1984), Harrigan (1985), and Kogut (1985a, b), among others. Figure 2–1 illustrates this model of the four dimensions of the business unit's overall strategy content.

The Substrategy Paradigm

Together, scope and competitive methods form the framework for the four different but related substrategies in figure 2–1. All four substrategies involve both scope and competitive methods, although each substrategy has different patterns of emphasis. Emphasis on different substrategies is manifest in the overall strategy of the business.

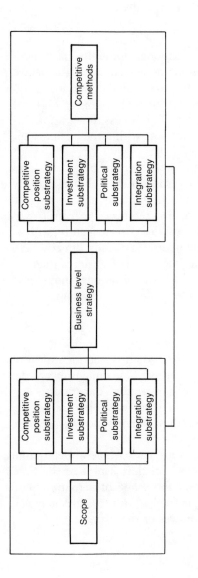

Figure 2–1. **Two Dimension and Substrategy Model of Business-Level Strategy**

Substrategies are implemented by different combinations of functional areas within the business. An investment substrategy can be defined as those policies determining the nature of the business's resource deployments. As such, investment substrategies are typically designed to support a business's competitive position substrategy. A political substrategy can be defined as those policies designed to maneuver the business within a given sociopolitical context. Political substrategies, although generally motivated by economic objectives, are based on influencing noneconomic relationships (Arndt 1983) to improve the business's overall context. Finally, an integration substrategy can be defined as those policies intended to configure both the internal and external functional relationships of the business. Integration substrategies formalize economic and political exchange within the business and between the business and its industry environment.

Remaining unspecified in the model are the particular strategic variables associated with each of the three substrategies that effectively discriminate businesses competing internationally. Unfortunately, none of the previously cited taxonomic research effectively captures the distinctive international activities posited along these dimensions.[2] Consequently, with a consideration of the potential scope and competitive methods dimensions of these substrategies, a review of both the international business theory literature and research on business strategy in highly international industries has identified substrategy variables deemed potentially discriminating. These variables are shown in the remaining tables.

Investment, political, and integration substrategies have all attracted little research attention, both in terms of scope and competitive methods, in the domestic classification research. The isolation and identification of domestic business strategies has generally ignored these dimensions or determined that variables associated with these substrategy dimensions are nondiscriminating.[3] This does not imply that these variables are not important in a domestic context, but rather that they do not appear to strategically differentiate organizations domestically.

Clearly, all four substrategies are inseparable in determining the overall strategy of a firm. Each explains a distinct aspect of the firm's internal or external activities. Depending on the scope of activities, particularly with regard to international activity, individual substrategies may play a greater or lesser role in determining the success of the firm.

The International Perspective

International business strategy can be conceptualized as uniquely emphasizing dimensions of strategy that are often nondiscriminating in a domestic, home nation context. Indeed, international business strategies are reflected in the composite of the national competitive strategies of individual business units.

As a result, it is essential that a study of international business strategies draw on the contributions of the domestic paradigm. However, even though considerable work has been done to identify patterns of domestic strategic behavior, little work has been done to synthesize these conceptual contributions into a typology of international strategies.

An apparent assumption made in domestic strategy research is that the resultant generic strategies are applicable in an international environment. Internationalization has been implicitly viewed as simply a contextual extension of the same basic strategic orientations. The broad environmental variance within the spectrum of international settings, however, raises serious questions about the applicability of the domestically generated paradigm in the determination of international strategy typologies (Doz 1980; Fayerweather 1982; Hamel and Prahalad 1985; Boddewyn 1986). Given our view that the fundamental notion of strategy is matching the organization with its external context, if the external context is altered through internationalization, it follows that the strategy will necessarily be changed to maintain the match. The next section of the paper reviews the substrategies posited as requiring an additional as well as altered emphasis in an international context.

Investment Substrategies

All businesses have investment substrategies in one form or another. Indeed, various universally applicable investment substrategies have been proposed in the literature (Hofer and Schendel 1978; Porter 1980; Harrigan 1980). In contrast to domestic investment substrategies, however, international business units emphasize unique investment tactics as outlined in table 2–2. These tactics are based primarily on the MNC's needs to (1) access cheap funds internationally, and (2) invest these funds in markets yielding the highest overall returns.

To the extent that membership in a larger corporate entity provides access to lower capital costs, the utilization of these capabilities is consistent with profit maximization objectives at the business level. Accessing the MNC's financial capacities as a means to lower overall capital costs is aimed primarily at profiting from financial market distortions. Financial market distortions combined with political forces also result in inconsistent tax rates across national boundaries. Internal financial transfers often disguise profits and bring them to low-tax-rate countries.

In addition to assuring an access to low-cost capital and minimizing exposure in high-tax-rate nations, international investment substrategies involve making location-specific capital investment decisions. Consequently, the other investment substrategy variables identified in table 2–2 include selecting host-nation investment sites according to low-cost factor endowments, labor costs, and/or tax bases as well as emphasizing management compensation based on overall international performance.

Table 2–2
International Investment Substrategy Variables

Source funds internationally	Rugman (1979); Doz (1980); Lessard (1985, 1986); Kogut (1985b); Porter (1986b)
Invest in countries with low-cost resources (e.g., labor, raw materials)	Buckley and Casson (1976); Dunning (1980, 1981); Calvet (1981); Hout, Porter, and Rudden (1982); Cvar (1984); Kogut (1985b); Casson (1986); Porter (1986a, b)
Invest in countries which offer investment incentives (e.g., low tariffs, grants)	Doz (1980, 1986); Porter (1980); Lindert and Kindleberger (1982); Cvar (1984); Lessard (1986); Encarnation and Wells (1986); Doz (1987)
Minimize tax liabilities through transfer pricing and choice of remittance channels	Rugman (1979); Lessard (1985); Srinivasan and Kim (1986)

Political Substrategies

Political substrategies involve a combination of often overlapping scope and competitive methods variables. Involved are variables determining where to compete and how to favorably influence national and international political actors. For international businesses, the tactical advantage attained through host-nation concessions is directly related to the political strategy engaged (Boddewyn 1986). The aim of a political substrategy is to obtain a competitive advantage through effectively interfacing with noneconomic actors, including the government, the public, special interest groups, and trade associations. Commenting on Porter's (1980) three generic strategies, Boddewyn (1986: 4) argues that "if a firm cannot be a cost, differentiation or focus leader, it may still beat the competition on another ground, namely, the non-market [political] environment."

At its broadest level, the overall political strategy of the business can be regarded as the rules by which particular tactics would be employed (Ansoff 1965). Utilization of particular political tactics, as outlined in table 2–3, would be contingent on the host nation's political environment. Typical political substrategy variables include emphasizing political risk forecasting, forming alliances with key host national officials, using strategic coalitions for political advantages, and emphasizing the development of political skills and international perspectives among management.

Integration Substrategies

Integration substrategies are manifest primarily in the scope variables of the firm's overall strategy. Scope-related variables determine where the organiza-

Table 2–3
International Political Substrategy Variables

Use international political risk forecasting	Fayerweather (1982); Kobrin (1982); Simon (1982); Poynter (1983); Boddewyn (1986)
Lobby for favorable host-nation government policies	Benson (1975); Tomlinson (1980); Boddewyn (1986); Doz (1986); Pfeffer (1987)
Develop international managers with political sensitivity skills	Miller (1977); Toyne and Kuhne (1983); Ondrack (1985)
Safeguard local operations from host-nation intervention	Fagre and Wells (1982); Poynter (1983); Kogut (1985b); Doz (1986); Encarnation and Wells (1986); Porter and Fuller (1986)

tion competes and which products it offers in particular markets. We posit that there is a direct linkage between integration substrategies and foreign direct investment (FDI); consequently, certain aspects of a firm's integration strategy take on unique importance internationally. These aspects include both where the firm operates on a nation-by-nation basis, and how the firm configures its operations, internally and with external agents. The following sections examine the integration substrategies of businesses competing internationally. Tables 2–4 and 2–5 summarize internal integration substrategies and external integration substrategies.

Internal Integration Substrategies. Both Kogut (1985a) and Porter (1985) have suggested the value-added chain as representative of the generic functional activities specific to the business unit. These activities can be classified as the "primary" and "support" functions that comprise the firm (Porter 1985). Primary activities include inbound logistics, operations, outbound logistics, marketing and sales, and service. Support activities represent the infrastructure of the firm, its technical development capacity, procurement, and human resource management. Although value chains are broadly determined by the industry, they are specifically controlled by the business unit.

Activities in a business unit's value chain are not discrete but are linked by a configuration and coordination that represent the business's strategic position. Factors determining the characteristics of an industry, such as economies of scale and the division of labor, are made evident in various degrees at the functional levels within the value chain. The geographic location of individual components of the value chain are thus strongly influenced by factors dictated by industry membership and host nation factors.

The competitive position of a business unit within an industry is affected by the interrelationships that exist both within a value chain and between value chains (business units) within the same corporate organization. Accord-

Table 2–4
International Internal Integration Substrategy Variables

Keep international tangible asset flows (e.g., intermediate/finished products) in-house	Kindleberger (1969); Doz (1980); Crookell (1984); White and Poynter (1984); Harrigan (1985); Porter (1980, 1985, 1986a, 1986b); Casson (1986); Flaherty (1986)
Keep international intangible asset flows (e.g., skills/technology) in-house	Kindleberger (1969); Hymer (1970); Johnson (1970); Rumelt (1974); Buckley and Casson (1976); Biggadike (1979); Doz (1980); Dunning (1981); Ohmae (1980); Porter (1985, 1986a, 1986b); Flaherty (1986)
Vertically integrate operations	Hymer (1970); Williamson (1975); Buckley and Casson (1976); Calvet (1981); Harrigan (1985); Beamish and Banks (1987)
Horizontally integrate operations	Hymer (1970); Williamson (1975); Buckley and Casson (1976); Calvet (1981); Harrigan (1985); Perlmutter and Heenan (1986); Beamish and Banks (1987)

Table 2–5
International External Integration Substrategy Variables

Secure long-term contractual agreements with buyers and sellers	Porter (1980, 1986a); Cvar (1984); Harrigan (1985, 1986); Ghemawat, Porter, and Rawlinson (1986); Perlmutter and Heenan (1986)
Secure local long-term contractual agreements with host-nation governments/agents	Tomlinson (1970); Porter (1980); Killing (1982); Poynter (1983); Harrigan (1984); Beamish (1985); Porter and Fuller (1986); Beamish and Banks (1987)
Establish formal international marketing/distribution agreements (e.g., joint ventures)	Porter (1980); Ohmae (1985); Hamel and Prahalad (1985); Porter and Fuller (1986); Ghemawat, Porter and Rawlinson (1986); Doz (1987)
Establish formal sharing agreements (e.g., joint ventures and licensing)	Porter (1980); Killing (1982); Cvar (1984); Harrigan (1985); Ohmae (1985); Porter and Fuller (1986); Ghemawat, Porter, and Rawlinson (1986); Reich and Mankin (1986); Perlmutter and Heenan (1986); Doz (1987)
Establish formal international production agreements	Ohmae (1985); Porter and Fuller (1986); Perlmutter and Heenan (1986); Reich and Mankin (1986)

ing to Porter (1985: 318): "Economic, technological, and competitive developments are increasing the competitive advantage to be gained by those firms that can identify and exploit interrelationships among distinct but related businesses."

Consequently, integration substrategies can take on several dimensions. For example, Harrigan (1985: 399–402) suggests four dimensions of business level vertical integration: (1) the number of stages in the span of integrated activities; (2) the degree of integration; (3) the breadth of integration or the extent of horizontal integration; and (4) the actual form of integration.

The advantages of integration are largely based on a combination of supply security, improved coordination, economies of scale, and cost economics based on internalization (Buckley and Casson 1976; Calvet 1981; Teece 1986). A combination of internalization advantages and market disequilibriums provides much of the incentive for foreign direct investment (FDI) (Calvet 1981). Consequently, reliance on a FDI integration substrategy is highly influenced by the degree to which internalization advantages can be achieved. Specifically, the stronger the advantage of internalizing transactions for the business unit, the stronger is its desire to use FDI (Lecraw 1984). Internalization encourages FDI in that it "allows business firms to transfer capital, technology, and organizational skills from one country to another where they may be more potent" (Hymer 1970: 443). The potency of the investment is necessarily reflected in ownership-specific advantages and location-specific advantages (Dunning 1980). Table 2–4 shows the related integration substrategy variables. The ability of the firm to capitalize on these advantages is directly related to the engagement of appropriate integration strategies.

Locational advantages are used by the firm to accentuate existing ownership-specific advantages (Dunning 1980: 10). This is particularly the case in market disequilibriums. Market disequilibriums and internalization advantages are most obvious in: (1) goods transfers; (2) technological and information transfers; and (3) funds flows and capital market transactions. These three areas form the basis of all internal integration substrategies. Given that integration substrategies encompass the scope of all the firm's activities, considerable overlap in the categorization of these three activities is expected. Fund flows and capital market transactions have been previously discussed. Attention now is turned to the transfer of goods and technological and information transfers as principal elements of the organization's overall internal integration substrategy.

Transfer of Goods. The flow of goods from one level of the business to another is perhaps the clearest manifestation of an integration substrategy. Several factors encourage the intrabusiness transfer of goods. These include (1) the competitive advantage of a novel division of labor; (2) concerns over quality control; (3) nonrecoverable investments or other commitments adversely affecting bargaining power in the marketplace; (4) risk reduction for some highly specific investment; and (5) exploitation of economies of scale (Casson 1986). Porter (1980: 303) suggests that production economies are manifest as economies of combined operations. In manufacturing efficiencies are gained by merging technologically distinct operations and thereby reducing the steps in the production process, by reducing handling and transportation costs, and by utilizing slack capacity throughout the organization's chain of activities. In marketing economies are achieved through such activities as shared brand names, shared advertising, bundled selling, and shared order processing (Porter 1985).

These potential advantages notwithstanding, trade among business units implies a structured integration substrategy or a more rigid linking of activities than would exist in the free market, and such rigidity implies certain costs. Kindleberger (1969: 13) asserts that if totally free markets and pure competition were in existence, direct investment would not exist. Even in existing markets, many instances of internalization have not been deferred to the marketplace (Coase 1937; Porter 1980; Harrigan 1985, 1986; Galbraith and Kay 1986). Consequently, FDI can be viewed as an equilibrating force among segmented foreign markets, whereby the advantages of internalization form the rationale behind the existence of the MNC and the competitive basis for international competition.

Technological and Information Transfers. The importance of using intangible organizational assets for the business unit is clearly evident in the literature, as shown in table 2–4. The content of intangible transfers by MNCs includes general organizational and managerial skills, marketing skills, the ability to differentiate products, and the development of new products and new production processes (Hood and Young 1979: 48–49). With regard to technological integration, Porter (1985: 349) suggests two broad strategic categories: "shared technology development" and "shared interface design for products with a technological interface." Both these categories involve efforts to reduce production costs or differentiate the product, thereby giving the business unit a competitive advantage in the industry.

External Integration Activities and Strategic Coalitions. With the growth in international trade has come a parallel growth in the use of external integration activities as elements of international business strategies (Cvar 1984; Ghemawat, Porter, and Rawlinson 1986; Porter and Fuller 1986). External integration activities take the form of coalitions or formal agreements linking one firm to another. Coalitions include joint ventures, licensing agreements, supply agreements, and marketing/distribution agreements (Porter and Fuller 1986).

Although interbusiness integration substrategies take several legal forms, the focus is on providing mutual benefits to the partners involved. These benefits may be available at every stage of a firm's value chain of operations but emphasis on two areas is most pronounced: R&D and distribution (Ohmae 1985; Porter and Fuller 1986). (See table 2–5.) Expenses for research and development can clearly be very high; given the rapid acceleration in the diffusion of new technology, it is essentially impossible for any business to indefinitely maintain a position of technological leadership in every related field. Coalitions can not only provide access to new sources of technology but also act as new conduits for technology initially developed for a domestic or regional market. According to Ohmae (1985: 17): "Since it costs dearly to develop a technologically advanced and differentiated product, the company must be able to sell simultaneously to the entire world in order to amortize the heavy front-end investment."

To benefit from the technological advantages coalitions can provide, businesses must also have access to an international marketing and distribution network. Distribution coalitions offer other advantages besides assisting in the amortization of sunk R&D costs. These advantages include circumventing host-government investment and trade regulations, gaining access to national markets whose cultural idiosyncrasies would otherwise be intimidating, and reducing overall sales costs through the utilization of world-scale distribution networks. Clearly, it is often more economical and timely to utilize the services of outside agents in moving products in culturally and geographically diverse locations.

Summary of Integration Substrategy. The choice to integrate operations extends beyond the make-or-buy decision inherent in the internalization concept (Porter 1980). Integration, consequently, takes on an organizational dimension extending beyond mere transaction cost analysis. Integration is also an element of strategy that extends beyond the business unit. At every level in the organization, strategy is formulated according to human perceptions, objectives, and nonquantifiable administrative constraints. Because firms maximize profits within a horizon extending into time and space, integration substrategies cannot be understood merely on the basis of a particular transaction (Lindert and Kindleberger 1982). Consequently, the strategic dimensions of business integration are extremely difficult to isolate.

Patterns of International Strategy

By identifying the variables associated with international strategy, it is possible to suggest certain patterns in the strategic behavior of firms competing internationally. Strategic patterns are posited to vary along a continuum from purely domestic strategies to purely global strategies (White and Poynter 1984; Crookell 1984). Figure 2–2 illustrates this framework.

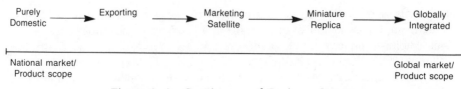

Figure 2–2. Continuum of Business Strategy

The position of a firm's strategy along the continuum in figure 2–2 depends on its emphasis on a subset of the strategy variables found in tables 2–1 through 2–5. Selection of which particular strategy variables to stress is a function of firm-specific factors, host-nation environments, and unique industry constraints. Industry constraints dictate in broad terms the nature of competition while the firm determines its overall scope and competitive methods. Consequently, contextual factors are critically important in determining which patterns of strategy variables are emphasized. Two contextual factors are critical in influencing the position of a firm's strategy along the continuum in figure 2–2: economies of scale and division of labor and standardization.

Economies of Scale. Certain products are more subject to economies of scale than others. The economy of scale concept is based on the reduction of the real unit cost of production of a particular product as the quantity produced increases (Caves and Jones 1973: 222). Other nonproduction scale economies are evident in marketing, purchasing, service, R&D, and transportation logistics (Cvar 1984; Porter 1986b).

Production economies of scale are based on the size of operations, length of the production run, and the learning curve effect. According to Child (1972: 7), increasing the size of operations offers more opportunities to reap the benefits of increased specialization. As specialization takes place, costs may fall for a number of reasons such as learning to make the product more effectively by repetition, or spreading a number of capital items of a lumpy character more thinly per unit of output (Lindert and Kindleberger 1982: 181). Production efficiencies due to scale economies encourage large-scale operations. When maximum efficiencies can only be achieved by producing beyond the consumption demands of the home market, there may be a considerable advantage in shifting the overall strategic position of the firm to the right along the continuum in figure 2–2.

Division of Labor and Standardization. The capability of firms to exploit economies of scale is represented by their vertical integration and division of labor (Casson 1986). Although each industry has its own distinctive pattern of trade, the location of production facilities away from home-market economies is contingent on the possible division of labor for that industry. Vernon (1979) postulated that a sophisticated new division of labor, and not a standardization of technology, encouraged a globalization of production. Components would be standardized but production location would be determined according to the exploitability of labor (i.e., its adaptability, trainability).

The division of labor is largely based on two contingencies: (1) the availability of adaptable and cooperative workers, and (2) the standardization of intermediate products. Intermediate products can be broadly thought of as raw materials, semiprocessed materials, and finished products awaiting distribution (Casson 1986: 8). Many businesses integrate all the way back to raw materials. Each stage in the integration process is subject to great refinement in the division of labor. Following Adam Smith's reasoning, the greater the sophistication in the division of labor, the greater the production efficiencies. When great efficiencies in the division of labor and standardization are possible, emphasis on investment, political, and integration substrategy variables is encouraged by the industry.

Patterns of Strategic Behavior in Global Product/Market Context

The availability of economies of scale and a maximization of the division of labor encourage particular strategic responses. When these forces are coupled with homogeneous worldwide product demand (Levitt 1983; Quelch and Hoff 1986), international transportation efficiencies (Karnani 1983), and overall low levels of government interference in the free trade of the industry's output (Scott 1973; Porter 1986b; Rutenberg 1981; Hamel and Prahalad 1985; Doz 1986; Boddewyn 1986), businesses typically respond with common patterns of global strategic behavior. This is seen at the right end of the continuum in figure 2–2.

Perhaps the most comprehensive discussion of the identification of global competitive strategies is found in Cvar (1984). In a review of eleven businesses engaged in global activities, Cvar (1984: 7) determined that "the central issue from an international strategy viewpoint is the nature and extent of required coordination of a firm's international activities." A global business strategy involves establishing a chain of globally integrated business operations that culminate in distributing a finished product to a geographically diverse customer base. Global business strategies are based on the tight integration of business activities on a global basis. According to Ghemawat and Spence (1986: 63): "International integration of some value activities is the essence of global competition. The competitive advantages of international integration necessarily rest on economies of coordination that spill over national borders."

Both internal and external integration variables are highly emphasized in businesses competing internationally. Other variables stressed include select-ing host-nation investment sites according to low-cost factor endowments, encouraging the compensation of managers according to overall international performance, and encouraging the development of managers with interna-tional perspectives.

Although not entirely risk-free, there are several advantages in competing globally. These include lower production costs due to integrated activities and economies of scale, reduced risk of expropriation, and simplified interna-tional management of operations through the identification of key sources of uncertainty (Doz 1980). Another advantage of a globally integrated operation is the ability of firms to respond quickly to "shifts in the relative factor cost competitiveness of various manufacturing locations by relocating their manufacturing facilities in different countries" (Doz 1986: 231).

Strategic Patterns in Host Nation Responsiveness Context

Unlike global business strategies based on global markets and broad value-added scope, host-nation strategies are based on local markets and narrow value-added scope. In industries where political forces isolate national markets, where national market demand is incompatible with global prod-ucts, or where transportation inefficiencies preclude international sourcing, businesses find it more attractive to pursue host-nation strategies. Such strategies isolate international business subsidiaries that are encouraged to pursue more politically sensitive strategies that invite favorable treatment by host nations.

The advantages of national responsiveness strategies include the pooling of financial risk, the transfer of intangible skills between like subsidiaries, the spreading of research and development costs over larger volumes than are available to strictly local competitors, and the coordination of export marketing among subsidiaries (Doz 1980; Porter 1985). International strategy variables emphasized include sourcing funds internationally, selecting host-nation investment sites according to government investment incentives, utilizing internal financial transfers to disguise profits, emphasizing the use of standardized political risk forecasting, establishing close relations with host-nation officials, integrating international operations to increase local bargain-ing power, and emphasizing intangible asset transfers between the parent and subsidiary. Competitive methods employed by businesses engaged are repre-sentative of similar patterns identified in the domestic literature.

Marketing satellites market products produced outside the host-nation's boundaries and not designed to meet particular local demands. Some marketing satellites become involved in packaging, quality control, service, and minor product assembly (White and Poynter 1984). Geographic scope, which is typically determined at the corporate level, is either national or subnational. Competitive methods are usually biased in favor of patterns dominant in the parent's home marketplace. Very little strategic autonomy is afforded the subsidiary.

In contrast, miniature replica businesses produce and market products developed by or related to the parent's product line. Miniature replica businesses work behind national tariff barriers and strive to be identified as domestic firms. According to Doz (1980: 29), "manufacturing is usually done on a local-for-local basis, with few intersubsidiary transfers."

Three distinctive strategic patterns can be identified for the miniature replica: (1) adopters directly take products and programs from the parent; (2) adapters adapt products from the parent to suit local tastes; and (3) innovators develop new, but generally related, products for local markets (White and Poynter 1984). The main difference between these patterns is the degree of autonomy afforded the subsidiary. Beyond this, the competitive methods employed are patterned after those identified in the domestic strategic management paradigm. Broad strategic issues such as host nation market selection and integration strategies are formulated at the corporate level. Political strategies are based on exploiting the subsidiary's identification with the host nation's marketplace. Typically, attempts are made to create a local identity for the subsidiary.

Conclusions

International business strategy is determined by a variety of factors including the distinctive competencies and capabilities of individual business organizations, the competitive methods dictated by industry membership, and sum of host-nation environments where the firm currently operates or where it may potentially operate. At its most basic level, international business strategy represents a blend of common factors identified by the domestic strategic management paradigm as well as elements uniquely emphasized in an international context. Investment, political, and integration substrategies all play a more vital role in the overall strategies of businesses competing internationally. Emphasis on particular patterns of strategic variables depends to a large degree on the positioning of the firm's overall strategy along the strategy continuum.

Increasingly, the international competitiveness of U.S. businesses is being challenged, both at home and abroad. According to one report, "fully 70 percent of [U.S.] industries, up from 25 percent only a dozen years ago, are under full-scale attack by foreign competitors" (Peters 1986: 11). Competitiveness is ultimately an issue of strategic responsiveness. Encouraged by historical success in enormous domestic markets, many U.S. businesses have failed to develop the capacity to adequately assess international threats and opportunities. Coupled with this perceptual myopia is the failure of some businesses to develop adequate internal capabilities necessary to effectively compete internationally. Increasing attention must be paid to improving the overall international responsiveness of U.S. businesses in investment, political, and integration capabilities. More specifically, however, heightened appreciation must be developed for the importance which particular substrategies play in the transcendent strategy of businesses. This means that businesses competing at opposite ends of the strategy continuum in figure 2–2 should place considerably different emphasis on developing internal substrategy capabilities.

This chapter has sought to synthesize the conceptually developed international strategy variables with those empirically generated in a domestic context. It is unfortunate that the conceptualization of international strategy has not itself arrived at the point of empirical validation. Also, although the domestic paradigm has moved both conceptually and empirically toward identifying patterns of strategic behavior that yield superior performance (i.e., generic strategies), no such approach has been attempted internationally. This chapter lays the foundation for such a study through the identification of the competitive methods and scope variables that form the basis of international business activity.

Notes

1. Variables selected were identified as discriminating, based on high factor loadings identified in at least two of the taxonomic studies reviewed.

2. We acknowledge that this research includes many studies which contain samples comprised of multinational organizations. However, in these studies, no explicit attempt is made to capture the essence of international business strategy.

3. For example, neither Robinson and Pearce (1985) nor Dess and Davis (1984) found that attention to specific geographic markets differentiated the strategies of businesses in their respective samples.

4. The authors recognize the helpful comments of James Chrisman on an earlier draft.

References

Andrews, K. 1986. *The concept of corporate strategy* 3d ed. Homewood, Ill.: Irwin.

Ansoff, I. 1965. *Corporate strategy: an analytic approach to business policy for growth and expansion.* New York: McGraw-Hill.

Arndt, J. 1983. The political economy paradigm: Foundation for theory building in marketing. *Journal of Marketing* 47, 44–54.

Bartlett, C. 1983. MNCs: Get off the reorganization merry-go-round. *Harvard Business Review* 61: 138–46.

Beamish, P. 1985. The characteristics of joint ventures in developed and developing countries. *Columbia Journal of World Business* 20: 13–20.

Beamish, P. and Banks, J. 1987. Equity joint ventures and the theory of the multinational enterprise. *Journal of International Business Studies,* Summer, 1–16.

Benson, J. 1975. The interorganizational network as a political economy. *Administrative Science Quarterly* 20, 229–49.

Boddewyn, J. 1983. Foreign and domestic divestment and investment decisions: Like or unlike? *Journal of International Business Studies,* Winter, 23–35.

———. 1986. International political strategy: A fourth "generic" strategy? Paper presented at the Academy of International Business meetings, London.

Bourgeois, L. 1980a. Performance and consensus. *Strategic Management Journal* 1: 227–48.

———. 1980b. Strategy and environment: A conceptual integration. *Academy of Management Review* 5: 25–39.

Buckley, P.J., and Casson, M. 1976. *The future of multinational enterprise.* London: Macmillan.

———. 1981. The optimal timing of a foreign direct investment. *The Economic Journal,* March, 75–87.

Calvet, A.L. 1981. A synthesis of foreign direct investment theories and theories of the multinational firm. *Journal of International Business Studies,* Spring/Summer, 43–59.

Casson, M. 1986. *Multinationals and world trade: vertical integration and the division of labour in world industries.* Boston: Allen & Unwin.

Caves, R.E., and Jones, R.W. 1973. *World trade and payments.* Boston: Little, Brown.

Child, J. 1972. Organizational structure, environment, and performance: The role of strategic choice. *Sociology* 6: 1–22.

Chrisman, J.; Hofer, C.; and Boulton, W. 1988. Toward a system for classifying business strategies. *Academy of Management Review* 13(3).

Coase, R. 1937. The nature of the firm. *Economica* 4(6): 386–405.

Crookell, H. 1984. Specialization and international competitiveness. *Business Quarterly,* Fall.

Cvar, M.R. 1984. Competitive strategies in global industries. Ph.D. diss., Harvard Business School.

Daniels, J.; Pitts, R.; and Tretter, M. 1984. Strategy and structure of U.S. multinationals: An exploratory study. *Academy of Management Journal* 27(2): 292–307.

Davis, P. 1986. An analysis of industry forces, corporate strategy, and business strategy as factors explaining business unit performance. Ph.D. diss., University of South Carolina.

Dess, G. and Davis, P. 1984. Porter's (1980) generic strategies as determinants of strategic groups membership and organizational performance. *Academy of Management Journal* 27(3): 467–88.

Douglas, S., and Rhee, D. 1987. Competitive strategies in international markets: Some generic types. New York University. Photocopy.

Doz, Y. 1980. Strategic management in multinational companies. *Sloan Management Review,* Winter, 27–46.

———. 1986. Government policies and global industries. In *Competition in global industries,* ed. M. Porter. Boston: Harvard Business School.

———. 1987. International industries: Fragmentation versus globalization. In *Technology and Global Industry: Companies and Nations in the World Economy,* eds. Bruce Guile and Harvey Brooks. Washington, D.C.: National Academy Press.

Dunning, J.H. 1981. *International production and the multinational enterprise.* London: George Allen & Unwin.

———. 1980. Toward an eclectic theory of international production: Some empirical tests. *Journal of International Business Studies,* Spring/Summer, 9–31.

Encarnation, D.J., and Wells, L.T. 1986. Competitive strategies in global industries: A view from host governments. In *Competition in global industries,* ed. M. Porter. Boston: Harvard Business School.

Fagre, N. and Wells, L. 1982. Bargaining power of multinationals and host governments. *Journal of International Business Studies,* Fall, 9–23.

Fayerweather, J. 1982. *International business strategy and administration,* 2d ed. New York: Harper & Row.

Flaherty, M. 1986. Coordinating international manufacturing and technology. In *Competition in Global Industries,* ed. M. Porter Boston: Harvard Business School.

Galbraith, C. and Kay, N. 1986. Toward a theory of multinational enterprise. *Journal of Economic Behavior and Organization* 7: 3–19.

Galbraith, C. and Schendel, D. 1983. An empirical analysis of strategy types. *Strategic Management Journal* 4: 153–73.

Ghemawat, P.; Porter, M.; and Rawlinson, R. 1986. Patterns of international coalition activity. In *Competition in global industries,* ed. M. Porter. Boston: Harvard Business School.

Ghemawat, P. and Spence, A.M. 1986. Modeling global competition. In *Competition in global industries,* ed. M. Porter. Boston: Harvard Business School.

Hambrick, D. 1980. Operationalizing the concept of business-level strategy in research. *Academy of Management Review* 5, 567–75.

———. 1984. Taxonomic approaches to studying strategy: Some conceptual and methodological issues. *Journal of Management* 10, 27–41.

Hamel, G., and Prahalad, C.K. 1985. Do you really have a global strategy? *Harvard Business Review,* July–Aug., 139–48.

Harrigan, K.R. 1980. *Strategies for declining businesses.* Englewood Cliffs, N.J.: Prentice-Hall.

———. 1984. Innovation by overseas subsidiaries. *Journal of Business Strategy* 5: 47–55.

———. 1985. Vertical integration and corporate strategy. *Academy of Management Journal* 28: 397–425.

———. 1986. Matching vertical integration strategies to competitive conditions. *Strategic Management Journal* 7, 535–55.

Herbert, T. and Deresky, H. 1987. Generic strategies: An empirical investigation of typology validity and strategy content. *Strategic Management Journal* 8, 135–47.

Hisey, K., and Caves, R. 1985. Diversification strategy and choice of country: Diversifying acquisitions abroad by U.S. multinationals, 1978–1980. *Journal of International Business Studies* 16(2): 51–64.

Hofer, C., and Schendel, D. 1978. *Strategy formulation: analytical concepts.* St. Paul: West Publishing.

Hood, N., and Young, S. 1979. *The economics of multinational enterprise.* New York: Longman.

Hout, T.; Porter, M.; and Rudden, E. 1982. How global companies win out. *Harvard Business Review,* Sept.–Oct., 98–108.

Hunt, S. 1983. *Marketing Theory: The philosophy of marketing science.* Homewood, Ill.: Richard D. Irwin.

Hymer, S. 1970. The efficiency (contradiction) of multinational corporations. *American Economics Review* 60(2): 441–48.

Jolly, V. (Forthcoming). Global competitive strategies. In *Strategy, organization design, and human resource management,* ed. C. Snow. Greenwich, Conn.: JAI Press.

———. 1988. Global competitive strategies. In *Strategy, organization design, and human resource management,* ed. C. Snow. Greenwich, Conn.: JAI Press.

Karnani, A. 1983. The tradeoff between production and transportation costs in determining optimal plant size. *Strategic Management Journal* 4: 45–54.

Killing, P. 1982. How to make a global joint venture work. *Harvard Business Review,* May–June, 120–27.

Kindleberger, C.P. 1969. *American business abroad: Six lectures on direct investment.* New Haven: Yale University Press.

Kobrin, S. 1982. *Managing political risk assessment.* Berkeley, Calif.: University of California Press.

Kogut, B. 1985a. Designing global strategies: Comparative and competitive value-added chains. *Sloan Management Review,* Summer, 15–28.

———. 1985b. Designing global strategies: Profiting from operational flexibility. *Sloan Management Review,* Fall, 27–38.

Lecraw, D. 1984. Bargaining power, ownership, and profitability of transnational corporations in developing countries. *Journal of International Business Studies,* Spring/Summer, 27–43.

Lessard, D.R. 1985. Transfer prices, taxes, and financial markets: Implications of international financial transfers within the multinational corporation. In *International financial management: Theory and application,* 2d ed., ed. D.R. Lessard. New York: John Wiley & Sons.

———. 1986. Finance and global competition: Exploiting financial scope and coping with volatile exchange rates. In *Competition in global industries,* ed. M. Porter. Boston: Harvard Business School.

Levitt, T. 1983. The globalization of markets. *Harvard Business Review* 61(3): 92–102.

Lindert, P.H., and Kindleberger, C.P. 1982. *International economics,* 7th ed. Homewood, Ill.: Richard D. Irwin.

McKelvey, B. 1975. Guidelines for the empirical classification of organizations. *Administrative Science Quarterly* 20, 59–70.

Miller, E. 1977. Managerial qualifications of personnel occupying overseas management positions as perceived by American expatriate managers. *Journal of International Business Studies,* Spring/Summer, 57–69.

Ohmae, K. 1985. *Triad power: The coming shape of global competition.* New York: Free Press.

Ondrack, D. 1985. International transfers of managers in North American and European MNCs. *Journal of International Business Studies* 16(3): 1–19.

Perlmutter, H. and Heenan, D. 1986. Cooperate to compete globally. *Harvard Business Review,* March–April, 136–52.

Peters, T. 1986. Competition and compassion. *California Management Review,* Summer, 11–26.

Porter, M.E. 1980. *Competitive strategy: Techniques for analyzing industries and competitors.* New York: Free Press.

———. 1985. *Competitive advantage.* New York: Free Press.

———. 1986a. Changing patterns of international competition. *California Management Review* 28(2): 9–40.

———. 1986b. Competition in global industries: A conceptual framework. In *Competition in global industries,* ed. M. Porter. Boston: Harvard Business School.

Porter, M., and Fuller, M. 1986. Coalitions and global strategy. In *Competition in global industries,* ed. M. Porter. Boston: Harvard Business School.

Poynter, T. 1983. The corporate management of government intervention: A survival plan. The University of Western Ontario. Photocopy.

Punj, G., and Stewart, D. 1983. Cluster analysis in marketing research: Review and suggestions for application. *Journal of Marketing Research* 20: 134–48.

Quelch, J.H., and Hoff, E.J. 1986. Customizing global marketing. *Harvard Business Review* 64(3): 59–68.

Reich, R. and Mankin, E. 1986. Joint ventures with Japan give away our future. *Harvard Business Review,* March–April, 78–86.

Robinson, R., and Pearce, J. 1985. The structure of generic strategies and their impact on business-unit performance. In *Academy of management proceedings,* San Diego, 35–39.

———. (Forthcoming). Planned patterns of strategic behavior and their relationship to business-unit performance. *Strategic Management Journal.*

Roth, K. 1986. Strategic behavior and organizational performance: Construct and antecedent variable analysis in a causal model framework. Ph.D. diss., University of South Carolina.

Roth, K., and McDougall, P. 1986. An empirical comparison of domestic and international strategic behavior. Paper presented to the International Management Division, Academy of Management National Meetings, Chicago.

Rugman, A. 1979. *International diversification and the multinational enterprise.* Lexington, Mass.: Lexington Books.

Rutenberg, David 1981. Global product mandating. In *International business: A Canadian perspective,* eds. K.C. Dhawan, H. Etemad, and R.W. Wright. Don Mills, Ontario: Addison-Wesley.

Schendel, D., and Hofer, C. 1979. *Strategic management.* Boston: Little, Brown.

Scott, B.R. 1973. The industrial state: Old myths and new realities. *Harvard Business Review,* March–April, 133–48.

Simon, J. 1982. Political risk assessment: Past trends and future prospects. *Columbia Journal of World Business,* Fall, 62–71.

Srinivasan, V., and Kim, Y.H. 1986. Payments netting in international cash management: A network optimization approach. *Journal of International Business Studies* 17(2): 1–20.

Teece, D. 1986. Transactions cost economics and the multinational enterprise. *Journal of Economic Behavior and Organization* 7: 3–19.

Tomlinson, J. 1970. *The joint venture process in international business: India and Pakistan.* Cambridge, Mass.: MIT Press.

Toyne, R., and Kuhne, R. 1983. The management of the international executive compensation and benefits process. *Journal of International Business Studies,* Winter, 37–50.

Vancil, R., and Lorange, P. 1975. Strategic planning in diversified companies. *Harvard Business Review* 53 (Jan.–Feb.): 81–90.

Vernon, R. 1979. The product cycle hypothesis in a new international environment. *Oxford Bulletin of Economics and Statistics* 42: 255–67.

White, R. 1986. Generic business strategies, organizational context and performance: An empirical investigation. *Strategic Management Journal* 7, 217–31.

White, R.E., and Poynter, T.A. 1984. Strategies for foreign-owned subsidiaries in Canada. *Business Quarterly,* Summer.

Williamson, O. 1975. *Markets and hierarchies: Analysis and antitrust implications.* New York: Free Press.

Wolf, A. 1926. *Essentials of scientific method.* New York: Macmillan.

Woo, C. and Cool, K. 1983. "Porter's (1980) generic competitive strategies: A test of performance and functional strategy attributes." Working paper, Purdue University.

3
Transnational Linkages and Strategy

Briance Mascarenhas

*F*irm A, from the United States, had a product clearly superior in quality and price to its competitors. When planning to enter some West
African markets, its managers naturally were optimistic. But the firm
has been unsuccessful, due largely to a French trading company, with ties
from the colonial days, which gave preference to French products. Managers
noted that in those markets the distribution system is fragmented, characterized by many small outlets, and is often efficiently serviced through a trading company which overcomes the inefficiencies associated with dealing with
many small accounts by handling numerous products. Colonial trading companies typically enjoy strong channel loyalty due to their longstanding relationships, their clout derived from representing many products, and the extensive contact associated with frequently restocking small wholesalers. [1]

Firm B's subsidiary in a Middle-Eastern country was having difficulty
obtaining consumer acceptance of its product, in part due to restrictions on
local advertising. Astute managers realized, however, that many local opinion
leaders listen to Radio Monaco and that its international advertising spillovers
could be used to develop consumer awareness and overcome the local restrictions.

Bank C's managers decided to make its French subsidiary a center for
information processing and computing to capture efficiencies of centralized
computing. After setting up the facilities and equipment, managers realized
that the German government would not permit client data to be sent to France
for processing because data protection laws in France are less stringent than
in Germany. The bank had no alternative but to open a separate data processing center in Germany and incur heavy duplication costs (Buss 1984).

Managers of firm D, a U.S. firm in the petroleum industry, were considering a joint venture in Indonesia, a predominantly Moslem country. In the
wake of an Israeli attack on an Iraqi nuclear reactor, top management felt that
should a similar crisis occur in the future, the firm with its association to the
United States which is supportive of Israel may get a backlash in Indonesia.
To reduce this political risk, top managers considered finding a Saudi Arabian
partner for its Indonesian operation.

These cases suggest the vital, if subtle role that linkages can play in the international context. Yet, American business has been less successful abroad than domestically because of its limited savvy about linkages in the international context (Thorelli 1986: 42). Further, organization theory has yet to tap the richness of thought of a network perspective (Fombrun 1982: 281).

This article first articulates the concept of transnational linkages. Second, it points out the potential advantages and disadvantages of linkages. Third, it identifies three basic transnational linkages—inadvertent, formal, and informal—together with their characteristics, conditions of occurrence, and significance for strategic decision makers.

Characteristics of Linkages

A linkage in this context is defined as a relationship other than trade and investment that exists between two or more units. By linkage we do not mean a similarity between two or more units but a connection or relationship between them. It is true that similarity between two units can sometimes spawn interaction, but not necessarily. Two markets, it is conceivable, may have similar local channels of distribution, per capita incomes, or forms of government, but there may be no special link between the two. In fact, two countries may have no similarity but a linkage may exist. For example, the market structure of Indonesia might be different from that of Holland but close ties between the two countries might exist nonetheless because of colonial ties.

The units among which linkages exist are diverse; they are not restricted to countries. Meaningful units also include individuals, firms, communities (Fombrun 1982), and supranational groups. Not all pairs of units join directly, and some join through multiple linkages (Tichy 1982).

By focusing attention on connections among units, an analysis of linkages provides a fuller understanding than a stand-alone view of a unit or a comparative view among units. For example, foreign market assessments may use surrogate indicators to predict market potential, but often do not consider linkages to and from a market that can be useful for penetrating it or using it as a base. There is also evidence that customer ties and market openness (Nigh et al. 1986) are more important than market size in explaining foreign investment patterns. Thus, the linkage concept provides an important and very different conceptual focus.

Attention needs to be focused not only on one unit's linkages with other units, but also on the relationships among the other units themselves. Consideration of a network of relationships provides a systemic view and can suggest complex strategies.

PepsiCo's current attempt to enter the Indian market is a case in point.

India is a potentially attractive market for Pepsi because Coca-Cola Company, its arch rival, is persona non grata there after leaving in the 1970s instead of acquiescing to government localization demands. Over the past ten years Pepsi unsuccessfully attempted to obtain a foreign investment permit. Soft drinks are not on the central government's list of foreign investment priorities. In its recent beverage business proposal, however, PepsiCo has added a fruit and vegetable processing plant to be located in the state of Punjab, India's breadbasket, where there is a growing Sikh separatist movement to secede from the country. PepsiCo's proposal has been enthusiastically endorsed by state government officials in Punjab. Some experts believe that this time the central government will approve the foreign investment proposal in part as a concession to the state of Punjab to dissipate their separatist demands. Such approval would also create jobs, reduce unrest, and show that the political climate in Punjab is safe for foreign multinationals to invest in and that the central government is in control of the country.

Advantages and Disadvantages of Linkages

Linkages can provide diverse advantages. They can provide economic benefits, such as lower costs and higher profits, reduce uncertainty, and improve control in transactions (Hakansson 1982). Improved communication that accompanies linkages may facilitate coordination among units and mutual adaptation (Hakansson 1982). The development and use of linkages forces a long-term point of view, beyond an individual transaction. Further, linkages may permit transactions without requiring all details to be worked out in advance. Linkages are valuable when transactions would be less efficiently carried out by the market or hierarchy in Williamson's (1975) framework (Thorelli 1986). They can also be valuable in explaining and predicting the spread of innovations in a system and the causes and consequences of organizational change (Aldrich and Whetten 1982). Finally, linkages may afford firms with the benefits of integration, diversification, or international market entry without the apparent resource commitments (Thorelli 1986).

There may also be shortcomings associated with linkages. Linkages may result in over-dependencies; institutionalization of a relationship may result in rigidity and a lack of awareness of outside opportunities, and possible exploitation by one of the partners when relationship asymmetry exists (Ford 1982). A relationship can constrain (Fombrun 1982) and can inhibit the search for other relationships. The barriers to entry into a relationship, such as uncertainty and switching costs, are also barriers to exit. To the extent that a relationship is exclusionary, it raises public policy questions of discrimination (Thorelli 1986).

Types of Linkages

Linkages in the international context involve three basic forms: inadvertent, formal, and informal. Table 3–1 summarizes the characteristics, conditions of occurrence, sources of information, and potential advantages and disadvantages associated with the three linkages.

Some linkages may involve more than one form. A linkage between two units, for example, may involve formal and informal ties. Forms of linkages may vary over time and there may sometimes be linkage dynamics. For example, inadvertent linkages may be formalized after discovery or asymmetrical linkages may gravitate to reciprocal linkages over time or disintegrate.

Inadvertent Linkages

Inadvertent linkages, or connections between units, arise due to physical and temporal factors and are not driven by formal or informal agreements between units. They are not preplanned and are thus unintended. These linkages may come to management's attention when products or problems spread to unplanned areas, for example through cases of parallel importing and distributor complaints. The challenge to management is to recognize these developments, even if it is after the fact, and reflect them in its strategy and organization.

Inadvertent linkages occur because of technological lines not matching national contours, a strategic location such as in a high-traffic sea lane or physical proximity, technological innovations which compress time and space, technological compatibility across units such as ports with similar capabilities for handling large ships, and population migrations.

Some examples and their strategic significance follow:

Media spillovers. Spillovers of media across political boundaries can create potential assets. Advertising spillovers, for instance, may permit market coverage in another country, bypass local media restrictions on advertising, and avoid cumbersome transactions with many different local media. This media spillover can also help to promote a uniform image or an international image and to prioritize countries for penetration and products for introduction. Philip Morris, Inc., for instance, recognized the advertising spillover by United States media over Canada after the fact and introduced its home brands there to exploit this externality (Keegan 1974).

Media spillovers, however, can also spread a problem from one market to another. Alert top management can use their knowledge of media spillovers to identify areas where a problem may spread so that preventive steps can be taken. When F. Hoffmann La-Roche & Company was involved in a public dispute with the British government regarding the pricing of its drugs, British

Table 3–1
Characteristics of the Three Linkages

	Inadvertent Linkages	Formal Linkages	Informal Linkages
Nature	Not preplanned Agreement may not exist	Written agreements Hierarchical ties	Tacit agreement
Conditions of occurrence	Space and time compression Technology does not match national contours Lack of restrictions	Across dissimilar or in low-context cultures Legal obligation and enforcement is desirable When visibility is desirable	Across similar or in high-context cultures When secrecy or ambivalence is desirable
Identification	After-the-fact analysis of unintended incidents, i.e., of parallel importing, distributor complaints, and unsolicited orders	Documentary evidence of agreements and structural arrangements, i.e., *Directories of Tax Treaties*, *Who Owns Whom*, *Stateman's Almanac*, *Treaties in Force*.	Use surrogate indicators to infer a linkage, i.e, patterns of behavior, similarity in culture, past colonializations, historical events, using observation, *Europa Yearbook*, *Stateman's Almanac*, or *Exporter's Encyclopedia*
Potential advantages	Economies of scale Bypasses local regulations	Specifies rules for coordinating the agreement Can be used to contain risk Can be used to manage outward appearance	Norms and trust facilitate coordination Loyalty serves as a buffer Facilitates extra firm transactions Can keep secrecy and avoid documentation costs
Potential limitations	May be too late to capitalize on linkages when discovered May spread problems	Agreements may not result in de facto linkages Linkages may not outlive agreement	Informal obligations and expectations create constraints.

media spillovers helped to encourage similar disputes in selected other countries ("A Drug" 1975; Leonhard 1981).

Overlapping media may also create a problem by spilling over the wrong audience, by projecting contradictory messages, or by stifling market segmentation. In the case of the Philip Morris advertising overlap in Canada, marketing research revealed that the spillover was a potential asset when it covered English Canadians but a liability when it covered French Canadians who resented English intrusions on their French identity (Keegan 1974).

Migrations. Migrations, involving the physical movement of people can be important in linking units. In many countries the presence of a dual economy with vastly different infrastructures presents a daunting challenge for building market coverage. In South Africa, for instance, it is difficult to reach the black population directly in their homelands because of limited media coverage. Astute marketeers, however, have targeted a segment of the black population that commutes to work to relay city advertising to the hinterland by word of mouth.

Transportation links. Geographical distance generally discourages international business. But transportation options and efficiencies can redraw commercial patterns, offsetting the distance effect. Often, what really matters is not only the distance between a firm's home base and a foreign country's major city, but also the transportation time from that major city to the hinterland location of a firm's project. Countries separated by large geographical distances might really be more attractive than they appear, if they are connected by superior transportation options, say, faster airplanes, more frequent flights, more direct shipping routes, or involve fewer transfers along the way which increase risk. For example, there are about twenty-five deep-water ports worldwide where nonbulk cargo is often consolidated and reassembled in an intermediate stage during shipment. Direct shipment is often slower and more expensive because of smaller ships and less frequent shipment. Thus, going a further distance may be quicker and cheaper; managers need to examine their location vis-à-vis the deep-water port, not the direct distance. As an oil-drilling company executive pointed out, a key factor in evaluating a foreign investment's feasibility was the company's ability to transport the roughneck crew to and from the rig site for their two-week shifts not only quickly but also avoiding the attractive tourist cities where the roughnecks were likely to create disturbances and disrupt the operating schedule.

Some countries provide more linkages than others because of their strategic locations along transportation lines or the range of transportation modes they can handle. Spain, for example, is strategically attractive as a supply base because it has two coastlines, the Atlantic and Mediterranean; these provide avenues for export in two major directions (Robinson 1985).

Formal Linkages

Formal linkages involve written administrative agreements or structural arrangements between units to develop and control interactions. Prescribed linkages per se, however, are not a guarantee that the intended interaction will take place. And if the interaction is driven by a formal linkage, it may not outlive that formal agreement or arrangement.

Formal linkages are more common in some contexts than others. An important characteristic of such an agreement is that they are more visible. Thus, when visibility is desirable, formal linkages are more common. For example, Kuwait formally reregistered its ships to fly the United States flag and thus obtain protection in the Persian Gulf. Many lesser known companies in developing countries, for instance, flaunt their ties with developed country multinationals for the sake of visibility and prestige. The visibility of formal linkages, however, may dissuade their use when secrecy or ambivalence is desirable. Strong antitrust pressures in the United States have deterred formal agreements between firms at home and have resulted in many executives being unprepared and ill at ease in developing agreements with organizations overseas. Some executives, however, have avoided visible formal agreements but managed to achieve the intended international market allocation through the more subtle and less visible means of selectively granting their patents to firms in different countries (Massel 1965).

Formal linkages are also more common in low-context and legalistic cultures where communication and contracts have to be made explicit to be understood. Formal agreements often include guidelines governing the rules of interaction, and are thus useful when coordination is required across different ideologies and cultures. For example, because the United States is a melting pot of immigrants, shared rules of conduct have been few and have had to be explicit to be clear to all. In many traditional societies overseas, in contrast, rules have had a chance to develop over time and may be informally understood by insiders.

Finally, formal linkages may be used when it is desirable to create legal obligations and enforcement. For example, Kennecott Corporation presold its Chilean copper mine's future output to diverse countries and borrowed from many countries' banks against these formal long-term supply contracts to reduce the attractiveness to the Chilean government of an expropriation (Moran 1973).

Some examples of formal linkages and their significance follow:

Political Agreements. Agreements among districts, states, or countries, such as regional economic integration plans, often result in strong business ties. Some countries also encourage international trade and investment through foreign policy incentives and aid programs on whose coattails firms can penetrate foreign markets. For example, the Marshall Plan—an assistance program to rebuild postwar Europe—was used by United States firms to develop a beachhead in Europe.

Tax Treaties. Bilateral treaties between some countries reduce capital gains taxes and withholding taxes on payments of capital gains, dividends, interest, and royalties between them. Such treaties can be exploited by strategies of selective routing of shipments between affiliates and by international ownership strategies involving the careful selection of countries to be used for parenting affiliates. Some international firms, for example, have developed advantages from such tax relationships by having a Dutch affiliate own other subsidiaries because Holland has a broad network of favorable bilateral tax treaties that reduce capital gains taxes on the sale of equity in foreign subsidiaries and withholding taxes on payments made to Holland.

Currency Ties. Some countries peg their currency to that of others in a formal agreement, such as the European snake. The significance of the currency linkage is that trading with firms based in nonlinked currencies is subject to greater foreign exchange risk and thus a deterrent to a long-term stable relationship. Firms that wish to develop a long-term relationship with foreign clients may, therefore, have to invest in diverse international sourcing capabilities to adjust to seesawing exchange rates or use a sourcing capability in a currency linked to the target market. Utilizing one base with a linked currency, however, has the added advantage of permitting economies of scale and close ties to develop between a dedicated plant and a foreign client.

Organizational Linkages. Organizations often involve some closely joined units and other weakly joined units. Of strategic importance is the delineation of loosely coupled subsystems within which units are tightly joined. Aldrich and Whetten (1982) have hypothesized that loosely coupled systems are less sensitive to external influence and are more adaptive in a complex, heterogeneous environment.

Some managers have carefully designed their firms' internal structural linkages to reflect the desired decoupling, formality, and associated control and responsibility, to achieve a strategic purpose. Organizations can be ordered on a continuum reflecting the extent to which they are perceived to be formally linked as opposed to having autonomy and separate personalities. At one extreme would be wholly-owned subsidiaries, somewhere in the middle would be joint ventures, and at the other extreme, independent organizations. Tactics such as the creation of a separate corporation instead of a branch, the use of different names, changes in the background of employees or the parent of an affiliate, can all serve to segment an organization or at least the perception of formal control and responsibility.

Recently, Fiat was seeking contracts from the United States Strategic

Defense Initiative Program. But its links with Libya, manifested through Libyan shareholders and board members, were awkward. United States' interests, it was felt, would not like it if profits and information generated by contracts in the United States found their way to Libya. So Fiat asked its Libyan shareholders and board members to divest themselves, and created a separate corporation in the United States, staffed by locals, to receive funds from government contracts with the restriction that they would not flow to other parts of Fiat ("Libya" 1986).

When a foreign project is risky, some managers have utilized mechanisms for segmenting that project from the rest of the organization, say, setting up a local limited liability corporation, so that the risk does not flow through to the remaining firm. Of course, this strategy works where it is difficult to pierce through the corporate veil under local law.

This decoupling strategy is also manifested by some United States firms who have used European joint ventures to circumvent United States' controls on exports to the Eastern Bloc. Their top managers know beforehand that when the United States administration pressures them to have their affiliates curb their exports to the Eastern Bloc they can respond that they could not comply, despite their intentions to do so, because of inadequate formal control over the joint venture. Further, they recognize that the United States government may not impose sanctions against the firm in cases where the parent makes a good faith attempt to control an affiliate. The Eastern Bloc buyers, meanwhile, also view the joint venture to be less formally controlled by the United States government, and thus less subject to its shifting policies.

Japanese strategists have used joint ventures to gain access to their Western partners' know-how and technology, when these are more difficult or costly to obtain directly (Beauchamp 1986). Again, these managers are really utilizing the closer links of the joint venture with their partner's organization than their firm's direct link with the partner.

Informal Linkages

Informal linkages involve ties based on shared beliefs, such as a common culture, language, religion, ideology, and historical past. These bonds can transcend national boundaries and develop or constrain international business. In informal linkages, the interaction between units is not driven by a formal agreement as much as by consensus in outlook, trust, and accepted norms; this helps to reduce conflicts and to resolve problems when they occur.

Informal linkages, by their nature are more likely to exist among similar high-context cultures than in low-context cultures or across dissimilar cultures. Informal linkages are often more subtle to detect than formal linkages because there may not be a visible agreement and because they are often below the surface or tied to some event buried in the past such as a military occupation or colonization. Nonetheless, informal linkages may be long-lasting, strong, and pervasive at the grass-roots level. Not only do they create entry barriers for others who may wish to participate in the exchange but also unwritten expectations and obligations may be exit barriers or constraints for the parties involved. There is a real danger, therefore, of either not detecting informal linkages because of their unobvious nature or of underestimating their strength.

For instance, before Toyota entered into a joint venture agreement with General Motors it broke off negotiations with Ford partly because Saudi Arabia was Toyota's second largest foreign market and Ford had a presence in Israel (Weiss 1987).

Informal linkages include:

Colonial Ties. Colonial ties often involve formal and informal linkages. But even with formal decolonizations and termination of official linkages, such as the expulsion of the British from Malaysia by Dr. Mahathir Bin Mohamed in the early 1980s, colonially-related firms continue to have informal ties in their former colonies. If for no other reason, it is because they were there first and have built up a relationship and trust at the grass-roots level (Levy 1986).

Cultural Ties. When culture, in the form of religion, language, or ethnic roots, spreads across political boundaries its bonds can translate into international business.

A case in point is Enka, a Turkish construction firm, which has been receiving a disproportionate share of business in the Arab World and North Africa. Certainly, this business can partly be attributed to geographical proximity between the parent base and its foreign markets. But Enka's top management has pointed out that the real key to its international business success has been a religious bond. They state, for example, that Enka obtained work contracts in Mecca and Medina because the Moslem religion of its workers was the only one acceptable there; other international contractors could not effectively meet that customer need (Reed 1985).

A close understanding of cultural distinctions can provide valuable insights into why particular trade and investment patterns occur. For example, Iran, despite its Moslem religion, has closer relations with Israel than many other Middle Eastern nations because it is not an Arabic-speaking nation and its population is composed of Shiite Moslems as opposed to the Sunni Moslems in other countries of the region. These factors were important in the transhipment of United States's arms to Iran via Israel.

Sometimes it is not a common dominant language, but a common second or a third language that stimulates international business ties. For example, executives have partially attributed the relatively heavy trade between West Germany and several Eastern European countries to the fact that the German language was spoken during the German occupation of Eastern Europe during the world wars. This common language facilitates the transfer of technology and training, which the Eastern Europeans have been keen on obtaining.

Ideological Ties. A common political ideology can translate into trust, support, and international business even when there are no formal agreements. For example, India's production of cashews is concentrated in the state of Kerala. Much of India's production is sold to the Soviet Union, at substantially higher prices for those grades than the world commodity market prices. Experts believe that the higher prices reflect a hidden subsidy by the Soviet Union to Kerala, which is the only state in India to have consistently voted communist over time (Jeannet 1981).

Informal Interorganizational Links. Astute managers realize that, through informal ties, control and coordination may be maintained even among formally separate organizations. A Japanese firm and a German firm utilized a long-standing, close relationship to engage in informal international market sharing. There was a legal reason for not placing this agreement in writing, and the close relationship was a substitute for a formal agreement. Such an arrangement would have been less likely with United States firms, given their desire to document everything in writing, their legalistic background, and the strong antitrust pressures they have faced at home.

Implications for Strategic Decisionmakers

As the scope of competition has become more international, strategists are increasingly concerned with trying to understand and find ways of competing in this expanded, unfamiliar, and complex arena. This article has argued that sensitivity to linkages embedded in the world economy provides valuable insights into business patterns and can be the basis for imaginative international strategies. Clearly, developing linkage-based strategies is a subtle and complex art. Yet, there are some general guidelines for exploiting linkages.

Focus on Multiple Connections and Units

Fundamentally, managers and researchers must refocus their attention and thinking away from views of independent units and toward multiple connections among diverse units. The traditional focus on the nation as the unit of analysis in international business is arbitrary and overly restrictive. This refocusing requires higher and deeper levels of analysis because multiple units must be examined simultaneously while being cognizant of each unit's details. Often, it is through the details that the connections become apparent. George

Christoph Lichtenberg, the great eighteenth-century philosopher, put it bluntly: "He who understands nothing but chemistry does not truly understand chemistry either!"

Examine Linkages of Current and Future Ventures

Strategists should be sensitive to the linkages associated with their existing and future ventures. Multiple linkages may foster stability and reduce uncertainty in ties among units (Aldrich and Whetten 1982).

In new international ventures, too often irrevocable commitments are made without considering their potential linkages. These linkages often become apparent only later. For example, Two-Ply Manufacturers entered into a joint venture on the Ivory Coast with a French partner; their agreement stipulated that profits of the joint venture would be shifted to France through transfer pricing on international sales. Later, however, it became apparent that Two-Ply should have retained its profits in the Ivory Coast because of a United States tax provision permitting profits from developing countries to be repatriated without double taxation. But by then, the joint-venture partner was unwilling to change the transfer price (Vernon 1971).

Earlier commitment may be warranted, however, when an investment is associated with numerous linkages that provide options in case the benefits of one or two are not realized. Recently, numerous firms have invested in Spain even before the country became an official member of the European Economic Community. Some of the reasons given, besides that of getting a head start, include Spain's ties to the Arab world, its ties to much of Latin America through culture, and its important transportation linkages (Robinson 1985).

Clearly, linkages also have implications for how companies should structure themselves to achieve the desired formality between units and to group together units with linkages to be emphasized. Many United States companies, for example, have wrongly excluded the United Kingdom from their European divisions in their organizational structures because of superficial geographical reasons, even though the United Kingdom has more in common with some of the countries included than others which are grouped together (Parks 1969).

There are parallel implications for government officials interested in encouraging foreign investment into their countries. Government officials need to uncover and promote the potential advantages of linkages associated with their countries. A country may represent a small market when viewed independently, but may be quite attractive from the perspective of other markets it opens up via inadvertent, formal, and informal linkages.

Hong Kong has often served as a go-between in trade among China, Taiwan, South Korea, and Japan because of the ideological, political, or historical differences between these countries.

Recognize the Different Linkages

The three linkages—inadvertent, formal, and informal—vary systematically in driving force, conditions of occurrence, visibility and identification method, and potential strengths and weaknesses. Strategists need to be sensitive to the systematic differences in the nature of these linkages. In some contexts, not all linkage types are present, appropriate, or equally exploitable by a particular firm. In other situations, different linkages may reinforce one another, or one type of linkage may compensate for the absence of another.

The identification methods also differ across linkage types. Inadvertent linkages require after the fact learning and the redesign of strategies and structures. Identifying formal linkages requires analysis of written, documentary sources of evidence and structural arrangements. Uncovering informal linkages, in contrast, requires inferring a relationship from similarities in culture, historical events, migrations, and behavior patterns.

Presently, the incorporation of linkages into strategic decision making is unsystematic and the preserve of a few experienced international managers. A senior international manager, for example, commented that when a problem occurs somewhere he intuitively thinks about "who around the world do we know that can get that job done in that country."

Given the excess number of possible linkages relative to the limited capacity of executives, the loss of historical knowledge as experienced executives retire, and the unsystematic and ad hoc use of linkages in current management practice, there is a real need and opportunity for developing data banks. These data banks would compile a vast number of linkage patterns which could readily be sorted and retrieved as decision aids in strategic decision making. Such banks would make an ad hoc pattern recognition process more systematic and expand its use among managers.

Notes

1. The cases that have not been specifically referenced otherwise are based on personal interviews with executives and government officials.
2. The author would like to thank Jean Boddewyn, Susan Douglas, Stephen Kobrin, and John Stopford for their helpful comments.

References

Aldrich, H., and Whetten, D.A. 1982. Organization sets, action sets, and networks: Making the most out of simplicity. In *Handbook of organizational design,* eds. P. Nystrom and W. Starbuck. New York: Oxford University Press.

Beauchamp, M. 1986. Use a long spoon. *Forbes,* 15 Dec., p. 122.

Buss, M. 1984. Legislative threat to transborder data flow. *Harvard Business Review,* 62(3): 111–118.

Deutsch, K.W. 1956. Shifts in the balance of international communication flows, *Public Opinion Quarterly*, 20(1): 143–60.

———. 1960. Toward an inventory of basic trends and patterns in comparative and international politics. *The American Political Science Review*, March, 34–57.

A drug giant's pricing under international attack. 1975. *Business Week*, 16 June 50–65.

Dunning, J.H. 1979. Explaining changing patterns of international production: In defense of the eclectic theory. *Oxford Bulletin of Economics and Statistics* 41: 269–96.

Fombrun, C.J. 1982. Strategies for network research in organizations. *Academy of Management Review* 7(2): 280–91.

Ford, D. 1982. Development of buyer-seller relationships in international markets. In *International marketing and purchasing of goods*, ed. H. Hakansson. Chichester: John Wiley & Sons.

Hakansson, H. ed. 1982. *International marketing and purchasing of goods*, Chichester: John Wiley & Sons.

Holt, J.B. 1977. Industrial cooperation in eastern Europe: Strategies of U.S. agricultural and construction equipment companies. *Columbia Journal of World Business*, Spring, 80–89.

Jeannet, J.P. 1981. Indian cashew processors case, Babson College, Wellesley, Mass.

Keegan, W.H. 1974. Philip Morris International, The George Washington University Case. Washington, D.C.

Leonhard, J. 1981. F. Hoffmann La-Roche & Co. In *Manager in the international economy*, ed. R. Vernon and L.T. Wells. Englewood Cliffs, N.J.: Prentice-Hall.

Levy, S. 1986. Ex-colonies ponder a return of Portuguese settlers. *Wall Street Journal*, 24 September, p. 33.

Libya sells 15.19% holding in Fiat S.P.A. 1986. *Wall Street Journal*, 24 September, p. 3.

Massel, M.S. 1965. Nontariff barriers as an obstacle to world trade. In *Legal problems and techniques*, ed. D. Thompson. The British Institute of Comparative and International Law.

Moran, T.H. 1973. Transnational strategies of protection and defense by multinational corporations: Spreading the risk and raising the cost for nationalization in natural resources. *International Organization* 27(2): 275–87.

Nigh, D.; Cho, K.R.; and Krishnan, S. 1986. The role of location-related factors in U.S. banking involvement abroad: An empirical investigation. *Journal of International Business Studies*, 17 Fall, 59–72.

Parks, F.N. 1969. Survival of the European headquarters. *Harvard Business Review*, 47 Mar.–Apr., 79–84.

Preskowitz, Jr., C.V. 1987. United States–Japan trade friction: Creating a new relationship. *California Management Review* 19(2): 9–19.

Reed, C. 1985. Turkish contractors: It's time to take them seriously. *International Management*, July, 41–45.

Robinson, J. 1985. Two-speed common market heading for heavy strains. *International Management*, 40(12): 24–30.

Savage, J.R., and Deutsch, K.W. 1960. A statistical analysis of the gross analysis of transaction flows. *Econometrica*, July, 551–72.

Sethi, S.P. 1971. Comparative cluster analysis for world markets. *Journal of Marketing Research,* August, 348–54.

Srivastava, R.J., and Green, R.T. 1986. Determinants of bilateral trade flows. *Journal of Business,* no. 4, part 1, (October): 623–40.

Taylor, C.L., ed. 1968. *Aggregate data analysis: political and social indicators in cross-national research.* Paris: Mouton and Company and International Social Science Council.

Teece, D. 1987. Can the United States compete? *Cal Business,* Winter.

Thorelli, H.B. 1986. Networks: between markets and hierarchies. *Strategic Management Journal,* 7: 37–51.

Tichy, N. 1981. Networks in organizations. In Nystrom, P. and W. Starbuck, eds., *Handbook of Organizational Design,* New York: Oxford University Press.

Tichy, N.; Tushman, M.; and Fombrun, C. 1979. Social network analysis for organizations, *Academy of Management Review,* vol. 4, no. 4, pp. 507–19.

Vernon, R. 1971. Two-ply manufacturers, Harvard Business School Case, #9–371–49.

Weiss, S. 1987. The General Motors-Toyota joint venture, paper presented at a New York University International Business Seminar.

Wilkins, M. 1974. *The maturing of the multinational enterprise: American business abroad from 1914 to 1970.* Cambridge, Mass.: Harvard University Press, 1974.

Williamson, O. 1975. *Markets and hierarchies: Analysis and antitrust implications,* New York: The Free Press.

4

Foreign Market Servicing Strategies and Competitiveness: A Theoretical Framework

Peter J. Buckley

T he central hypothesis of this chapter, and the research project which it introduces, is that the competitiveness of British firms is dependent on an appropriate set of foreign market servicing strategies.

The foreign market servicing strategy of a firm is the set of decisions on which production plants should be linked to which specific foreign market and the methods or channels through which this should be achieved. The three main generic types of foreign market servicing strategy are exporting, licensed sales abroad, and foreign direct investment. The foreign market servicing decision is a complex one both theoretically (Buckley and Casson 1985) and in practice (Buckley and Pearce 1979, 1981, 1984).

Competitiveness may be defined as "the immediate and future ability of, and opportunities for, entrepreneurs to design, produce and market goods worldwide whose price and non-price qualities form a more attractive package than those of foreign and domestic competitors" (European Management Forum 1984).

The links between competitiveness and market servicing strategy need to be established. It is clear that an optimal foreign market servicing strategy impacts on price by reducing costs to the firm and hopefully to the consumer and on nonprice factors, most obviously in improved quality, delivery, after sales, and product adaptation terms.

This chapter lays the theoretical groundwork by briefly examining the elements of foreign market servicing, taking a macro or national cross section view, presenting a time series analysis of the market servicing decision, and relating these findings to competitiveness. Finally we point out the implications for decisionmakers.

Elements of a Foreign Market Servicing Strategy

The three main generic elements of a foreign market servicing strategy are exporting (X), licensing and other contractual relationships, (L), plus foreign direct investment (I). All three cover a spectrum of types of arrangement in which the channels of distribution and relationship with the buyer vary within type.

Exporting covers the indirect export of goods; through agents, distributors, merchant houses, trading companies, and a variety of other intermediaries, as well as the direct export of goods and services. Its essential feature is that production activities are carried out in the home country although marketing may well be carried out in the host country, separated by a transport cost barrier.

Exporting is often regarded as merely the first step into a foreign market, but its persistence as a viable strategy mode even in the largest multinationals suggests that it still has a role to play. The sequentialist school has made much of the observed pattern of servicing a foreign market over time which goes X → L → I or X → I. Indeed exporting itself has been analyzed as a sequential process (for a review of this literature see Buckley 1982). Its role in internationalization is well documented but exporting's role in the market servicing pattern of established multinationals is less well understood. To be adequately modeled, the relationship between exporting and other forms of market servicing must be carefully specified as must the factors influencing multiplant operation (Scherer et al. 1975). New thinking and modeling on strategic trade policy and the new international economics should reintegrate exporting into realistic models of the multinational firm (see Krugman 1986; Dunning and Buckley 1972).

Licensing is a generic term covering a variety of indirect investment production operations involving arm's length cooperation with an external agency or agencies. Some element of market transfer is included in this packaged sale of asset services. A spectrum of relationships is possible ranging from the rate, simple sale of embodied knowledge or assets (brand name, patent) through franchising, turnkey operations, contract manufacturing, and management contracts.

A typology of these forms of international operation is provided in Buckley (1985) where they are classified in five dimensions: (1) equity or nonequity ventures, (2) time limited or unlimited, (3) space limited or unlimited, (4) extent of transfer of resources and rights, and (5) internal or external mode of transfer. See also Young (1987) for a survey and Luostarinen (1980) for an alternative approach.

As a mode of market servicing, licensing is often regarded as a transitory mode, perhaps utilized for learning or market testing purposes before a move is made to a foreign direct investment. A minority of firms are regarded as specialist licensors and licensing is often seen as a peripheral activity contingent on peculiar extraneous eventualities, such as government restrictions, as a second best choice.

It is conceivable that changing world competitive structures make this view outmoded. The new forms of international operation may be uniquely well-suited to the competitive conditions prevailing in many world markets, including political uncertainty, government restrictions, idiosyncratic markets, and residual technologies. Moreover licensing allows international companies to avoid head-to-head competition by cross licensing, joint marketing and production agreements, and knowledge pooling. These cooperative devices may be genuine or may be methods of reducing competition by collusive behavior (Buckley and Casson 1987).

Foreign direct investment, too, covers a range of operations. The normal image of a foreign direct investment is a production facility involving a huge capital outlay. This is not necessarily so. A foreign direct investment can be the creation of a sales subsidiary—one man with a car delivering stock from his basement. The key feature of foreign direct investment is not scale but control from the parent. This control, exercised most usually through equity ownership, enables direct management of a foreign facility rather than control through a contract. These issues are widely debated in the internalization literature (Buckley and Casson 1976, 1985; Dunning 1981; Hennart 1986 among many others).

Direct investment thus covers marketing operations and production operations: both sales subsidiaries and production subsidiaries ranging from assembly to full production. Moreover, there are other important distinctions in mode of entry between a greenfield venture and a takeover and in organizational form between a joint venture and wholly owned subsidiary.

Direct investment is regarded as the most risky form of entry in capital committed, but as the most effective in securing market share and strategic competitive advantage. This is confirmed, for instance, in two recent articles on entry into the Japanese market (Buckley, Mirza, and Sparkes 1987; Simon and Palder 1987). It also confers prestige as an internationalized company and is seen as the key weapon in a global strategy as for instance in the triad concept (Ohmae 1985; Buckley, Mirza, and Sparkes 1984).

It is, however, far too easy and incorrect to assume that direct investment is always the correct form of market servicing. External conditions and internal capabilities often suggest otherwise.

Cross Section Analysis of Foreign Market Servicing

The total foreign sales (TFS) of British firms are made up of exports from the United Kingdom (X), sales abroad licensed by U.K. firms (L), and sales arising from British foreign direct investment.

$$TFS = X + L + I$$

The amounts of each of these can be measured at a point of time, over time, and in particular markets, as we later show.

At its most simple, X can be differentiated from the other two methods by the location effect, as with exports the bulk of value adding activity takes place in the home country, while the other two methods transfer much of value adding activity to the host country. Similarly, L can be differentiated from X and I by the externalization effect. L represents a market sale of intermediate goods or corporate assets by the firm. In licensing the firm sells rights and the use of assets to a licensee. In X and I such activities are internalized (Buckley and Casson 1976, 1985). This has important implications. Broadly then, the internalization and location effects separate the three generic forms of market servicing.

$$
\begin{array}{c}
\text{Internalization} \\
\downarrow \quad \text{Effect} \quad \downarrow \\
TFS = \quad X + L + \quad I \\
\uparrow \quad \uparrow \\
\text{Location} \\
\text{Effect}
\end{array}
$$

In practice these simple differentiations are highly complex. First, comparative costs are not easily calculable or obvious. In multiproduct, process, and functional firms, the internal division of labor and the costs associated with each activity are difficult to assess accurately. Further, there are many complex interactions between the activities involved. Location abroad of some activities has knock on effects on home costs and those of third countries within the firm's international network. Second, the costs and benefits of internalization are nebulous and difficult to measure. Both sets of complication are entirely contingent on circumstances. The difficulties and intellectual excitement of these calculations is that the situation is dynamic and the determinants of choice of optimal market servicing strategies are continually shifting.

Cross section analyses of market servicing are snapshot pictures at a moment in time of a continually changing process. The makeup of total foreign sales into X, L, I, at the macro level can give us a crude picture (Buckley and Davies 1980) but this pattern is continually changing as the nature of international competition alters. Further, it is difficult to get meaningful comparative measures of the three modes, although this is usually done by estimating final foreign sales in aggregate (Buckley and Davies 1980; Luostarinen 1978).

A major complicating factor in the analysis of foreign market servicing policies is that the forms are often complements, not substitutes. This fact means that a careful analysis of the relationship between modes is essential.

For instance, Hood and Young (1979) point to the existence of anticipatory exports (goods exported from the source country in anticipation of building the foreign plant), associated exports (complementary products exported by the parent after establishment of the subsidiary), and balancing exports which result when the first plant built abroad is operating at capacity. Also foreign direct investment has a dynamic effect in maintaining the worldwide competitive position of the investing firm. (Hood and Young 1979: 313–15).

This suggests that a dynamic analysis is essential. Assumptions in modeling not allowing for changes in demand conditions—for instance, the existence of a presence effect which results in an increased demand after the establishment of an investment presence (Buckley, Newbould, and Thurwell 1987)—are clearly inappropriate. Similarly models ignoring the competitive process, in particular the role of defensive investments established to protect a market share, are unlikely to capture the nuances of strategy. Models must be organic rather than static and capable of specifying the relationship between exports, licensing, and foreign direct investment.

Time Series Analyses of Foreign Market Servicing Strategies

A number of theoretical models of firms' foreign market servicing strategies are extant. They are almost entirely concerned with the switch from exporting to a foreign market to investing in it. Licensing is a largely neglected phenomenon in modeling (see though Davies 1977; Buckley and Davies 1980).

Comparative Static Analyses

The model used in the product cycle approach (Vernon 1966) is a cost-based formulation:

$$\text{invest abroad when } MPC_X + TC > APC_A$$

where MPC_X is marginal cost of production for export

TC is transport cost to target market

APC_A is average cost of production abroad.

The argument here is that marginal costings are appropriate for exports because domestic production would be undertaken anyway while the foreign unit must bear the full average costs of production.[1]

This move in the maturing phase of the cycle can be triggered, or reinforced, by the desire to defend a market established through exports; most analysts agree that this is best done by a direct investment.

Several other approaches have been suggested for the switch from exporting—or less usually, licensing—to investment. Two comparative static approaches are given by Horst (1971, 1972) and Hirsh (1976). Hirsh's analysis is based on cost minimization; he derives the following inequalities to give firms in country A simple decision rules on the best way to service the foreign market B, either from source country A by export or by direct investment in B. (Subscripts *a* and *b* indicate location.) Therefore, for firms in A:

$$\text{Export to B if} \qquad P_a + M < P_b + K \qquad (4.1)$$

$$\text{and } P_a + M < P_b + C \qquad (4.2)$$

$$\text{Invest in B if} \qquad P_b + C < P_b + K \qquad (4.3)$$

$$P_b + C < P_b + M \qquad (4.4)$$

Where P_a and P_b are production costs in the two countries, M is the difference between export and domestic marketing costs, C represents the extra costs of controlling a foreign rather than a domestic operation, and K represents firm specific know-how and other intangible income producing assets. All quantities are present values of costs covering the life span of a specific investment project. The meaning of inequalities (1) and (2) is that exports should be undertaken if costs of domestic production and export marketing costs are below costs of doing business abroad. Inequalities (3) and (4) suggest that investment should be undertaken when total costs of production abroad (including control costs) are below costs of utilizing the firm specific advantages (K) in production abroad and below the costs of exporting from the parent country A.

Hirsh's analysis assumes that demand is insensitive to the location of supply and can, therefore, be ignored. The analysis is also concerned with an initial investment abroad assuming no excess capacity in the parent country A (otherwise this would mean exporting until marginal costs of further exporting exceeded revenues). It is thus applicable to the siting of a new additional production facility. No analysis is given of the generation of K (firm specific know-how) and thus no idea of relative costs of investing in R and D (to attempt to generate K) versus other types of investment. K is given as a return from a past sunk cost. No light is shed on the timing of the investment and demand factors are removed by assumption.

Horst's (1971) analysis concentrates on the influence of tariff and tax rates in the invest-versus-export decision. Rather than being able to throw up simple rules, Horst shows that the analysis breaks down into special cases according to the conditions under which the firm is operating and the level of taxes and tariffs in home and foreign countries. Horst notes the interesting finding that high tariffs are a mixed blessing for multinational enterprises (MNEs); on one hand they make exporting more costly. On the other, they enhance the firm's prospects for increasing profits by allowing increased price discrimination between markets. If the price elasticity of demand is lower in the protected market than elsewhere, an increase in the tariff allows the firm to raise its price locally, thereby reducing demand and discouraging investment. Investment policy is further influenced by the conditions of production of the firm and market size: the sensitivity of foreign investment to tariff policy being greatest when the marginal cost of production is decreasing with respect to output. If the protected market is a relatively large one, there is a certain tariff level beyond which it is optimal for the firm to concentrate *all* production in that market, even if resource costs are higher in the protected market, because saving of tariff costs outweighs additional resource costs. The complexity of decision rules even in this simple model is illuminating. Horst adds industry-specific influences on foreign investment (firm size, R&D intensity, concentration of the industry, and desire for resource control) to the preceding firm-specific factors in a further paper (1974).

The analyses of Hirsh and Horst highlight different aspects of the foreign investment decision. Hirsh's emphasis on marketing and technological costs is complementary to Horst's inclusion of tariff and tax rates. Both include relative production costs at home and abroad, although Horst emphasizes returns to scale. However, neither approach is particularly concerned with the timing of the switch to foreign direct investment (FDI).

The Timing of the Switch to FDI

Analyses concerned with the dynamics of foreign expansion of the firm should be able to specify those factors governing the timing of the initial FDI. Aliber (1970) attempts to do this by reference to the capitalization of returns from the firm's alternatives: exporting, licensing, and foreign investment. Aliber assumes that the firm possesses a patent or monopolistic advantage. He argues that the costs of doing business abroad prevent investment from being the preferred strategy until a certain market size. Only at a particular size of market does the higher capitalization ratio that applies to source country firms overcome the cost advantage of a local producer (which can be exploited via licensing the patent to a local firm). In Aliber's system, the source-country firm is always a higher cost producer than the host-country firm, provided the latter has access to the patent at competitive rates. This limits the analysis by ruling out those situations where the source country firm (through familiarity with the technology and firmwide economies of scale) has compensating advantages vis-a-vis host-country competitors.

The dynamics of the switch from exporting to licensing and then to FDI are thus dependent, according to Aliber, on the host country's market size and the differentials in capitalization ratios between assets denominated in different currencies. The latter is determined by the currency premium in the capital market—the compensation investors require so that they bear uncertainty concerning fluctuations in exchange rates. Tariffs are easily incorporated into this framework—an increase in the host-country tariff biases the foreign patent owner toward use of the patent in the host country; the choice between its use in licensing or internally via FDI remains unchanged, the choice depending on whether host market size allows the capitalization factor to outweigh the cost of doing business abroad.

In a theoretical paper, Buckley and Casson (1985) provide a model specifying the optimal timing of a switch to direct investment by reference to the costs of servicing the foreign market, demand conditions in that market, and host-market growth. The market servicing decision is more complex than it appears at first sight, particularly when the initial costs of setting up a foreign investment are time dependent.

A simple model of a firm facing a growing market is illustrated in figure 4–1. This model specifies two kinds of costs, fixed and variable, and two forms of foreign market servicing: exporting which has low fixed but high variable cost, and foreign direct investment which has high fixed but low variable cost. Licensing is an intermediate state; in this example it is never the preferred option. Should foreign market size become greater than Q_1, then the firm switches its mode of market servicing to investment in the market.

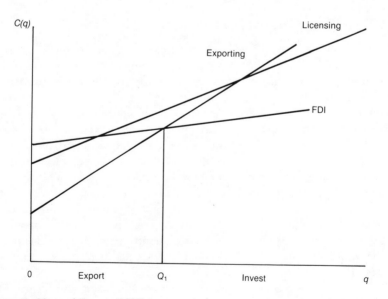

Source: Buckley and Casson (1985)

Figure 4–1. Foreign Market Servicing Policies

Removal of tariffs may, therefore, lead to a switch, not to exports (or to exports only as an intermediate stage), but directly to foreign investment by the multinational firm.

This model enables specification of the optimal timing of a switch in modes by reference to the key variables (1) mode related costs, (2) demand conditions in the host market, and (3) target market growth. The introduction of time dependent set up costs, in particular, makes the decisions very complex. A similar model has been developed by Giddy and Rugman (1979).

Location Decisions

The location decisions of multinationals have been examined by Dunning (1972) and Casson (1985). Dunning's pioneering work on the location decisions of international firms in an enlarged European Communities (EC) isolated several variables likely to influence switches of location. Among the most important were (1) the extent to which products required special adaptation to different national markets; (2) the product and process structure of the firm, in particular the extent to which it was horizontally or vertically diversified; (3) the size and significance of tariff reductions; (4) quantities of output supplied before tariff reduction; (5) elasticities of demand and supply in the various locations; (6) economies or diseconomies of scale in production; (7) transport costs; (8) availability and prices of inputs in the various locations; and (9) government policies on trade and investment.

Casson (1985) in a paper which extends and formalizes the work of Dunning and others also gives the theory of location a radical twist. First, Casson suggests that factor substitution has a very limited role in the location of production. The effect of this proposition is that the Ricardian theory of comparative labor costs assumes great significance. If capital is mobile, then the only significant margin is that at which labor is allocated between industries. As this margin differs at different locations, it will be a prime determinant of the pattern of international production.

Second, Casson argues that technical progress results in reductions in transport costs, greater economies of scale, and promotion of the division of labor rather than factor saving advances in production. In particular, the promotion of the division of labor has profound implications for the location of the activities of multinational firms. The subdivision of a productive activity creates a market for an intermediate product linking the first activity to the second. The division of labor can, as Casson notes, create a pyramid of activities in which both horizontal and vertical specialization occurs—the activities at the bottom produce components which are then combined in assembly processes higher in the pyramidal structure. When the intermediate products are tradable, it becomes possible to separate spatially the activities and to replace one plant by two different ones, on which different location pressures now operate. The resulting increased specialization enables cost reductions in economies of scale, lower input costs, and transport costs.

Third, Casson suggests that proprietary technology where access to knowledge is restricted, is an important barrier to entry, which encourages monopoly or oligopoly in the supply of new products. It is often advantageous for the monopolist to integrate backwards to control supplies of inputs or components embodied in the final product. This leads to the control of international production of new products by vertically integrated monopolistic MNEs.

The Nature of the Industry

A recent study of multinationals and world trade (Casson 1986), concentrating on vertical integration and the nature of the division of labor in world industries suggests an interesting typology of industries. Table 4–1 shows the type of industry and the nature of intraindustry trade. Type I industries are New Product Industries as identified in Raymond Vernon's product cycle hypothesis (Vernon 1966). The major intrafirm trade is final goods between advanced developed countries marketed through the agency of the multinational firm and its distribution networks. Type II industries are Mature Product Industries where technology is codified and transferable. Exports of specialized components and capital equipment to affiliates are important and the parent firm exports finished products to smaller, fragmented markets. However, foreign affiliates of the parent firm also undertake exports where they are favorably placed to do so. In the third type of industry, designated Rationalized Product Industries, the intrafirm division of labor is developed so that component specialization can take place and offshore production and assembly is undertaken, based on low labor costs in newly industrializing countries. Resource based industries' (Type IV) trade is dominated by the export of raw materials or semiprocessed intermediate products from countries with large endowments of raw materials to more developed countries for finishing and marketing. Type V industries, Trading Services, are international wholesale and retail operations, confined to more advanced countries and newly industrializing countries. Here a large volume of finished products is either exported or imported by the parent company. Finally, in Type VI, Nontradable Services, no trade in intermediate products takes place.

Casson makes the point that analysis of intrafirm trade statistics is hazardous if aggregations are made without regard to the mix of products and the type of intrafirm trade. This strongly suggests that a case by case, firm or industry analysis is necessary to establish the amount and nature of intrafirm trade and, therefore, to trace the development of intrafirm division of labor.

Internationalization and Globalization Models

Two parallel, yet distinct, models of the development of foreign market servicing strategies over time are the internationalization model, developed largely in Scandinavia[2] and used in European-based studies and the globalization model, developed largely in U.S. business schools and used in models of international business strategy.[3]

The internationalization models, as a generic type, suggest an incremental approach to foreign markets: "deepening involvement" or "creeping incrementalism" being terms used to describe a step-by-step penetration of foreign markets or foreign market segments. This contrasts with the more grandiose, planned globalization of U.S. Porter-type models.

The cautious evolutionary model has been widely applied to small and medium-sized companies, often those investing abroad for the first time (Buckley, Newbould, and Thurwell 1987; Buckley, Berkova, and Newbould 1983). The reaction to risk and uncertainty is a primary determinant of this cautious approach—determining being influenced by the time taken to collect appropriate information, a phenomenon well described by Aharoni (1966). This information gathering and the biased search implied by the managerial literature has a cost implication. The costs of managerial time are a major constraint on the smaller firm planning an effective foreign market servicing strategy. An effective model of market servicing should include such costs.

The applicability and relevance of this model should clearly be limited in scope. Young (1987: 39) suggests that "rapidly changing high technology sectors" should be an exception because the time scale to foreign manufacture should be shortened. The phenomenon of shortening product life cycles was noted by Giddy (1978) ten years ago. Industries with rapid competitor reaction are also an exception as are industries dominated by firms capable of global scanning.

Alternatively, how widely applicable is the globalization model? In its pure form, with implications of a global product, standardized marketing techniques and centralized control, the answer is probably not many sectors, industries, or product divisions conform to a homogeneous worldwide strategy. Perhaps the model is an idealized view of the market servicing policies at the opposite end of the spectrum of size and international experience from naive first time investors? (It is also not without its normative elements). National markets in many areas remain firmly idiosyncratic. The focus on successful multinational leads us to ignore the many failed attempts to impose a foreign, international, or global product on an unwilling national market. Moreover, the existence of market niches leaves global marketers vulnerable to competitors' nonstandardized products.

Table 4–1
Schematic Representation of the Structure and Content of Foreign Trade in Six Industries

From	To			
	Source Country	Other Developed	Newly Industrializing Country	Undeveloped
I. New product industry				
Source country	—	Finished products	—	—
Other developed	—	—	—	—
Newly industrializing country	—	—	—	—
Developing	—	—	—	—
II. Mature product industry				
Source country	—	Key components and capital goods	Finished products	Finished products
Other developed	—	—	Finished products	Finished products
Newly industrializing country	—	—	—	—
Developing	—	—	—	—
III. Rationalized product industry				
Source country	—	Key components and capital goods	Key components and capital goods	Finished products
Other developed	Key components and capital	—	Key components and capital	Finished products
Newly industrializing country	Finished products	Finished products	—	Finished products
Developing	—	—	—	—

IV. Resource-based industry				
Source country	—	Finished products	Finished products	—
Other developed	—	—	—	—
Newly industrializing country	—	—	—	—
Developing	Raw materials and semiprocessed materials	—	—	—
V. Trading services				
Source country	—	Finished products	Finished products	—
Other developed	Finished products	—	Finished products	—
Newly industrializing country	Finished products	Finished products	—	—
Developing	—	—	—	—
VI. Nontradable services				
Source country	—	—	—	—
Other developed	—	—	—	—
Newly industrializing country	—	—	—	—
Developing	—	—	—	—

Source: Reproduced from Casson 1986. *Multinational and World Trade.* London: Unwin Hyman.

A more cautious version of the globalization model is now the norm. Porter's recent work (1986) suggests that there is not a single global strategy (Young 1987). Rather a strategy is constrained by the value chain (vertical integration), configuration (location costs of interrelated activities internalized within the firm), and coordination issues. This leads to a typology of global strategies. A related categorization by White and Poynter (1984) distinguishes the types of integration among networks of foreign affiliates (miniature replica, marketing satellites, rationalized manufacture, product specialist, strategic independent) which have much in common with Casson's typology in table 4–1.

Strategy Considerations

There remains a final consideration in the time series analysis of market servicing policy. This is the issue of management discretion. How far are such policies the result of planned management decision making and how far are they market determined? Further, does planning extend to an overview of foreign market servicing or are decisions made on an ad hoc basis taking each market separately, producing incremental decisions with no strategic overview? What is the value of an overall coordinated market servicing policy? This links closely with the centralization versus decentralization debate on decision making within multinationals (Brooke 1984) and brings in to the calculus the organizational structure of decision making in such firms.

A final challenge is to encompass coalition behavior—see relevant readings in Porter (1986) or cooperative strategies (Buckley and Casson 1987)—into models of market servicing.

The Impact on Competitiveness

Given a crude definition of competitiveness, "delivering the right product, at the right time to the right place under the right conditions," why should we expect the method of market servicing to influence competitiveness?

It is clear that an optimal choice of market servicing strategy can (1) reduce costs, (2) more adequately meet demand conditions, (3) improve intelligence and information gathering on the target market, and (4) provide a crucial competitive weapon.

Cost Reduction

Choice of the optimal mode of market servicing can reduce costs by providing cheaper inputs and by reducing marketing outlays. A crucial relationship here is between the sourcing network of the firm (where inputs are drawn from) and the market servicing network. The evolution of these two sets of relationships over time needs to be balanced and coordinated.

Adaptation to Local Demand Conditions

Market servicing must be designed to relate to local demand conditions as closely as possible. Here, fine tuning within modes may be as important as between modes.

Improved Intelligence and Information Gathering

Market servicing modes are not one-way transmitters of goods and services, they are also receptors of information on markets, technologies, and competitors. The choice of market servicing mode has a crucial role to play in this imbibing of information. The function of foreign investments as trading posts is well established and sensitivity to local market conditions is a crucial attribute of any successful market servicing policy.

Market Servicing Policies as a Competitive Weapon:
A Question of Timing

Formal models of market servicing often fail to encompass the crucial features of the competitive process. In this, as in all dynamic phenomena, the timing of strategic moves is crucial. Competitiveness depends not only on making the right strategic moves, but also on making them at the right time. This is a difficult process to model.

The preceding theoretical frameworks have a limited dynamic content and it is in this direction which theory must develop to encompass the complexities of market servicing strategies. Interaction with competitors' moves also may need to be treated more explicitly.

A further positive feedback mechanism from market servicing policies to competitiveness may arise from reverse transfer; that is, learning or skills derived from foreign experience which improve products or operations internationally. Examples of such reverse transfer are extant in research on European direct investment in Japan (Buckley, Mirza, and Sparkes 1987).

Implications for Management

The theoretical literature on market servicing contains important implications for decisionmakers within enterprises.

First, the foreign market servicing decision is a key element in acquiring and retaining a competitive edge. An appropriate mix of market servicing tools enables a company to cut costs, to keep in close touch with demand conditions and to keep ahead of competitors. It is, therefore, worthy of top management attention. Indeed, it is only at the level of top management that market servicing decisions can be taken and a coherent policy formulated.

Second, the foreign market servicing policy of a company needs constant monitoring and fine tuning. Changes in cost conditions and demand conditions in particular foreign markets and the policies of competitors must be monitored. An intelligence gathering system on the key indicators must be carefully integrated into the policy-making framework. Marginal adjustments to market servicing strategies can be very important and within-type shifts (e.g. from a distributor to an agent with exporting or from a sales subsidiary to a production subsidiary) can be as important as between-type shifts.

Third, interrelations and complementarities between policies in different national markets and between types of market servicing must be noted and acted on. A foreign investment in country or market A may enable country or market B to be serviced by that facility, thus reducing exports from the home base, for example. The myriad of interdependencies of this type in large multinational companies form the basis for a true global strategy, based on incremental adjustment of policies toward markets, coordinated centrally but driven by local conditions. (This approach contrasts greatly with more grandiose, standardized global strategies that fit few cases). Similarly, a foreign investment has all kinds of implications for exporting from the parent company—in some cases it substitutes for the exports of final goods but encourages the export of semifinished or other intermediate products. These interdependencies must be built into the planning process.

Fourth, the dynamic environment of the world economy must be recognized. At any one time, the pattern of market servicing is a snapshot of a changing process. No market servicing pattern can be perfect and were it to be so it would rapidly become imperfect! The policies are not entirely under management's control. The pull of changes in demand and cost conditions gives market servicing a dynamic of its own which should not be ignored. It is a fallacy to believe that a strategy can be imposed, rather, sensitive response and anticipation of trends is the appropriate stance. Modeling of these processes is extremely difficult as the earlier theoretical sections show. Consequently, the large element of judgment in formulating strategies is likely to remain because of the uncertainties surrounding the key variables which drive market servicing strategies.

This leads to the final point which is that although exact modeling of the market servicing decision is difficult, there are broad rules or indicators that can be followed in designing a strategy. The growth of demand in a particular market, the relevant costs (1) of production, which are largely location dependent; (2) of distribution and marketing; and (3) transactions costs influencing the mode of market servicing can be monitored and built into the international corporate plan. Product innovation and development can be coordinated with a planned attack on particular markets and market segments. It is essential that past experience and knowledge of individual markets and methods that have proved successful elsewhere be drawn on in the formulation of today's policies. By reference to the key variables, internal knowledge of product development within the company, past experience, and clear company objectives, a market servicing policy can be designed to enhance competitiveness.

Conclusion

Theoretical models of foreign market servicing require consolidation and need the clarification of certain important issues as well as more careful specification. There are grounds for the belief that the choice of the optimal mode of servicing a foreign market can have a significant impact on the firm's international competitive situation through cost reduction, increased sensitivity to local demand conditions, improved intelligence, and an improvement in competitive posture.

Empirical verification of the links between competitiveness and market servicing is required as is the production and testing of a tractable theoretical model.

Notes

1. Vernon.

"As long as the marginal production cost plus the transport cost of the goods exported from the United States is lower than the average cost of prospective production in the market of import, United States producers will presumably prefer to avoid an investment. But that calculation depends on the producer's ability to project the cost of production in a market in which factor costs and the appropriate technology differ from those at home." (Dunning, ed. 1972: 313).

2. A selection of references are: Carlson (1975); Johanson and Vahlne (1977); Luostarinen (1978); Welch and Wiedersheim-Paul (1980a, b); Wiedersheim-Paul (1972); Cavusgil (1972); Juul and Walters (1987).

3. References are available in Porter (1986b).

4. Previous versions of this chapter were given at the European Institute for Advanced Studies in Management (EIASM) Conference on Internationalization and Competition, Brussels, June 11–12, 1987, and at the Marketing Education Group (MEG) Conference, University of Warwick, July 7–10, 1987. The author is grateful to the participants of both conferences for their comments.

This chapter is part of a three-year project at the University of Bradford Management Centre on "The Foreign Market Servicing Strategies and Competitiveness of British Firms" funded by the Economic and Social Council (ESRC) (Grant F 20250027).

References

Aharoni, Y. 1966. *The foreign investment decision process.* Boston: Harvard Graduate School of Business.

Aliber, R.Z. 1970. A theory of foreign direct investment. In *The international firm,* ed. C.P. Kindleberger. Cambridge, Mass.: MIT Press.

Brooke, M.Z. 1984. *Centralization and autonomy.* Eastbourne, England: Holt, Rinehart and Winston.

Buckley, P.J. 1982. The role of exporting in the market servicing policies of multinational manufacturing enterprises: theoretical and empirical perspectives. In *Export management,* eds. M.R. Czinkota and G. Tesar. New York: Praeger.

———. 1985. New Forms of International Industrial Cooperation. In Buckley and Casson. *The economic theory of the multinational enterprise.*

Buckley, Peter J.; Berkova, Z.; and Newbould G.D. 1983. *Direct investment in the United Kingdom by smaller European firms.* London: Macmillan.

Buckley, Peter J. and Casson, M. 1976. *The future of the multinational enterprise.* London: Macmillan.

———. 1985. *The economic theory of the multinational enterprise: Selected readings.* London: Macmillan.

———. 1985a. The optimal timing of a foreign direct investment. In Buckley and Casson. *The economic theory of the multinational enterprise.*

———. 1987. A theory of cooperation in international business. In *Cooperative strategies in international business,* ed. F.J. Contractor and P. Lorange. Lexington, Mass.: Lexington Books.

Buckley, Peter J. and Davies, H. 1980. Foreign licensing in overseas operations: Theory and evidence from the United Kingdom. In *Technology transfer and economic development.* Greenwich, Conn.: JAI Press.

Buckley, Peter J.; Mirza, H.; and Sparkes, J.R. 1984. *European affiliates in Japan.* Tokyo: Report to the Japan Foundation.

———. 1987. Direct foreign investment in Japan as a means of market entry: The case of European firms. *Journal of Marketing Management* 2(3): 241–58.

Buckley, Peter J.; Newbould, G.; and Thurwell, J. 1987. *Foreign direct investment by smaller United Kingdom firms.* London: Macmillan.

Buckley, Peter J. and Pearce, R.D. 1979. Overseas production and exporting by the world's largest enterprises—A study in sourcing policy. *Journal of International Business Studies* 10(1): 9–20.

———. 1981. Market servicing by multinational manufacturing firms: Exporting versus foreign production. *Managerial and Decision Economics* 2(4): 229–46.

———. 1984. Exports in the strategy of multinational enterpises. *Journal of Business Research* 12(2): 209–26.

Carlson, S. 1975. *How foreign is foreign trade?* Uppsala, Sweden: University of Uppsala.

Casson, M. 1985. Multinationals and intermediate product trade in Buckley and Casson. *The economic theory of the multinational enterprise.*

———. 1986. *Multinational and world trade.* London: George Allen & Unwin.

Cavusgil, S.T. 1972. Some observations on the relevance of critical variables for internationalization stages. *Export management,* eds. M.R. Czinkota and G. Tesar. New York: Praeger.

Davies, H. 1977. Technology transfer through commercial transactions. *Journal of Industrial Economics* 26(4): 161–75.

Dunning, J.H. 1972. *The location of international firms in an enlarged EEC: An exploratory paper.* Manchester, England: Manchester Statistical Society.

———. 1972. *International Investment.* Harmondsworth, England: Penguin.

Dunning, John H.; and Buckley, P.J. 1977. International production and alternative models of trade. *Manchester School* 65(4): 392–403.

European Management Forum. 1984. Report on Industrial Competitiveness 1984. Switzerland.

Giddy, I.H. 1978. The demise of the product cycle in international business theory. *Columbia Journal of World Business* 13(1): 90–7.

Giddy, I.H., and Rugman, A.M. 1979. A model of trade, foreign direct investment and licensing. New York: Columbia University. Mimeo.

Hennart, J.F. 1986. What is internalization? *Weltwirtschaftliches Archiv.* 122(4): 791–804.

Hirsh, S. 1976. An international trade and investment theory of the firm. *Oxford: Economic Papers* 28: 258–70.

Hood, N., and Young, S. 1979. *The economics of multinational enterprise.* London: Longman.

Horst, T.O. 1971. The theory of the multinational firm—Optimal behavior under different tariff and tax rates. *Journal of Political Economy* 79(5): 1059–72.

———. 1972. Firm and industry determinants of the decision to invest abroad: An empirical study. *Review of Economics and Statistics* 54: 258–66.

———. 1974. The theory of the firm. In *Economic analysis and the multinational enterprise,* ed. John H. Dunning. London: George Allen & Unwin.

Johanson, J., and Vahlne, J.E. 1977. The internalization process of the firm—A model of knowledge development and increasing foreign market commitments. *Journal of International Business Studies* 8(1): 23–32.

Juul, M., and Walters, P.G.P. 1987. The internationalization of Norwegian firms— A study of the United Kingdom experience. *Management International Review* 27(1): 58–66.

Krugman, P.R. ed. 1986. *Strategic trade policy and the new international economics.* Cambridge, Mass.: MIT Press.

Luostarinen, R. 1978. Internationalization process of the firm. Working Papers in International Business 1978/1, Helsinki School of Economics.

———. 1980. *Internationalization of the Firm.* Helsinki School of Economics. Photocopy.

Ohmae, K. 1985. *Triad power: The coming shape of global competition.* New York: Free Press.

Porter, M.E. 1986a. Competition in global industries: A conceptual framework. In *Competition in global industries,* ed. Michael E. Porter. Boston: Harvard Business School Press.

———. 1986b. *Competition in global industries*. Boston: Harvard Business School Press.

Scherer, F.M., et al. 1975. *The economics of multi-plant operation—An international comparison study*. Cambridge, Mass.: Harvard University Press.

Simon, H., and Palder, D.M. 1987. Market entry in Japan—Some problems and solutions. *Journal of Marketing Management* 2(3): 225–39.

Vernon, R. 1966. International investment and international trade in the product cycle. *Quarterly Journal of Economics* 80: 190–207.

Welch, L., and Wiedersheim-Paul, F. 1980a. Domestic expansion—Internationalization at home. *South Carolina Essays in International Business*. University of Carolina. 2.

———. 1980b. Initial exports—A marketing failure. *Journal of Management Studies* 17(3): 333–344.

White, R.E., and Poynter, T.A. 1984. Strategies for foreign-owned subsidiaries in Canada. *Business Quarterly* Summer, pp. 59–69.

Wiedersheim-Paul, F. 1972. *Uncertainty and economic distance*. Uppsala Studies in International Business. Uppsala, Sweden: Uppsala University.

Young, S. 1987. Business strategy and the internationalization of business: Recent approaches. *Managerial and Decision Economics* 8(1): 31–40.

5
Five Organizational Typologies for Developed and Developing Nations: A Stage of Development Contingency Framework

Carl A. Rodrigues

H istorically, many multinational enterprises (MNEs) have existed in a relatively stable environment. In recent years, however, a global economy with multinational competition has evolved. To improve their firms' competitive edge in the global economy, managers of MNEs must develop a greater cross-cultural managerial perspective. This perspective should include the knowledge of how organizations and individuals in them behave and how behaviors change over time. Armed with this knowledge, managers can develop effective and efficient short- and long-range managerial strategies enabling them to reduce costly cross-cultural blunders and thus enhance their respective enterprises' competitive edge.

This chapter describes five organizational behaviors: the task orientation, the relationship or social orientation, the task and social orientation, the responsive orientation, and the scanning orientation. The general economic conditions in a nation affect the behavior of individuals, and individuals' behavior affects organizational behavior. The ideas presented in this chapter draw from the stages of economic development society passes through theory (Rostow 1967), the hierarchy of needs theory (Maslow 1943), and general organizational and behavioral theory, as well as from various other disciplines.

A foundation of these ideas is that developing nations are now importing technology from developed nations at a rapid rate (Basche and Duerr 1975). New technology has a dramatic effect on a nation's economic development (Gee 1981; Singh 1983). Technology also changes culture (Hall 1973). Basically, culture includes the economic, social, and political forms of behavior associated with humankind (Heilbroner 1962). According to Maslow (1943: 370–96), as society makes social and economic progress, new needs of employees arise. As these needs change, organizational behavior, in a broad sense, also changes.

The objective of this chapter is to provide managers of foreign investments and managers in foreign countries with a general framework for making decisions relative to the organizational behavior likely to work best in organizations at various stages of development in developed and developing countries. Ultimately, however, the decisionmaker must analyze more specifically the type of technology being exported or imported, as well as the particular economic, social, and political aspects of each individual country. To help illustrate the ideas presented in this chapter, the economic progress and some of the evolving organizational theories in the United States are used. Foreign investors and managers should be aware that the term *technology* includes organizational and managerial know-how. When developing countries import new technologies from developed countries to help with their development, these countries often import organizational and managerial know-how as well. For example, scientific management, which resulted from the Industrial Revolution, was predominant in the United States around 1900. Developing European countries eventually imported and implemented scientific management into their organizations.

Contingency Organization

Research within the past two decades or so indicates that, in establishing the appropriate organizational design, many organizations respond to their environment. The fundamental basis for organizations runs on a continuum from the classical or mechanistic approach (Taylor 1911; Weber 1947; and Fayol 1929), which tends to be efficiency- and production-oriented, to a human relations (Mayo 1933) or organic (Miner 1973) approach, which tends to be people-oriented and seeks to maximize flexibility and adaptability (Likert 1967).

Burns and Stalker (1961) found that organizations functioning in a stable environment use the mechanistic form and that organizations existing in a dynamic environment use the organic form. Woodward (1965) looked at the impact of the industry on the organizational form. She found that mass-producing firms tend to be mechanistic and that firms producing specialized or prototype goods tend to be organic.

Lawrence and Lorsch (1967) looked at the internal aspects of the organization. They found that some subunits use the organic form, for example, the marketing division, and that some subunits use the mechanistic, for example, the production division. These and other studies led to the contemporary thinking that the appropriate organization design is contingent on the situation. That is, the appropriate form, mechanistic or organic, is dictated by the environment. The environment consists of the social, cultural, legal, political, economic, competitive, supplier, and technological forces. These forces generally influence organizational behavior (Carlisle 1973: 29). For example, the sociocultural factors, which include the prevailing attitudes, values, and customs of a culture, influence the organizational form. Culturally, some individuals prefer a structured form and others prefer an organic form.

Another present thought on organization typology is the matrix approach. This form aims to attain a balance between functional and departmental bases (Daft 1983: 237). The objective of the matrix form is to maximize the strengths and minimize the weaknesses of both the mechanistic and organic designs. Another contemporary idea on organizational design deals with uncertainty and information processing. This type of organization receives, processes, and acts on information to achieve performance. A basis of this typology is that the faster change occurs, the greater the requirement for information and the greater the necessity for flexible and innovative organizational design (Galbraith, 1982: 5-25).

Many of these contemporary theories can be applied mainly in the more developed, more educated, wealthier nations. For example, in discussing the uncertainty and information processing approach just described, Galbraith (1977) suggested that the need for information can be reduced by creating "slack resources" or by creating "self-contained units." Creating slack resources means stockpiling materials and personnel, thus enabling an organization to respond to uncertainty. Many organizations in the poorer, less-developed nations lack the ability to stockpile. Creating a self-contained unit means providing each unit with its own personnel, marketing, and manufacturing; that is, by decentralizing. Generally, young organizations in less-developed nations cannot apply a decentralized approach to management; this is because young, growth-oriented organizations are normally managed by a strong leader who centralizes decision making (Greiner 1972: 37–46; and Mintzberg 1973: 44–53). Individual behavior in many of the poorer, less-developed nations is likely to generate a structured organizational behavior; individuals in those nations often prefer a mechanistic-oriented approach, especially if they are seeking to sastisfy their lower-level needs. Also, individuals in less-developed countries tend to lack the education required to function effectively in advanced forms of organization. Therefore, the structured form generally works best in those nations.

For example, Hofstede (1980) researched national differences in work related value patterns in forty countries. One of the values was power distance. Power distance, as a characteristic of a culture defines the "extent to which the less powerful person in a society accepts inequality in power and considers it normal" (Hofstede 1984: 390). The study revealed that the less-developed nations studied tended to have a large power distance, that is, subordinates have strong dependency needs and expect superiors to behave autocratically. On the other hand, the study revealed that the more-advanced nations tended to have a smaller power distance, that is, subordinates usually expect participation or at least consultation (Hofstede 1984: 394).

The study also revealed that less-developed societies tend to be collectivist or group-oriented, and the more developed societies tend to be individualist-oriented. People in individualistic societies place task before relationship and individuals in collectivist societies consider the group more important than the task. The type of organizational behavior that a foreign investor or a foreign manager applies in a foreign country is, therefore, contingent on many factors, including the stage of development.

Foundation for this Chapter

A foundation for the ideas presented in this chapter is the economic environment. The economic environment has an effect on the industry, the organization, and on the individual. During difficult economic times, organizations become more task-oriented and individuals in such an environment are generally more willing to accept authoritarian or paternalistic organizational behavior. During prosperous times, individuals prefer a more organic- participative- relationship-oriented form (Stoken 1980: 14–18). However, as previously indicated, some individuals culturally prefer the structured orientation and others prefer the organic form, regardless of the situation. And, there are leaders who prefer an authoritarian, structured form, regardless of the situation.

As it was pointed out earlier, the introduction of new technology into a nation affects its economic development dramatically (Gee 1981; Singh 1983); it also changes the nation's culture (Hall 1973: 85). Culture influences an organization's social, political, and economic systems. Therefore, when a nation's culture is changed, the other systems are likely to change as well. Maslow (1943: 370–96) suggested that as society makes social and economic progress, new needs of employees arise. This implies that as nations progress, new organizational forms are required. Hofstede (1984: 395) has observed that cultures change over time from collectivism to individualism and that the change occurs after an increase of wealth in those countries.

Maslow's Hierarchy of Needs Theory

Maslow's theory proposes that certain individual needs serve as motivators. He contended that individuals are first motivated by activities satisfying their basic needs. Once these needs are reasonably satisfied, they seek to satisfy the next level, their safety needs. Subsequently, they satisfy the next higher level, their social needs. Once the social needs are reasonably satisfied, the individuals satisfy their esteem needs, the next higher level of needs. And once these are reasonably satisfied, they satisfy their self-actualization needs, which, according to Maslow, is the highest level of the needs hierarchy.

Maslow's theory has not been empirically verified. In fact, it has been widely criticized. Such terms as *belonging* and *esteem* are vague. The meaning of satisfaction is unclear. For example, after a big meal an individual may be full; he or she, however, has a memory and the ability to anticipate the future when hunger could occur again. There is no evidence that gratification of one need activates the next higher need, and there is little support that a level of satisfaction of a need diminishes its importance as a motivator (Williams 1982: 80–81). In an international context, the hierarchy has been criticized as being based on Maslow's personal value choice—U.S. middle class values (Hofstede 1984: 396). A study by Haire, Ghiselli, and Porter (1966) concluded that workers in different cultures tend to have a different hierarchy of needs. For example, managers in the United States and Italy ranked security as being relatively less important than other needs (basic needs were omitted from the study); in India, Spain, and Germany, security ranked relatively more important. However, Hofstede has observed that culture changes rapidly; therefore, the results of the 1966 study may not be the same today.

Nevertheless, Maslow's theory does have application. There may not be a need hierarchy which applies to everyone; hierarchies do exist within individuals, however. The ability to motivate an individual depends on one's awareness of that individual's need hierarchy. Maslow's proposition about how needs become active may lack validity; however, within certain persons some needs are more active than others. The motivational appeals should thus be to the active needs. Hungry employees, for example, may not be motivated to increase productivity by the anticipation of challenging work; they may, however, be motivated by the anticipation of higher wages that they could use to buy food. Also, one should expect shifts and changes in needs, and therefore vary motivational appeals, fitting them to individuals as much as possible (Williams 1982: 91). What this suggests is that the progression of organizational behavior established in this chapter does not necessarily apply to all nations. However, it also suggests that as a nation progresses economically, change in organizational behavior can generally be expected. It is a matter of identifying the nation's broad scheme and applying the appropriate organizational typology—bearing in mind that, ultimately, the immediate environment must also be considered in establishing the appropriate organizational typology.

Stages of Economic Development Society Passes Through

Rostow (1967: 11) developed a theory that society passes through five stages of economic development. The first stage is "the stage of traditional society." At this stage there is little hope for economic progress and agriculture is the greater part of a nation's resources. The traditional society operates on past societal precepts; technology is basically static, occupations are passed down from one generation to the next, and social and economic systems remain fundamentally closed to change (Heilbroner 1962: 10–16). Stage two is "the establishment of preconditions for takeoff." To break out, entrepreneurs in finance and manufacturing are required and the government must invest in changing the nation's infrastructure. In the third stage, takeoff begins. Investments rise; manufacturing becomes a leading growth sector; political, social, and institutional structures are transformed to help sustain the rate of growth. Stage four is "the drive to maturity." The most advanced technology available is used. At stage five, high mass consumption occurs. Emphasis is given to production of consumer goods and services aiding the greater part of the nation's population to attain a relatively high level of living.

As in the case of Maslow's theory, Rostow's theory is not without its critics. The stages are not readily distinguishable from one another in practice. Empirically, testable characteristics are not displayed. The dynamic characteristics that generate movement from one stage to another are not readily identifiable. Rostow's theory is confusing as to whether agricultural improvements are achieved as part of the takeoff or whether they must occur before a society can enter the preconditions for takeoff, or whether they are attained as part of the takeoff. The theory does not consider foreign trade, and the suggested time frame from stage to stage applies only to a few industrialized countries; it cannot be generalized across many of today's less-developed countries. Notwithstanding the criticism of the theory, it is a very useful framework for analysis. There is no doubt that the theory is here to stay (Stoever 1985: 4).

The fifth organizational typology discussed in this chapter is speculative. This is because it is tied to the speculative postindustrial society—a stage of development that many individuals feel some advanced nations, such as the United States, Japan, and a few West European countries, are on the threshold of entering. In the postindustrialized society, it is expected that individuals will exist in a state of instability and uncertainty, and that change becomes a way of life. In this society, levels of affluence, education, and leisure are high. This society requires new organizational, political, and cultural values (Trist 1970). Figure 5–1 illustrates the relationship between organizational typology, the stages of economic development, and the hierarchy of needs. The objective of figure 5–1 is not to show exact relationships; rather, it is to show that there is a relationship, that is, change in one generates change in another. The following sections explain the relationship.

Type One: The Task-Oriented Organization

The Industrial Revolution brought new technology to the United States in the late 1800s; this technology caused social, political, and economic changes

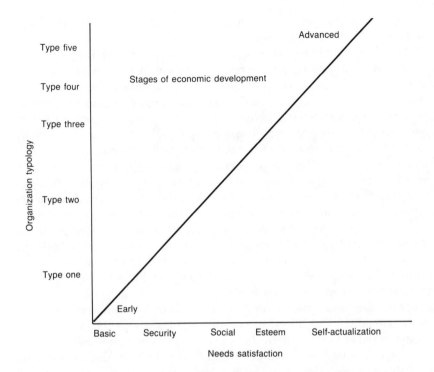

Figure 5–1. Organization Typologies, Hierarchy of Needs, and the Stages of Economic Development

(see White 1965; and Morrow 1975). The U.S. political system changed to the extent that government began becoming heavily involved in economic and other matters. This would relate to stage two of Rostow's theory. The social system changed: Individuals began urbanizing—which also affected the political structure—and they became less self-sufficient than they had been in the agrarian economy. The economic system changed; greater wealth began emerging. A result of the greater wealth and individuals' declining self-sufficiency was that society placed a demand on enterprises to increase productivity. Around 1900, scientific management pioneers, such as Frederick W. Taylor (1911), sought to determine how productivity could be increased. He proposed rearranging the task as a way to increase productivity. Taylor also proposed the differential piece rate approach whereby employees producing more than a set amount of units, would be paid for the excess units at a higher rate. The philosophy at that time was if employees produced more, they would benefit more. More pay would enable individuals to better satisfy their basic and security needs. The movement has been criticized as being too mechanistic-oriented; that is, managers were concerned mainly with the task and production and treated people as if they were machines—the social aspects of individuals were ignored.

Many U.S. individuals were no longer self-sufficient and living in masses caused poor conditions for a great number of them; if Maslow's theory were applied to that situation, many of those individuals would be motivated to satisfy their basic and security needs. The task-oriented organization philosophy predominant at the time seems to have worked well economically for the United States because prosperity began rising rapidly. It satisfied individuals' basic, and to some extent, security needs fairly well. The proposition here is that if a nation is in a stage where economic progress is little, and if the nation begins industrializing, the most appropriate form of organization is likely to be an authoritarian- paternalistic task-oriented one. If people in that country are hungry, based on Maslow's theory, they are likely not to be seeking to satisfy their higher level needs. These individuals are likely to prefer an efficiency-oriented approach aiming to maximize production to enable the greatest possible number of individuals to satisfy their lower level needs. This organizational typology is not likely to be resisted by individuals who are hungry and confronted with new technology. New technology often generates conditions of uncertainty in an organization. Where there is uncertainty, individuals generally prefer directive, task-oriented leadership (Halpin 1954).

As pointed out earlier, individuals in economically poorer countries tend to accept centralized power more so than individuals in the economically wealthier countries. Also, individuals in economically poorer countries tend to be more collectivistic, that is, they place relationship before task more so than individuals in economically wealthier countries. This should not be taken to mean that all collectivistic societies are less productive than individualistic societies. For example, Japan is a collectivist society more productive than most individualistic cultures. So that the group may benefit more, Japanese workers are motivated to produce more.

Type Two: The Relationship- or
Social-Oriented Organization

As the new technology takes root, the nation begins prospering economically and individuals generally become adapted to the technology. Once individuals become adapted to the new technology, they are likely to feel more competent. Once an individual feels competent, he or she usually prefers a less structured form of leadership and less leader direction (Filley, House, and Kerr 1976). According to Maslow's theory, after an individual's basic and safety needs are reasonably satisfied, that individual's social needs begin to motivate. In this situation, an organization that motivates its employees by placing greater emphasis on their social needs is likely to work best.

The efficiency aspects of the U.S. scientific management movement did produce great wealth from which the workers benefitted greatly; they also created many problems, however. The task-oriented approach to management caused much dissatisfaction, leading many employees to join unions as a means of protecting their interests. A sort of collectivist orientation thus began evolving into a previously highly individualistic culture. The movement also provoked strong protests from humanitarians concerned with the problems of the workers. These problems led to certain events producing the "human relations movement" that emphasized concern for the social needs of people. Nonauthoritarian forms of leadership were sought (Williams 1982: 11). Whereas the effectiveness of organizations in the scientific management movement was measured by production, the effectiveness of organizations in the human relations movement was measured by the morale of the employees—high morale could increase productivity. Informal groups, which restrict productivity, evolve in structured organizations.

The Hawthorne studies (Mayo 1933) had a great influence on the human relations movement. These studies concluded that friendly supervision, a cooperative nonthreatening work environment, and the special attention given to workers increased their motivation and subsequently productivity. What this suggests is that once their basic and safety needs are adequately satisfied, individuals tend to become less tolerant of centralized power. Many organizations which adopted this philosophy found that productivity was often partially ignored, however. Nevertheless, what this means to managers in developing nations is that after the task-oriented organizations in the nation have provided for the individuals' basic and safety needs, many of those individuals are likely to prefer the relationship-oriented form of organization. It also suggests that many of those individuals will want to participate more in organizational matters or at least be consulted and involved more. Foreign investors and managers should bear in mind that many of the powerful people in organizations where these changes have taken place will not readily give up their power, therefore creating turbulence in the organization. For example, if many of the powerful people in United States organizations had been less resistant in giving up some of their powers, many of the unions in the United States probably would not have evolved so powerfully.

Type Three: Task- and
Relationship-Oriented Organizations

As nations progress in their economic development stages, new technology generates greater wealth; however, it also generates complexity, which often creates ambiguous or unclear conditions. When individuals cannot tolerate ambiguous or unclear conditions—which is the case in most cultures—they generally prefer that leadership provide much structure (Burack 1975). On the other hand, applying Maslow's theory, an individual whose social needs have been reasonably satisfied seeks to satisfy self-esteem needs; the individual wants greater opportunities and more challenging work, as well as greater recognition.

Responding to technological changes in the 1950s in the United States, the behavioral science movement, for example, came into major focus in the 1960s. The philosophy was that organizations could not ignore production, that is, the task, nor could they ignore the social aspects of individuals. The movement thus sought to integrate both aspects into organization philosophy. For example, Blake and Mouton (1964) developed a concept proposing that managers ought to strive toward a leadership style where there is both a strong task and relationship orientation. Likert (1967) developed "the linking-pin" concept of organization, where there is strong vertical and horizontal communication in the organization.

The concept of management by objectives (MBO) also came into focus (see Raia 1974). In MBO together the subordinate and the superior establish those objectives the subordinate will accomplish. These approaches allow managers to remain production-oriented; at the same time by involving the subordinates in the decision-making process, they can help satisfy their higher needs. As nations progress in their development stages by adopting more complex technologies, managers of organizations in those nations need to change the organization philosophy accordingly. As organizations become more complex, managers often need the assistance of others in making decisions—subordinates with hands-on experience are usually valuable sources.

Foreign investors and foreign managers are cautioned that many individuals in some countries that have reached an advanced stage of economic development—for example, France and Belgium—have developed an individualistic culture while maintaining a preference for paternalistic leadership. Some countries have advanced economically, yet strong individual motivation is security-seeking—Japan, for example. Also, based on Rostow's theory, in order for a country to progress economically, the country's institutional structures are supposed to be changed. What this suggests is that countries such as France and Japan will eventually either change by becoming less paternalistic, or reach stagnancy. Indications are that both France and Japan are modifying their institutional systems, such as education, to eventually develop a less-security seeking orientation in individuals, and thus, to develop a less paternalistic system.

Type Four: The Environmental, Responsive Organization

As more nations progress in their economic development stages, and they implement new technologies, advanced nations find themselves in a more dynamic, fast-changing environment. Organizations in this environment are forced to change often; they must remain very responsive to the demands of the environment. The United States, for example, was for many years techno-logically far ahead of other nations. Firms in the United States thus enjoyed a relatively stable environment. In recent years, however, several nations have been catching up to the United States (Cateora 1983: 25). Many U.S. firms have thus been forced to change to respond to these environmental changes.

In a dynamic, changing environment, effective organizations utilize an open-systems approach (Miller and Rice 1967); they make wise use of their resources (inputs) by processing them into something useful (outputs) for society. As the outputs are placed in the environment, the effective organiza-tion changes in response to new demands from the environment. Quite often this means using different inputs and processes, which means changing insti-tutional structures.

As was stated earlier, Burns and Stalker (1961) found that organizations existing in a dynamic, changing environment use an organic form of organiza-tion. Miner (1973: 270) observed that effective organizations adapt readily to environmental changes and they are organic in nature. He listed the following characteristics of an organic organization: (1) The expectations of individuals and organizational goals bear a close and direct relationship; (2) what is expected of individuals is continually redefined through discussion; (3) the response of "it's not my responsibility" as an excuse for failure is rejected; (4) individuals want to contribute to the larger organization without having to always receive specific inducements for accomplishing specific tasks; (5) the needed information at the appropriate places in the organization is available; (6) there is horizontal communication, that is, peers take care of problems without orders from above; and (7) rather than maintaining what already exists, individuals are committed to goals that further the organization. An individualistic culture such as the United States is likely to encounter consider-able resistance to the organic form of organization. This is because of the strong self orientation individuals in this culture possess. Collectivist cultures are likely to be more adaptable to this form because of their members' concern for the group's well-being.

This organization would be functional when a great many of its em-ployees are motivated by the pursuit of their upper level needs. For example, when they are motivated by the need for recognition. As more and more indi-viduals are developed in the Type Three organization, this is likely to be the situation in the Type Four environment. As developed nations begin encoun-tering heavy competition from developing nations lagging a bit behind, man-agers in those nations have to change the organization typology accordingly; they have to change their institutional structure. Some social theorists have proposed that organizations in the United States might be more in tune with the times if individuals were taken out of their individual offices and placed together in a single area. This would develop group cohesiveness. Individuals in organizations usually organize informally to satisfy certain needs which the formal organization cannot satisfy. For example, reduction of tension and fear, reduction of boredom, and improved communication. In these groups, informal leaders emerge. The informal leaders perform the roles of representative to management, technical expert, information source, the enforcer of group norms and values, the tension reducer, and the crisis manager (Williams 1982: 127–33). Policies and change introduced formally are often sabotaged.

If there is proper communication between the formal managers and the informal leaders, strong support for new policies and change can often be generated because there is less resistance to change. Greiner (1972) has proposed that organizations eventually grow to such a size that the structured form of management becomes ineffective. He suggested that at this point social control and self-discipline take over from formal control. The Japanese, with a strong group orientation, are very productive. Americans, on the other hand, with a very strong individualistic orientation, are very innovative. The effective manager thus seeks a balance between the individual and the group orientation.

Type Five: The Scanning-Oriented Organization

As more and more nations progress along their economic development stages and reach the postindustrial stage, individuals exist in a state of instability and change becomes a way of life. When affluence, education, and leisure are high, individuals generally seek to satisfy their upper-level needs. The scanning-oriented organization has an innovating capability and a huge capacity for global scanning (Vernon 1985: 20). Due to technological advancements, global communication becomes relatively inexpensive; information is digested and interpreted at low cost; market ignorance or uncertainty is no longer attributed to distance; markets, regardless of their locations, have an equal opportunity to stimulate firms to innovate and produce. The global-oriented organization is in a position to service any market in which it is aware that a demand for a product or service exists (Vernon 1985: 21). This organization monitors the environment and based on the information gathered, when it predicts that incomes and demands will rise in a certain market, it innovates and produces for that market.

The uncertainty and the rate of change in the environment are so extensive that continuous information processing and coordination in both vertical and horizontal directions are essential in many organizations. The matrix (Daft 1983) and the uncertainty and information processing (Galbraith 1977, 1982) approaches discussed earlier are applied in the scanning-oriented organization. These approaches are appropriate when the task environment of the organization is complex and uncertain, and external changes are frequent (Davis and Lawrence 1977: 11–24). The scanning-orientation resembles the cybernetic form. In the cybernetic form, a central unit continuously monitors the system and acts—either reactively or proactively—as the situation requires it; politics and bureaucracy diminish, however (Schick 1971: 214–33).

Because it is challenging and professionalism is high, this organization generally satisfies individuals' upper-level needs. The need for structured leadership which uncertainty has stimulated in the past is mitigated because information is quickly compiled to reduce uncertainty and ambiguity and because individuals in the organization have been institutionalized to cope with change more rapidly than individuals in organizations in an earlier stage of development.

Conclusion

The proposition in this chapter is that the introduction of new technology into a nation changes that nation's sociocultural, economic, and political systems. Therefore, as a nation progresses through its economic development stages and new technology is introduced, the level of individuals' needs and the organizational typology in that nation—in a broad sense—change. Figure 5–1 illustrates the relationship between organizational typology, the stages of economic development nations pass through, and the hierarchy of needs. As it was pointed out earlier, the objective of figure 5–1 is not to depict exact relationships; rather, it is to show that there tends to be some relationship. For example, individuals in poorer, early development nations that have begun industrializing, are likely to be motivated by activities to satisfy their lower-level needs. Therefore, a centralized organization orientation with major emphasis on task and efficiency, that is, major emphasis on producing goods to satisfy those needs, is likely to work best. On the other end of the spectrum, individuals in economically advanced nations are likely to be motivated by activities to satisfy their upper-level needs. These upper-level individual needs may be different from one culture to another. In any case, an organizational typology that satisfies those needs would work best. According to Greiner's (1972: 37–46) theory of the evolution of organizations, in the early stage of organizational growth, centralized leadership works best; however, as the organization grows, individuals in the organization eventually want autonomy—which can, in a general sense, be equated with the satisfaction of the upper-level needs. Many individuals in some cultures may prefer centralized paternalistic leadership even after the nation has advanced economically. Because new technology changes culture, individual needs in these cultures eventually change.

Not all nations progress at the same rate. The speed of development is contingent on many factors, including the economic conditions, the leaders, and the people in the nation. Rogers (1962) indicated that the diffusion of technology process is influenced by the nature of four major, interrelated constructs: (1) the innovation, (2) relevant social systems, (3) time, and (4) communications about the innovation.

Organizations in a country adopt new ideas at a different rate. Rogers and Shoemaker (1971) categorized the adopters of any innovation into five groups, according to the order they adopt the innovation. The order is as follows: the innovators, the early adopters, the early majority, the late majority, and the laggards. The innovators are venturesome, thus they readily try new ideas. The early adopters eventually adopt new ideas, and as opinion leaders, they influence others to use a new idea. The early majority is characterized by their ability for deliberation, they adopt the new idea only after other respected individuals have done so. The late majority tends to be skeptical, and they proceed only after public opinion strongly favors the new idea. Laggards generally take the past and traditions as their point of reference; generally older, they tend to be suspicious of new ideas. What this suggests is that a new organizational typology is accepted first by innovation-oriented organizations and subsequently by other organizations. This also suggests that organizations with similar objectives and subject to the same environmental changes may use different typologies at the same time.

Some nations have internal environments enabling them to adopt new technology faster than other nations. Therefore, their development is likely to occur at a faster pace. It is not improbable that some social systems may totally reject innovation and thus never take off. Such systems are likely to eventually become extinct, however.

As some individuals can bypass a level or levels in their hierarchy of needs, some nations may possibly be able to bypass a stage or stages of development. For example, the oil-rich, less-developed nations may be able to afford advanced technology to help them bypass some of the stages of development, or at least to help them progress through the stages much more quickly. To reiterate, the objective of this chapter is mainly to provide a framework for analysis to foreign investors and managers in foreign countries relative to the type of organization likely to work best in a country at a certain stage of development. It also suggests that as a country progresses economically, the motivational needs of individuals in organizations are likely to change, and that the type of organizational behavior required to satisfy those needs changes. Foreign investors and foreign managers are again cautioned that this is a general concept and not a necessary condition in all situations. Investors and managers thus need to analyze each situation individually.

By considering each situation, managers can develop managerial strategies appropriate for that situation. Developing and implementing suitable strategies reduces costly cross-cultural managerial mistakes. Fewer mistakes are likely to improve a firm's competitive edge in the global economy.

References

Basche, J.R., and Duerr, M.G. 1975. *International transfer of technology: A world-survey of executives.* New York: The Conference Board.

Blake, R.R., and Mouton, J.S. 1964. *The managerial grid.* Houston: Gulf Publishing.

Burack, E. 1975. *Organizational analysis: Theory and application.* (Hinsdale, Ill.: Dryden Press.

Burns, T., and Stalker, G.M. 1961. *The management of innovation.* London: Tavistock.

Carlisle, H.M. 1973. *Situational management.* New York: American Management Associations.

Cateora, P.R. 1983. *International marketing.* Homewood, Ill.: Richard D. Irwin.

Daft, R.L. 1983. *Organization theory and design.* St. Paul, Minn.: West Publishing.

Davis, S.M., and Lawrence, P.R. 1977. *Matrix.* Reading, Mass.: Addison-Wesley.

Fayol, H. 1929. *General and industrial management,* trans. J.A. Conbrough. Geneva: International Management Institute.

Filley, A.C.; House, R; and Kerr, S. 1976. *Managerial process and organizational behavior,* 2d ed. Glenview, Ill.: Scott, Foresman.

Galbraith, J.R. 1977. Organizational Design. Reading, Mass.: Addison-Wesley.

———. 1982. Designing the innovative organization. *Organizational dynamics,* Winter, 5–25.

Gee, S. 1981. *Technology transfer, innovation, and international competitiveness.* New York: John Wiley & Sons.

Greiner, L.E. 1971. Evolution and Revolution in Organizations. *Harvard Business Review,* July–August, 37–46.

Haire, M.; Ghiselli, E.E.; and Porter, L.W. 1966. *Managerial thinking: An international study.* New York: John Wiley & Sons.

Hall, E.T. 1973. *The silent language.* New York: Doubleday/Anchor Books.

Halpin, A.W. 1954. The leadership behavior on combat performance of airline commanders. *Journal of Abnormal Psychology* 195: 19–22, 49.

Heilbroner, R.L. 1962. *The making of the economic society.* Englewood Cliffs, N.J.: Prentice-Hall.

Hofstede, G. 1980. *Culture's consequences: International differences in work related values.* Beverly Hills, Calif.: Sage Publications.

———. 1984. The cultural relativity of the quality of life concept. *Academy of Management Review* 9 (3): 390.

Lawrence, P.R., and Lorsch, J.W. 1969. *Organization and the environment* (Homewood, Ill.: Richard D. Irwin.

Likert, R. 1967. *The human organization.* New York: McGraw-Hill.

Maslow, A.H. 1943. Theory of Human Motivation. *Psychological Review,* July, 50, 370–396.

Mayo, E. 1933. *The human problems of industrial civilization.* Cambridge, Mass.: Harvard University Press.

Miller, E.J., and Rice, A.K. 1967. *Systems of organization.* London: Tavistock.

Miner, J.B. 1973. *The management process: theory, research, and practice.* New York: Macmillan.

Mintzberg, H. 1973. Strategy-making in three modes. *California Management Review,* Winter, 15, 44–53.

Morrow, W.L. 1975. *Public administration: politics and the political system.* New York: Random House.

Raia, A.P. 1974. *Management by objectives.* Glenview, Ill.: Scott, Foresman.

Rogers, E.M. 1962. *Diffusion of innovations.* New York: Free Press.

Rogers, E.M., and Shoemaker, F.F. 1971. *Communications of innovations.* New York: Free Press.

Rostow, W.W. 1967. *The stages of economic growth: A non-communist manifesto.* New York: Cambridge University Press.

Schick, A.T. 1971. Toward the cybernetic state. In *Public administration in a time of turbulence,* ed. D. Waldo. New York: Chandler Publishing.

Singh, V.N. 1983. *Technological transfer and economic development: models and practices for the developing countries.* Jersey City, N.J.: Unz and Co., Division of Scott Printing Corp.

Stoever, W.A. 1985. The stages of developing country policy toward foreign investment. *Columbia Journal of World Business,* Fall, Vol. XX, no. 3, 3–11.

Stoken, D. 1980. What the long-term cycle tells us about the 1980s: The kondratieff cycle and its effects on social psychology. *The Futurist* 14(1): 14–18.

Taylor, F.W. 1911. *The principles of scientific management.* New York: Harper & Row.

Trist, E. 1970. Urban North America: The challenge of the next thirty years (A social psychological viewpoint). In *Organization Frontiers and Human Values,* ed. Warren Schmidt. Belmont, Calif.: Wadsworth Publishing.

Vernon, R. 1985. The product cycle hypothesis in a new international environment. In *Strategic management of multinational corporations: The essentials,* eds. H.V. Wortzel and L.H. Wortzel. New York: John Wiley & Sons.

Weber, M. 1947. *The theory of social and economic organization,* trans. A.M. Henderson and T. Parsons. New York: Oxford University Press.

White, L.D. 1965. *The Republican era.* New York: Free Press.

Williams, J.C. 1982. *Human behavior in organizations.* Cincinnati: South-Western Publishing.

Woodward, J. 1965. *Industrial organization: theory and practice.* London: Oxford University Press.

Part II
Strategic Decision Making
in an International Setting

6

Challenges to Strategic Planning Processes in Multinational Corporations

Peter Lorange

Most corporations that want to remain truly excellent and to be continuously successful have little choice but to be firmly commited to the international or global perspective in their business philosophies. The alternative is that a company might slow down and become relegated to the role of a provincial national company. Loss of offensive momentum might result. Strategic planning processes can play a significant role in facilitating better global strategic management for meeting international competition. Our contention, however, is that many planning systems unfortunately fall short of offering realistic support for an effective international competitive focus.

In the following chapter we offer guidelines for strengthening strategic planning systems to cope with a global competitive strategy approach. First, we review several emerging reasons for a corporation to pay more attention to the international strategic dimension and discuss implications for the corporate strategic planning process. Second, we suggest ways in which further modification of critical management processes, not only strategic planning but also strategic control, can be achieved. The new professional roles and challenges of the corporate strategic planning department in the global firm are also reviewed in this context. Third, we discuss how the global strategizing process can be further expedited through new cooperative modes for the establishment and growth of international business activities, such as through strategic alliances and joint ventures. Finally, we close our discussion by reviewing the key implications of these international cooperative strategy forms for strategic planning. In an earlier article (Lorange 1976), we articulated several principles for delineating strategies in multinational corporations. These seem largely still valid. Additional emphasis on the issues addressed in the present article need to be added, however, to reflect the changing context of the multinationals (Chakravarthy and Perlmutter 1985). This seems particularly critical given the added intensity of international competition and the important changes in market and industry structures now facing the international firm.

Reasons for Pursuing Multinational Strategy Today and Resulting New Challenges for Strategic Planning

Let us briefly review six reasons for pursuing a multinational strategic approach on a stronger and more determined basis than before, and examine the implications that the resulting shifts in strategic focus might have on strategic planning.

Choosing Emerging Growth Opportunities on a Global Basis

The economic outlook in many countries of the world has been one of a general flattening out in terms of often no longer seeing clear, strong future growth prospects. Even so, time and again we see that there are plenty of pockets of growth opportunities that can represent very attractive business niches for successful firms of the future. These niches must be sought out systematically and carefully. The successful corporation must choose the most attractive battlegrounds for deploying its organizational energies, know-how, and capital. Without reasonable expected growth in the new business niches, and thus a reasonable potential volume for a new business investment, it will be difficult to recoup the money, time, and other efforts expended to launch sustained business self-renewal.

It will be crucial to look as broadly as possible for growth opportunities; a global view is most likely to offer the best chances—anything else would be too unnecessarily constraining. This implies that more than before the planning process must have available data bases providing inputs on a large number of countries' demographical trends and shifts, as well as sectorial economic development outlooks. Socioeconomic patterns may be fundamental in helping the proactive corporation spot good opportunities at an early stage. The global understanding of such socioeconomic scenarios or patterns, along with an overall view of demographic developments, can significantly increase the likelihood of finding good growth opportunities. To limit the planning process to assessing only the environment of one national market may unnecessarily diminish the likelihood of finding the best growth opportunities. Inceased emphasis on comparative socioeconomic analyses is called for as a way to strengthen the planning process, to enhance the picking of better growth targets (Prahalad and Doz 1987).

Establishing Relevant "Listening Posts" to Changing Customer Needs and Preferences.

No one disagrees that the world is becoming smaller, meaning that global trends in consumer preferences and needs are becoming increasingly critical. One must understand shifts in customers' attitudes on a global basis to crack these complex patterns of movement and gain a proper understanding (Levitt 1983). For instance, what is happening in the Japanese food industry with its development of new health-oriented products, say, based on new biotechnological processes? This movement can have significant impacts on U.S. and European product preferences, due to a global desire for more healthy diets. Similarly, what are the innovations in developing new total service packages to satisfy the emerging customer? Other than only narrowly developing new products, how can one get clues from observing sophisticated customers from around the world regarding what such a future, more broad-based service package might look like? One must have an overall global view on these issues to get the best possible impulses for new business concepts and developments from a balanced, leading edge sample of customers. Without such an overall understanding, a company can easily miss new opportunities, and become overly exposed to threats from taking a too confined view of what the customers' needs are. One must understand customers in the fullest sense, that is, on a global basis.

In addition to the socioeconomic data needs emphasized earlier, the planning process must also attempt to gather global intelligence regarding consumer preferences, needs, and shifts, and increasingly emphasize a comparative analysis of such data. Today many planning systems address these issues inadequately, in that the data is often provided on a bottom-up basis from each country or region. Such data is analyzed in isolation, based on an implicit assumption that the more limited country—or region—definition for what constitutes the unit for business strategy analysis might suffice. Ironically, therefore, even though much of the data may be available, frequently it is not examined and analyzed in an overall global manner. The strategic planning process should ensure that the data is lifted up one level, away from the focus of the bottom-up driven, geographically well-defined business strategy kingdoms, to get a global picture of emerging consumer preferences.

Spotting Early Technological Changes and Radical Innovations

It is, perhaps, more critical than ever to be as fully aware as possible that technological breakthroughs can take place in many parts of the world, and that such innovations increasingly can be spearheaded by players that we traditionally may not have considered as active participants in our business. This trend of a more globally dispersed innovation pattern is likely to accelerate, nontheleast due to the expansion of sophisticated basic technological bases to larger parts of the world. Who would have thought, for instance, that the People's Republic of China would be de facto competitors in the commercial space satellite launching business, with a competitive edge being held by a French-led consortium, and with the United States at least temporarily being somewhat behind as a viable competitor!

Even in businesses normally considered quite traditional from a technological perspective, there are changes. Japanese corporations, for instance, have pioneered the application of bioengineering for new ways of manufacturing of foods. Many new packaging concepts have revolutionized the world, some of them initially coming from small European markets, such as the Swedish (now Swiss) Tetrapak Group. Critical technological innovations must be spotted early and integrated into a company's own business approach when possible, to create a new business opportunity and help ameliorate a potential threat. An attitude of isolationist indifference in this respect can be dangerous; to counteract such moves requires early action when the options are still available.

This challenge to strategic planning must be met by strengthening the emphasis on global scanning of new technological developments, applied to monitoring technologies at large, not only to what one's traditional competitors seem to be doing. The challenge to strategic planning is thus to allow for such points of emphasis to take place, not to let it be suppressed within a dominating classical competitive product-market driven planning context. Important in this context would be the inclusion of technologists from around the world in one's creative planning team discussions on a broader basis. One way of achieving this might be to create networks of contacts with outside organizations such as universities and independent scientists. Other approaches might include the creation of technology advisory boards. Thus, businesses must have a multitude of channels established to be able to determine the critical technological issues and to be able to pursue these.

Strengthening the Ability to Fight Increasingly Global and Universal Competitors

Increasingly, in many industries a relatively small number of corporations compete against one another on a more or less global basis. Competitors must understand the global strategies of these companies and interpret their country-based moves in this global context. To look at competition simply on a country-by-country basis, as it pops up from market to market, without understanding the underlying, unifying dimensions that might explain a particular company's global behavior, can easily give an incomplete picture. Counteracting global competitors on a global basis prevents them from having an excessively strong competitive advantage. To fight such competitors only in one's own home markets is becoming increasingly difficult, given the resources this global competitor typically can muster (Doz 1986).

International corporations may be ready to exhibit more flexibility than traditionally has been the case in involving themselves in new businesses. For instance, we might see pharmaceutical or chemical firms enter into the consumer food business, based on their know-how in bioengineering. The entry of new competitors from less-than-obviously traditionally related business areas should provide another strong incentive to keep a close eye on global competitors. There may be some unpleasant surprises if such new entrants are allowed to move on their own for too long.

Analysis of key competitors on a global basis must consequently be part of the strengthening of the strategic planning process. Assessment of what can create global competitive advantages, not only in the more traditional economies of scale factors upstream in the value-chain, but also much more important sources for gaining downstream economies of scope, should be done for a relatively broadly defined set of competitors. Too narrowly defined competitive analysis on a bottom-up, country-by-country basis will probably not suffice. It is important in this context to establish an understanding of which global strategic advantages each major competitor is attempting to create, upstream as well as downstream. This in turn might allow one's strategic planning to come up with responses that are meaningful, not only in a more narrowly focused sense, say by responding in a given country, but also to ensure that this response fits into a globally coordinated pattern of responses across countries. Without such an overall appreciation of the global master plans of the competitors, it is easy to end up fighting strategic battles against competitors on the wrong fronts. It is critical, therefore, that the strategic process allows for competitor assessments on a global basis, not only on the basis of bottom-up, country-by-country competitive analysis.

Establishing and Taking Advantage of Global Upstream
or Downstream Strategic Thrusts

In the previous paragraph we discussed how to strengthen the strategic planning process to defensively meet global offenses from competitors. In this section, we discuss how to offensively take the initiative in creating global strategic advantages, upstream and/or downstream.

Let us begin by discussing in more detail one aspect of the challenge of establishing global downstream competitive advantages, namely the potential benefits from global brand names. Brand names are, of course, difficult, expensive, and time-consuming to establish. It is particularly challenging, but also potentially more rewarding, to establish global brand names. Brand names can be used in several ways to gain competitive advantages. They can play a key role in facilitating and leveraging new product introductions. They can serve as platforms for establishing families of synergistically related products and services. They can also be vehicles for joint ventures or franchising. Here care must be taken not to confuse a loyal customer base by using a proprietary brand name carelessly, associating the brand name with a partner's image rather than one's own. It is important to take advantage of the opportunity to extend brand names globally to gain unique and potentially significant competitive advantages. Global brand recognition can also be strong protection against competitors; it is usually difficult to duplicate or defuse a strong brand recognition.

Other downstream global advantages might be created through common sales force approaches, coordinated distribution systems, and global service organizations. The purpose in all cases is to develop an economy of scope advantage by coordinating and pooling various aspects of the downstream value creation activities.

Let us now turn to the creation of upstream global advantages. This can take place in several forms: For instance, one might coordinate research and development among many business activities globally to create an economy of scale advantage. Similarly, manufacturing of parts as well as assembly activities might be coordinated globally. The importance here is to be clear about how far one might go in creating global economies of scale without sacrificing too much of the needs to adapt locally (Porter 1985).

One of the key purposes of strategic planning is to facilitate the allocation of scarce strategic resources to the most advantageous applications. Most planning processes have, perhaps, focused relatively too heavily on the allocation of financial funds as particularly critical. Although this is always going to be a key for future success, it may be useful to take a somewhat broader view of what represents critical strategic resources in a multinational corporation, and which consequently also should be more explicitly and carefully dealt with in the allocation process—critical managerial human resources. Where do we put our best movers and shakers? Regarding unique technological know-how, to which business opportunities do we particularly apply these unique technological advantages? In this context, how do we allocate the uses of brand names on a systematic, global basis, so as to not over-tax them, nor dilute their image vis-a-vis the consumers? How can we take full advantage of opportunities to establish business families of related, synergistic products and services?

Many planning processes fall short of these global value-creating considerations around one's broader sets of key strategic resources, good-will, and know-how. It is thus critical that the strategic planning process is able to facilitate the identification of which upstream and/or downstream synergies can be established, say, through more globally coordinated activities leading to economies of scale and/or coordination leading to economies of scope in the marketplace. Resources should then be allocated in such a way that these global advantages are effectively developed.

Managing Risk

It is clear that economic forces, to a greater or lesser extent, impact national economies differently. Macroeconomic comparative advantages that certain countries may enjoy with respect to energy, currency, or trade surplus, and/or underlying productivity and demographic issues, can significantly impact one's own success. It is, therefore, important to take advantage of this global differentiation by developing a business portfolio that allows for maximum response flexibility by being meaningfully positioned in major markets. In this connection, it is important to underscore the word *major;* a strong position in the key European, Far Eastern, and U.S. markets probably offers the best risk hedging (Ohmae 1985). Of course, this can be complemented by positions in other, at times more turbulent, markets such as some of those in South America, the Middle East, or South Asia. An explicit global risk-taking perspective should be applied to a firm's international business activity profile, however. Too often mere historical circumstances dictate the global portfolio mix.

A thorough understanding of the local economies is necessary to manage risk in this way, so that one can have a better ability to develop a balanced global portfolio and to take ameliorating actions in time to shift the balance when necessary.

Even though many firms have taken steps to assess their businesses globally from such a global risk perspective, it seems as if their planning processes often can be strengthened further to deal with this by incorporating more systematically national economic outlooks and/or sectorial economic forecasts and by doing more comprehensive comparative international economic analysis. More systematic inclusion of political risk dimensions might also be included in a planning process approach for strengthening the portfolio global perspective. In general, although portfolio strategies have been emphasized more recently (Rappaport 1986), a national bias often prevails when it comes to such portfolio value creating approaches. The international aspects of the portfolio are often seen as representing appendix issues. In our opinion, it is necessary to take an entirely global point of view in delineating an appropriate corporate portfolio for creating the best stockholder values.

The six emerging internationalization issues just discussed and the corresponding needs they create for strengthening the strategic planning processes in many multinational corporations are, of course, not new. They are stronger reasons today than ever before, however, for the multinational corporation to meet the challenge of developing a more appropriately strengthened strategic planning process. It seems difficult to see how an excellent company can plan to maintain its leadership position and project its momentum into the future without relying heavily on strategic planning processes that are truly adapted to such a multinational context. Consequently, a first step for many multinational corporations in strengthening their strategic planning processes would be to review how they cope with the issues just outlined, and to make the necessary evolutionary modifications of their planning processes accordingly.

There is also, however, a need for more fundamental changes in strategic planning approaches in many corporations to allow them to pursue more effective multinational strategies. We now discuss a set of such fundamental general design issues that often need to be modified to achieve more effective global strategic planning. This includes ways to strengthen the strategic control process so that its focus is more global. Also the strategic planning department's commitment, ambition, and organizational culture may represent particularly critical factors for a strengthened global strategic plan to emerge. There is often a broader agenda of items for top management to consider in making its global strategic vision come through, by more fundamentally modifying management processes to make a globally directed corporate strategy approach more of a reality.

Fundamental Challenges to the Strategic Planning System

Strategic planning in some form or another is, of course, a reality in most well-managed corporations. Many such strategic planning processes, however, need to be modified in at least two fundamental ways to make them more well-adapted to global strategy development.

Global Strategic Planning Support to the CEO

A first requirement deals with the communication dimension in planning, particularly upper management's top-down communication which typically must be more carefully delineated to the various business activities worldwide (Lorange and Probst 1988). It is absolutely key for the CEO to be seen as relevant throughout the organization. The CEO must provide a meaningful vision to a broader constituency of executives, and give more prompt and meaningful feedback to a more heterogeneous group of business strategists. Thus, the CEO must pay particular attention to fulfilling the inspirator role in the global strategic planning process to insure meaningful top-down global visions. With a more passive and reactive approach, it is unlikely that a truly meaningful global strategy can emerge.

In particular, the time-spending patterns of the CEO must be very carefully worked out. The most energy must be spent on creating global strategies. In this connection, it should be pointed out that the sum of local initiatives from around the globe, put together into a corporate strategy, is not a global strategy. Thus, the CEO should not be under the illusion that effectively pushing a global approach simply means traveling extensively worldwide. By spending time and energy in gaining insight into what constitutes an overlying global value-creating dimension, the CEO will not lose track of such an overall vision. Strategic planning must be an ally in facilitating this. The CEO's commitment to a truly international approach thus becomes a fundamental prerequisite to good multinational strategic planning. Beyond this, however, the strategic planning process must be formulated to allow the CEO to play an effective role as an internationalist, rather than being bracketed into the role of running the company from a host country perspective, treating the strategic planning for the rest of the company as a secondary activity (Heenan and Perlmutter 1979).

International Strategic Task Forces and Think Tanks

A second commonly fertile area for improvement of the strategic planning process is to emphasize how to make better use of creative, ad hoc task forces in the strategic processes, with broader participation from talented executives from several countries to help delineate more potent global business strategies. It continues to be important in this connection to come to grips with whether the basic organizational direction should be along geographic lines or global business lines. For instance, should a particular business be run as a global strategy, with the consequence that in a given country there will be several global business strategies executed in parallel? Alternatively, should each country be driven by its own integrated strategy, with the consequence that global business strategies become more or less the sum of various country-based business strategies? The answer to this seemingly difficult trade-off is often not either/or, but that both issues must be dealt with. The planning process might thus be structured in such a way that what makes sense to focus on as the most dominant of these two dimensions in any given case should be adhered to as the prime driving force behind the development of the plans. In addition, however, task forces should be established with a de facto mandate to allow the other dimension to be addressed (Hedlund 1980).

For instance, let us assume that we have a capital-intensive producer of various metal products. For such a company, one might argue that each of the basic metal products should be seen as global businesses and have their separate global strategies. However, particularly important regions such as the North American market also represent critical strategic dimensions in that there would be a lot to gain by strategically coordinating, say, the North American activities between these global strategies. A task force with representation from each of the global business strategies might thus be formed to delineate the coordination needs. For a globally operating food company, on the other hand, it might be typical that the country-based local consumer preferences might be dominant. Consequently, its international strategy might be largely developed on a country-by-country basis. Still, it may become increasingly evident that coordination of particular business strategies should also take place on a global basis, across the various country strategy boundaries. Here again, global task forces might be established for the key businesses, with representatives for the most important countries involved.

It is critical to get broad based acceptance for the working form of executive task forces which must cooperate on developing meaningful global strategies. CEOs should be realistic about the fact that it typically takes a lot of time and energy for many executives to develop such strategies. Consequently, careful attention must be given to setting the agendas and to running the meetings efficiently, to scheduling the planning calendar and meetings so that travel can be minimized. In short, to pay utmost attention to spending time cost efficiently. Also, truly key people must be involved in the committees, not junior executives or staff assistants. Choice of a good chairman for each committee also means much. To be effective, nonetheleast politically, the committees should be given clear mandates, articulated from the CEO and backed up by CEO visibility. On an overall basis, the planners should do their best to secure a realistic working context for the committees, so that they can function in a task-fulfilling, viable way.

Why are these cross-organizational committees so critical? Probably the most important reason is that they can add the critical dimensions of being effective think tanks, providing the necessary vitality and vision in the strategic thinking of the global corporation (Lorange 1983). Without such cross-functional impetus to lift executives out of their more narrow operating contexts, it is quite likely that the global strategy will become nothing much more than the sum of various minikingdoms' perspectives. The overall commitment by the members of the organizations to be responsible for developing a truly ambitious global corporate strategy which is more than the sum of the strategies of each operating organizational entity is therefore vital.

Strategic Control

Traditional management control systems often have several dysfunctional impacts on the development of global strategies. First, many control systems put relatively unilateral emphasis on monitoring short-term performance. As such, traditional management control can reinforce a bias toward short-term bottom line results and return on investment considerations. This can create mixed signals and doubts in the organization regarding the true viability of investing for the longer-term in global strategies. It is, therefore, particularly important that during the routine monthly or quarterly reviews of operating performance the long-term perspective is kept in mind, so that as little as possible unnecessary doubt, misunderstanding, and confidence undermining are created regarding the international strategies long-term viability. The control process should not distract or disrupt the organization's longer term global strategic frame of mind (Lorange, Scott Morton, and Ghoshal 1987).

Also, the management control process should be sufficiently tailor-made to realistically cope with local circumstances. A uniform global treatment of all country operations can again easily lead to difficult strategy implementation dysfunctionalities for local managers in a given country. The way proper control discipline should be exercised must differ in accordance with local conditions. For instance, when it comes to business operations in some particular high inflation country settings, it may be difficult to see how a tight control of cash flows from operations can be separated from capital structure controls. It should be an opportunity to take advantage of the interplay between short-term financing/borrowing/capital placement tactics and managed ups and downs in the cash flow streams stemming from operations. For instance, when a major devaluation is expected—a phenomenon which normally can be more easily detected by astute local management—it may make sense to intensify selling activities, accelerate the shipping of products through the distribution channels, and increase promotional efforts to realize a strengthened temporary in-cash flow on an immediate basis. This can then be placed on a forward basis in the local short-term capital market to gain from the devaluation. Financial tactical gains might more than offset short-term disturbances in operations (Jacque and Lorange 1984). Many strategic processes are so general that they disallow the kind of flexibility described in this example, however. Overly standardized stereotypic approaches to the design of a firm's strategic processes can thus be detrimental to local strategic success.

Beyond such pragmatic but typically nondramatic modifications of the traditional management control systems as the ones just discussed, it typically is very important to add a more fundamental strengthening of the strategic control approach, through what can be seen as a more proactive global strategic control. Two aspects of such a strategic control approach seem particularly important: First, shifts in growth patterns in various market niches across the world might be more closely and systematically monitored. It is critical for the success of the company to pick the right niches to emphasize, that is, the battlegrounds that have the strongest future potentials and offer a relatively long-term basis of return for the efforts expended to develop such business niches. It is also important to spot early signs of decline in growth rates in particular business niches. A monitoring of underlying critical factors such as demographics and socioeconomic trends should be carried out on a routine basis for this purpose.

The other critical aspect of strategic control is the systematic monitoring on a global basis of news regarding one's key competitors. Most control approaches might involve signals from one's local business managers on how they see a move from a given competitor. Such signals, seen in isolation, do not necessarily reveal a true picture of the underlying strategies of global competitors; they must be seen in an overall context to highlight a clearer understanding of key competitors' strategies. Spotting and detecting major shifts in the competitive arena is essential.

To add such control of critical competitive and environmental factors can improve judgments regarding when to accelerate the pursuit of certain niche opportunities that are opening up, and when to deemphasize certain other niches that may be softening and flattening out. A successful track record in managing the in and out decisions—to achieve good timing—is critical in global management. Strategic control processes should be able to significantly contribute to this need.

The Strategic Planning Department's Ambition and Commitment to Global Strategic Excellence

To remain a viable and successful company, there must be a true willingness in a firm's culture to develop new business opportunities for the future. The strategic planners can be particularly important catalysts in this respect, to help the corporation to strengthen its ability to spend energy, time, know-how, management involvement, and capital today, to build up legs on which to stand on in the future. As discussed, this expenditure of energy should be directed toward global opportunities for the highest likelihood of a successful return. Applying a strict return on investment criteria to this building strategy will probably not lead to a sufficiently strong international commitment. There might always be more easy marginal investment opportunities to be realized by extending present business activities "in the small." However, the problem is that in the long run, failure to build these new global legs might lead to a loss of opportunity "in the large." Safe, marginal incremental and internally focused myopic investments can only carry the momentum for so long. One's real competitors of the future are certainly likely to do better than that.

The strategic planners must, therefore, be prepared to challenge the pattern of incremental extension of already established businesses based on competent but conventional bottom-up strategic plans. Such reliance on extending the strategic momentum is normally not ambitious enough—the strategic planning group should be lead advocates in cultivating more radical global adaptive aspirations.

Another critical dimension of organizational ambition that the strategic planning team must have is to fully recognize that for it to be able to contribute to the really first-class ideas and creativity that must take the company into the global future, the team will have to possess both a broad eclectic set of substantive skills, as well as solid behavioral, political, and cross-cultural understanding. The challenge for such an advanced team of planners is to facilitate the interfacing among creative executives from all over the world, so as to see develop an eclectic cross-fertilization regarding how better to create new global business opportunities, and to stimulate the realistic implementation that will have to take place in the heterogeneous global contexts. It can be argued that many a strategic planning department often has too much of a predominantly domestic outlook. Rather than stimulating good global strategy development, such planners can, with some likelihood, impact a firm's retrenchment into more of a domestic, even parochial culture. It will be less likely than ever that such a firm will be at par with the best global thinking that can be found.

Consequently, for the strategic planners, the global organization is all; they must commit to a global strategic approach so that their firm will remain a truly excellent company. Thus, a high level of organizational ambition on the part of the planners should be a key driving force in making a successful strategy based on global premises a reality. Too often the strategic planners are not fully up to this catalytic challenge. What is called for, therefore, is a strengthening of the strategic planning team to have the necessary skills and ambitions to cope with the emerging strategic issues facing the multinational firm. Above all, emphasis on ability to enthuse and stimulate must be key—not parochial, negative, passive, or analytically review attitudes.

In this section we have argued that, with strengthened strategic planning and control processes in place, complemented with a strong, committed strategic planning team, the corporation should now be in a position to better pursue specific actions to speed up the evolution of its global strategies. Specifically, the four suggested changes in the strategic management approach outlined in this section tend to be more dramatic than the six evolutionary strategic planning process changes suggested in the first section of the chapter. We feel that a planning process might be backed up by, and tailored to, the globally committed CEO. It must be based on international think tank executive teams, it must be complemented by a strategic control process emphasizing global reach, and it must be nurtured along by a corporate strategic planning team that must be global in its commitment.

Let us now move our focus to a more detailed discussion of various modes of growth and new revenue generation in the global firm, together with a discussion of which types of tailor-made strategic planning process support the various growth modes might require. There are particular business moves that might typically accelerate the globalization process, by stimulating growth from scratch in certain markets, considering international acquisitions, or pursuing various forms of cooperative ventures. Let us now discuss each of these growth mode issues and also review the strategic planning process tailoring that typically must be faced by top management and their planners in connection with each.

Global Strategic Expansion Moves— And Their Planning Implications

Internally Generated Growth

The most apparent vehicle for implementing a global strategy would be to establish and grow businesses from scratch. The advantage of this is that such a business position often can be developed relatively inexpensively over time, avoiding major resource outlays. However, an often critical problem is that it might take too much time to develop viable business positions in this way internationally. When the appropriate opportunity is there, it generally makes good sense to implement such a greenfield approach. When it comes to the major markets where strong competitors typically already have been well established, however, it may be too much of an uphill battle to follow this approach. On the other hand, in secondary markets which are not necessarily so overly filled with heavy competition already, one may have more of a first mover success. Of course, such peripheral markets are not necessarily of the highest priority in one's global strategy. Accordingly firms must focus their resources where it matters the most, typically in the main markets. Strategy means making choices, and the choice should be to pursue what one considers the key major international markets. Thus, although building from scratch may be feasible, it may not make much strategic sense in some such instances.

We have already emphasized several challenges that a planning process must cope with to facilitate the establishment of new businesses in foreign niches. The emphasis on seeking out such growth opportunities must be stressed in the planning process in particular. Stimulation of communication with the new and fledgling organizational entity must be done in such a way that needed support for strategy modifications can be given on a prompt basis. It would be important to tailor-make the planning process to the foreign start-up situation in such a way that the weight of the formalized planning approach which has to be carried out in large, established foreign subsidiaries would not be felt as a bureaucratic burden.

Growth through International Acquisitions

A second option, therefore, is to make a number of selected acquisitions. This strategy has an obvious potential major advantage in that it can lead to a more rapid buildup of a global strategic presence. However, there are at least two potentially serious limitations to this approach: First, it may not be easy to execute the number of acquisitions that have to be made in such a way that they are interrelated in a manner leading to the establishment of global viability in a particular business area. It is not enough to simply acquire a company in a given country and leave it alone; it must be put into a larger strategic context. That a whole string of meaningfully related acquisitions will be required can be a major area of potential failure for many companies wanting to move rapidly in further strengthening the international dimension. They end up acquiring a number of companies in various countries that do not add up to much, if anything at all, beyond being merely the sum of the individual companies they are.

A second issue along the acquisition route is the price question. Given that a number of global competitors can be expected to have canvassed the world for good acquisition candidates for quite some time, it may already become increasingly difficult to find meaningful acquisitions sufficiently cost beneficial to be worth pursuing. Also, in such a situation, it is probably better to consummate a small number of relatively large acquisitions, rather than a larger number of smaller ones. If a premium has to be paid, it might be better to pay it for such larger acquisitions that can then more realistically become new launching pads for further multinational growth and development. Thus, the overall international momentum gained through a few large acquisitions may be more valuable than the sum of "mini-momentums" that would come from smaller, cheaper acquisitions. Top management capacity constraints further underscore the wisdom of selectively going big.

To support a multinational acquisition strategy the planning process needs to scan acquisition candidates systematically and evaluate their potential for offering synergy to global business strategies. Planners should pay particularly strong attention to the quality of the human resources being acquired. Often, the emphasis on the physical assets tends to dominate the evaluation, when considerations having to do with compatability in management style and ability to motivate the acquired management team are relatively much more important.

The postacquisition phase needs to be supported through the planning process. Here, it is critical that plans are developed that bring the new management team into the action on an effective basis as early as possible. It is key that inputs from the acquired firms must be reflected in the new plans. Also, the planning process acts as a common language between the existing businesses and the newly acquired entities. This facilitates the development of common ways of talking about these strategies, minimizes misunderstandings, and lessens the cost of communication. Significantly, this might speed up the implementation of the anticipated synergistic plans.

Global Cooperative Ventures

A third and often increasingly viable mode of establishing multinational strategies involves the pursuit of cooperative strategies, such as joint ventures, franchising, and licensing (Lorange 1988). The advantages of such strategies can be manifold. First, they can facilitate access to a local partner who better understands the local situation, who has the necessary local legitimacy, relevant government contacts, and access to local market know-how. This can significantly increase the odds of success. Second, it can facilitate the build-up of the business more quickly than doing it alone. Third, it may be a cost-efficient approach, in that many of the required investments are carried out by the partner, and that often already existing complementary resources are being utilized. Finally, it represents a way of sharing risks among several participants in developing a global strategy.

However, there are also several potential problems that should be kept in mind. First, one must have a clear architecture regarding how a particular cooperative venture is supposed to work, delineating who is supposed to contribute with what and how the overall competitiveness of the joint venture is intended to be achieved. An understanding of how this joint venture is intended to dynamically develop and adapt to new environmental circumstances is critical. Too often joint venture agreements are agreed on in principle but not thought out thoroughly enough in delineation of roles nor in how cooperation is intended to evolve and adapt over time.

Second, it is critical to address how to protect one's own core strategic competence in the cooperative venture. If, for instance, a parent bringing a unique technology to the joint venture wishes to maintain its position of strength in this cooperative arrangement, it is key for that parent company to continue with research and development on its own. That way, the other partner knows that violating the joint venture runs the risk of isolation from the benefits of future R&D insights. Proper legal agreements and patent protection are, of course, necessary. In this connection, no legal agreement should be so rigid that it might handicap the actual working of the joint venture as a business—the agreements must be flexible enough to adapt. A know-how base consisting of a system of components—not merely a simple product— probably can be more easily defended. One might control the most critical know-how components behind this broader concept. Finally, the employees in the joint venture must be motivated to continue to be loyal to the parent company; that is, the parent should provide some type of career planning to support executives working for the joint venture so they know they have a future in the parent organization.

A key aspect of cooperative venture success has to do with delineating proper planning and control processes so that the cooperative venture can better adapt over time to new opportunities, and so that strategic progress can be controlled (Lorange and Probst 1989). Too often, cooperative ventures stagnate, become bogged down in legal static, and respond too slowly to environmental threats or to take advantage of environmental opportunities. A clear set of procedures for conflict resolution should also be developed as part of such a planning and control process, so that conflicts of interest can be dealt with in an unemotional and expedient manner, rather than being put under the rug for too long until a potentially highly dysfunctional blow-up might occur.

Perhaps the most critical consideration that can increase the odds of a successful cooperative venture is to search for partners compatible in style so that a management form based on mutual trust can be developed. Too often, problems in cooperative ventures end up taking a disproportionate share of top management's time and energy; as such, they can be quite expensive when considering the opportunity costs of bogging down the key managers. Therefore, it is crucial to find compatible, easy-to-work-with partners who can see common interests in pursuing a joint strategy. The strategic planning process can play a particularly important role in maintaining such a management culture of common purpose. A final side of the strategic planning process of cooperative ventures would be to develop mechanisms for the joint venture's dissolution once it no longer satisfies the overall objectives of each partner. Of course, it follows that it is an advantage to be clear about what objectives each partner is actually pursuing. There is, of course, nothing wrong with encouraging the dissolution of a cooperative venture when it no longer satisfies a mission congruent with the objectives of both partners. It is an advantage to work out such closure mechanisms beforehand.

General Conclusions

A general conclusion regarding the strategic planning process roles in the multinational firm of the future is that to fully pursue the various opportunities that internationalization and globalization now represent, it may be particularly necessary to strengthen strategic planning in several ways. First are the six evolutionary issues for strengthening the strategic planning process to become more effective as a vehicle for implementing global strategies. Needless to say, a particular firm may already have made sufficient steps to strengthen its strategic planning process in one or more ways relative to these issues; explicit care should be taken, however, to make such a self-examination. Second are the four fundamental changes in approaching strategic management issues; these have to take place, to a greater or lesser extent to facilitate better global strategies. These issues range from facilitating a better global push regarding strategic factors by the CEO, allowing for more flexible task force participation from globally composed task force teams, allowing for more sensitive strategic control, and allowing a globally committed strategic planning staff to prevail. Finally, we feel that the strategic planning process may have to be tailored differently to business revenue generating challenges stemming from growing new businesses globally from scratch in contrast to growing through international acquisitions, again in contrast to growing by means of strategic alliances and joint ventures. Success in developing a global strategy may depend to a great extent on the ability to have the necessary professionalism and know-how in one's own organization to address the complex issues raised in an effective manner. Most important, the planning process must be tailor-made to allow top management to interact with its global organization in an effective and useful manner to nurture an adaptively evolving set of global strategies.

A global strategic approach should be focused not merely on a set of somewhat random international moves. Strategy means choice; to be successful there must be carefully chosen battlegrounds to be pursued, attacked, and implemented by means of appropriate entry and build strategies. These activities must be managed and monitored through meaningful planning and control. The challenge is still great, but the potential payoff for the professionally run and appropriately motivated global organization seems to be higher than ever.

Note

I am thankful to Peter Hagstrom and Per Aman for comments on an earlier version of this chapter.

References

Chakravarthy, B.S., and Perlmutter, H.V. 1985. Strategic planning for a global business. *Columbia Journal of World Business* 20(2).

Doz, Y. 1986. *Strategic management in multinational companies.* Oxford: Pergamon Press.

Hedlund, G. 1980. The role of foreign subsidiaries in strategic decision making in Swedish multinationals. *Strategic Management Journal* 1(1).

Heenan, D. and Perlmutter, H. 1979. *Multinational organizational development.* Reading, Mass.: Addison-Wesley.

Jacque, L., and Lorange, P. 1984. Hyperinflation and global strategic management for multinational corporations. *Columbia Journal of World Business* 19(2).

Levitt, T. 1983. The globalization of markets. *Harvard Business Review,* May–June.

Lorange, P. 1976. A framework for strategic planning in multinational corporations. *Long Range Planning* 9(2).

———. 1988. "Cooperative strategies: planning and control considerations." In *Strategies in Global Competition,* eds. N. Hood and J-E. Vahlne, London: Croom Helm.

———. 1983. Implementing strategic planning in two Philippine companies. *The Wharton Annual.* Philadelphia.

Lorange, P., Scott Morton, M., and Ghoshall, S. 1987. *Strategic control,* St. Paul: West Publishing.

Lorange, P. and Probst, G. 1989. "Effective strategic planning processes in the multi-national corporation." In *Managing the Global Firm,* eds. C. Bartlett, Y. Doz and G. Hedlund. London: Routledge.

Omahe, K. 1985. *Triad power,* New York: Free Press.

Porter, M. 1985. *Competitive advantage,* New York: Free Press.

Prahalad, C.K., and Doz, Y. 1987. *The multinational missions,* New York: Free Press.

Rappaport, A. 1986. *Creating shareholder value,* New York: Free Press.

7

Strategic Issues in Corporate Planning in United States- and United Kingdom-Based Multinationals

Norman Coates

This chapter presents a report on the findings of a study of strategic issues affecting corporate planning in multinationals in the United States and the United Kingdom. The focus of the study was on the environmental factors that have affected corporate planning, especially those factors in the headquarters environments of multinational corporations (MNCs) in both countries over the ten-year period: 1977–1986.

Environment refers to the broad economic, political, social, and cultural aspects of a society, rather than to any narrower perception of the planning environment. The planning process refers to the steps taken by the key actors in an organization to formulate corporate strategy, the ultimate output being a corporate strategic plan addressing environmental realities. Strategic issues are defined as developments, events, and trends that may affect an organization's strategy (Dutton and Duncan 1987a). For our purposes, the MNC is a business firm based in a particular headquarters country, but planning for, producing, and selling its products or services on a worldwide basis; the overall coordination remains in the home country.

Among the basic questions our study sought to answer are the following:

1. What is the strategic planning process in MNCs and how does the MNC strategic planning process differ from planning in non-MNCs?
2. To what extent does strategic planning in the MNCs provide a competitive edge in a global economy?
3. To what extent is the process of decision making in planning part of the political process?
4. Over the last decade, what have been the problems and issues facing MNC top management in the two countries?

5. What has been the planning environment in these two countries, and has this environment affected the outlook of, and the strategy chosen by, top management?

6. Have any influences in the headquarters environment had an impact on strategic issues or on their formulation and diagnoses?

Methodology and Scope. In-depth interviews were held intermittently with the general managers and strategic planners of selected MNCs in both United States and United Kingdom headquarters locations, principally in or around New York and London, in the period 1977–1986. Given the proprietary nature of plans, and, indeed, of the planning process itself, face-to-face interviews were considered to be superior to more comprehensive questionnaires, permitting the researcher to capture the nuances characteristic of each subculture studied. The small, but representative, sample of twelve companies represented the energy, chemical, pharmaceutical, and computer industries on both sides of the Atlantic, and selected other airlines and steel companies.

It was hypothesized that the immediate, national environment of headquarters staffs would have some measurable effects on the strategic planning process, as reflected in the strategic issues characteristic of each respective domestic environment and that, therefore, there would be distinctive differences in the strategic issues affecting the strategic planning process in MNCs based in the United States and the United Kingdom. In this context, the headquarters' environment was hypothesized to be sensitive and overly responsive to the political, economic, and cultural currents pervading the headquarters' society over a given period of time.

Organization of the Chapter. First, we draw on the relevant literature on the environment-strategic planning interface and examine the planning processes in the MNCs studied. Second, certain differences are identified in the planning processes of MNCs as opposed to non-MNCs. Third, the data are presented on the central issues perceived by the key actors in each MNC in the United States and the United Kingdom. Finally, some conclusions are drawn on the similarities and differences between the planning environments in the two countries.

Background

A good case can be made for the idea that the MNC represents the current stage in the evolution of organizations as efficient learning systems adapting to changing global environments. Given the environmental forces at work, in particular the enormous growth and diffusion of scientific and technological knowledge and their applications, and the increasing interdependency of the nations tied inexorably together on a planet, only a large, complex, global, international organization could cope effectively with such environmental challenges. In this sense the learning capabilities of the MNC are seen as exceeding those of other institutions in society today, including those of government, thus giving rise to the avowed apolitical character of MNCs and the frictions arising between MNCs and home or host governments. Nonetheless, it is likely that indigenous managers in the headquarters environment of any given MNC are susceptible to and influenced by factors peculiar to that environment.

To understand how MNCs cope with their immediate and far-flung environments, we examine the planning process in MNCs. Our interviews with key actors sought to link the processes of strategic planning in MNCs to major political, economic, and related trends to determine the degree to which purely domestic issues affected strategic thinking and decision making. On the surface, the normal expectation is that the perspective of the multinational manager is increasingly global. Accordingly, at first glance, it would appear contradictory to suggest that the headquarters environment should have significant effects on strategic planning. We need to turn to the literature, and then to the data in our study, to clarify this and related matters.

Review of the Literature. A recent review of the literature on planning by Negandhi (1987), in which he cites the work of Steiner and Cannon (1966) among others, concludes that U.S. and European MNCs had very similar planning structures: typically three- to seven-year plans; subsidiaries enjoying autonomy in the process; headquarters staffs engaged in planning; and the same thought process being used in all companies. Negandhi (1987: 235) concludes his survey by noting that all MNCs studied are using strategic long-range planning and environmental scanning to coordinate their global activities. Dutton and Duncan (1987b) demonstrate the contextual influences, especially organizational factors influencing how strategic issues are diagnosed.

Davidson (1984) established that the administrative orientation of the MNC affects planning choices between centralized, decentralized, and customized approaches. Kennedy (1984) concluded that there is a quantitative increase and qualitative change in the institutionalization of external environmental analysis by U.S. MNCs. Dymsza (1984) derives a model of planning for MNCs and puts into context the role of strategic issues in such a model. As Dymsza's study (1984: 176) demonstrates, some companies ask country managers to identify strategic issues that may have an impact on their businesses in the planning period. This analysis does not examine the headquarters country's strategic issues, however.

A number of studies of decision making in MNCs, with reference to investments, have been carried out by Aharoni (1966) and Zwick (1966). Aharoni found human factors were as important—if not more important— than financial and economic considerations. Zwick's findings appear to be similar, identifying the gap between top managements' strategic intentions and the implementation by lower-level management. Hoffman (1987) upheld the proposition that in strategic decision making, both political and rational decision models may apply. Bower (1970a,b) established that capital project decisions are subject to the administrative context in which they are proposed and evaluated. Kolde (1985: 277) has pointed out that it is important to differentiate between types of MNCs: the established ones may be seen as equity-based, with managerial control emanating from equity ownership; however, newer MNCs are nonequity MNCs that may be technology-based with managerial control exerted through technology. Our sample includes both types.

Negandhi (1987: 24) proposes the hypothesis that

> The lack of congruence between the demands of the home and host countries and the headquarters' and subsidiaries' strategies will be reflected in tensions between headquarters and subsidiaries, between headquarters and host, as well as home countries, and between subsidiaries and host countries.

Planning in the United States and the United Kingdom

In general, apart from the studies just cited, the literature on planning has focused on firms in a domestic rather than a global environment. Because we are examining U.S. and U.K. headquarters' environments, it may be useful to assess country studies shedding light on planning in these two countries. Generally speaking, here, also, the literature would suggest widespread use of common approaches to this aspect of management in the United States and the United Kingdom. Higgins and Finn (1977), for example, in a survey of fifty-six U.K. companies established that 75 percent of these companies had practiced corporate planning for ten years or less, with about half of these having adopted planning between the year 1966 and 1977. In the United States, in a small sample of firms, Henry (1967) found that thirty-eight of the forty-five companies studied had formal planning organizations. In a later survey, the same author found the same high incidence of planning in U.S. companies, although many companies had apparently redesigned their planning systems in the 1970s. In a comparative study Sim (1977, cited by Fayerweather 1982) established that planning and budgeting in a sample of U.S. firms invited more headquarters involvement and was a top-down process. British subsidiaries tended to have less headquarters attention and the process was more a bottom-up one.

The ever-expanding body of literature on planning confirms current experience that the incidence of formal planning is high. Davidson (1982), in a review of the literature, concludes that an increasing number of U.S. firms are adopting strategic planning systems. As the complexity of the environment increases, the more likely it is that firms adopt formal planning (Lindsay and Rue 1980). Litschert (1968) established a relationship between planning, company size, and technological factors. A more recent study on ninety-seven manufacturing firms found strategic planning positively correlated with high levels of organizational performance, confirming the findings of earlier studies (Pearce, Robbins, and Robinson 1987).

MNCs are no less impervious to prevailing trends than are other corporations. Just as companies operating within a single domestic environment have been influenced to use planning as a key to success, so have multinationals. As Garland and Farmer (1986: 34) point out, planning on a global basis is an extension of the conventional planning techniques of domestically oriented firms but is more complex, having to deal with the problems of geographic diversification around the world, country and foreign exchange risk analysis, and methods of entering foreign markets.

Planning in MNCs

The prevailing pattern of strategic planning in the MNCs surveyed is characterized by a formal process for which planning guides, manuals, and headquarters staffs are available to assist in the process. In its broad outlines, that process is not much different from, and follows closely, the process characteristics of large nonmultinational corporations. In most instances, a corporate-level management committee or, specifically, a planning committee, meets periodically to carry out a sequence of planning functions as determined by the planning process.

A major difference between the non-MNC and the MNC is that, for the latter, there is a higher degree of decentralization of the planning process on a geographic basis, corresponding to the structure of the firm's operations. There is also a greater degree of negotiation between managers indigenous to those countries where the decentralized operations are located and the headquarters staffs and chief executive officers (CEOs' staffs). In the majority of cases in the sample, the headquarters' staffs were conscious of the fact that in dealing with their overseas regional headquarters, or with specific country managers, it was usual to expect a local, and sometimes a nationalistic, viewpoint upholding values and attitudes prevailing in the decisionmakers' own environment. As a result, there was a delicate process of clarification and negotiation as headquarters' staffs sought to have what they perceived to be their global viewpoints prevail.

From the standpoint of the country manager in the MNC, however, the headquarters' staff were seen as being affected by the national policies, values, and attitudes of their home environment: the United States or the United Kingdom, as the case may be, for the American or British MNCs respectively. Therefore, in arguing their cases for their particular points of view, the country managers were not only indulging in defending their turf, so to speak, or in attempting to win more in the resource allocation game vis-à-vis other divisions, subsidiaries, or countries, but they were also attempting to reason with headquarters' staffs so that they could "see the light." In this respect, the regional headquarters manager, and the MNC CEO are often cast in the roles of mediator and multicultural facilitator attempting to bring about a consensus among the many nationalities comprising the management team globally.

Typically, the headquarters gathers intelligence from subsidiaries around the world. In the case of one company, this meant data were collected from 130 countries. Based on these data and on country forecasts, headquarters provided all its divisions and subsidiaries with a global return on investment (ROI) target which, in this case, was planned to average about 20 percent per annum over the seven-year strategic planning period.

A Model of the MNC Planning Process

A model of the planning process derived from our survey of U.S.- and U.K.- based MNCs is portrayed in figure 7–1. Headquarters' planning staffs, sometimes with the aid of counterparts in regional headquarters and national subsidiaries, prepare long- and short-range environmental forecasts affecting the various businesses in which that particular group may be engaged, identifying specific strategic issues for review by top management. These forecasts, and the issues identified, affect management's definition of its ROI and other corporate objectives from time to time. Subsequently, as noted earlier, the resulting judgments on corporate objectives are communicated to divisions providing basic assumptions around which proposals for strategy are developed for corporate approval. In some cases, a portfolio model, using a modified Boston Consulting Group matrix, was utilized to provide an indication of how different businesses might be classified. In other cases, a simulation had been utilized initially but was subsequently abandoned for a more traditional approach. In a number of cases, scenario building was utilized as a well-developed tool by management at top and middle levels to provide a picture of where the companies were headed.

Division managers were asked to recommend a range of strategic options—and in some instances contingency options—for their industry, product lines, or area. Some managers were asked to identify, or comment on, strategic issues. The options and issues were reviewed and evaluated by planning staffs at headquarters and were sent to top management for review and approval. There is a process by means of which gaps between corporate expectations and divisional recommendations are closed by a negotiated

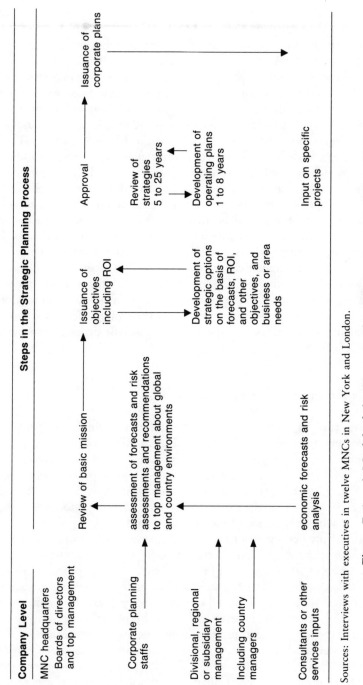

Figure 7–1. A Model of the Strategic Planning Process in Selected MNCs

Sources: Interviews with executives in twelve MNCs in New York and London.

agreement before particular strategies are decided on, approved, and communicated to divisional levels.

Once these corporate plans and divisional strategic plans were approved, these documents became the basis for another process. In this instance, typically, divisions developed short-range plans of one-to-seven years' duration, depending on the nature of the industry; once more, these were sent to top management for approval. (Energy companies on both sides of the Atlantic had twenty-five-year strategic planning horizons, with an operating time frame of seven or eight years.) In practice, at this stage approval was pro forma, as a good deal of latitude was permitted different national and regional groups to achieve overall strategic plans through local implementation. Clearly, any variance from plans, especially in those companies with a predetermined portfolio matrix, or with real-time computer-based information systems, permitted top management to immediately raise with operating groups any questions as to why such variances occurred; these, as well as quarterly and annual reviews, permitted further modifications to plans. A few companies had developed contingency, as well as operating strategies, and these were committed to writing to permit rapid shifts to other modes in the light of rapid changes in the environment. Since the so-called energy crisis of 1973, the need for contingency thinking at the strategic level had made itself felt in a number of industries, especially those heavily dependent on petroleum or its derivatives.

MNCs Headquarters' Environments

We now turn to an assessment of the differences in the respective headquarters' environments of MNCs based in the United States and the United Kingdom. Britain is a country with only over a quarter of the population of the United States. The factor of size is important to productivity, especially in the ability to effect economies of size and scale. Granick (1972) predicted in the early 1970s that the then current trend in Europe to mergers of companies to achieve American-style bigness would not bring about the desired results. His predictions would seem to be borne out by our data. The classic case of the efforts in the U.K. steel industry—where such mergers and economies were sought as a matter of national policy—have produced substantial financial losses. In the 1980s a similar phenomenon, evolving in significantly different ways, occurred in the U.S. steel industry. Here the competition from foreign steel prompted requests by the steel industry for government intervention in the form of tariff protection and resulted in conglomerate diversification of steel companies into oil and other unrelated areas.

In the decade 1977–1986 other striking similarities emerged in the U.K. and U.S. environments. The Callaghan Labour government was replaced in

1979 with the Thatcher Conservative government, which was reelected twice again in 1984 and 1987. In the United States, the Carter Democratic administration was replaced in 1980 by the Reagan Republican administration and this administration was reelected in 1984. Thus, in the period under study, the political climates changed significantly in both countries with significant effects on the perception of strategic issues identified over time in each headquarters location.

Central Issues Identified

In a comparative assessment of the issues in the two countries' environments, the following central issues emerged: British managers were unanimous in their criticism of the tax structure in their country, which they perceived as a serious disincentive to British management. In 1977 the effective tax rate on earned income of £50,000 was over 70 percent; on investment income it was over 85 percent, rising to 91.8 percent on incomes over £100,000. In 1986 as a result of the Conservative government's efforts, tax rates on £50,000 were about 40 percent with the effective tax rate on incomes of £100,000 or more at about 50 percent.

In the United States, the effective corresponding tax rates did not exceed 50 percent, but changes by the Reagan administration lowered the rates on income. Over the decade, there have been concerns with inflation, although in recent years the rates of inflation in both countries have declined substantially.

Other issues perceived as confronting top managements of the MNCs surveyed included the following: employment and unemployment; research and development in the home-based country or abroad; movement of capital; exchange rates and fluctuations in those rates affecting corporate profit; employment of indigenous managers in overseas subsidiaries and the views of those managers, and their ability to use local shareholders' influence to obtain leverage vis-à-vis headquarters organizations; geographic as well as product diversification; left-wing political parties espousing broad-based nationalization or other programs perceived as injurious to business and market forces; labor unrest; stagnant economic growth; and protectionism versus free trade, including hidden tariff barriers, orderly marketing arrangements, and other restrictions on free trade. Depending on the individual manager's point of view, other issues were also perceived as central, for example: energy, its availability and cost; government control of prices; international attempts at regulation of MNCs; competition from Japan; the drop in oil prices; and other factors which were tied to current events at the time each manager was interviewed.

In both countries a certain degree of satisfaction has emerged in recent years about the privatization of formerly state-owned, or nationalized, companies. The drift toward a free-market philosophy in both countries stimulated the sale to the private sector of businesses that had been operated as government enterprises.

Principal Findings

Bearing in mind the limited sample of MNCs studied, some strong reservations are in order about any generalizations drawn from the data. Whatever the many issues, national or global in scope, in their forecasting the MNCs tried—as a basic step in long-range planning—to encompass political, social, cultural, technological, as well as economic changes, trends, likely scenarios or new developments, both in the headquarters' environments and outside. Many of the key actors articulated their satisfaction with the evolution of strategic planning away from purely economic factors, and away from earlier optimistic computer-based simulations which extrapolated economic data, to a more comprehensive planning framework encompassing political, social, and technological variables.

For example, one major United States energy company, whose headquarters was separate geographically from domestic operations headquarters, anticipated the public sensitivity in the United States in the late 1970s to the number of inside, as opposed to outside, members of its board of directors. In response to weak signals in the headquarter's environment, this company expanded its outside director membership substantially. Not only were more outside members included but also women and minorities were represented. Corporate officers saw this action as an intelligent response to environmental change in the United States, carried out in a responsible way long before any compelling necessity mandated it. On the other hand, the counterpart energy company in the United Kingdom was sensitive to different issues. In that case the government owned shares in the company and the attempt was to anticipate developments which might involve lesser governmental involvement, through the sale of its holdings of shares in this energy company.

The energy company in the United Kingdom, could not possibly follow the pattern in the U.S. industry by diversifying into other energy sources, such as coal, for the simple reason that, in the United Kingdom coal was a nationalized industry. But this British company did purchase control of coal companies outside the United Kingdom, suggesting that there is a high degree of imitation in strategy formulation within an industry on a global basis.

It would appear that the problem facing the MNC strategist is to adapt corporate strategy to changing conditions and to institute in the organization some mechanism by means of which commitments to a given strategy, and some flexibility in adopting alternative contingency approaches, can survive, side-by-side. Moreover, it is apparent from our analsyis that the environment is not simply one of competitive market forces but includes monopolies, cartels, oligopolies, political, governmental, attitudinal and other constraints, making the job of the corporate strategist very complex indeed. In the practice—as opposed to the espousal—of planning, the personalities of the key actors; the social, cultural, and political environment of headquarters; incumbency changes in key positions; and the natures of the company and the industry in which it operated served to produce pragmatic and immediate reactions, resulting in a complex interplay of factors and strategic issues, some of which were cited in this study. A wide range of sensibilities, particularly in the immediate human environment of headquarters, confronts the MNC decision-maker, suggesting that responses are as much to the political pulse as to economic, company, and industry conditions.

We now summarize the answers to the basic questions raised initially.

1. What is the strategic planning process in MNCs and how does the MNC strategic planning process differ from non-MNCs? Our study would seem to confirm the findings of other studies that the planning process in MNCs follows quite closely the process of planning in non-MNCs. In planning as in other matters, the prevailing patterns and practices in the headquarters environment have a bearing on how the company plans. There are some significant differences between planning processes in MNCs and non-MNCs.

Clearly, in any one country, especially the United States and the United Kingdom, vast amounts of data are available from official and private sources about the environments of the two countries. A non-MNC in each of these respective countries does not have to go too far to get domestic data. On the other hand, MNCs based in New York or London have to develop elaborate intelligence systems to gather data from around the planet because of the problem of the reliability and availability of these data. In recent years, of course, a number of services have emerged providing either published or consulting advice on political and/or economic risks associated with investments or joint ventures in selected countries. At the same time multinational financial services companies serve the needs of MNCs for data in the financial area. Thus one major distinguishing characteristic of the MNC planning process is the degree to which data are collected on a planetary basis pinpointing areas in which the corporation has or plans future operations.

2. To what extent does strategic planning in the MNCs provide a competitive edge in a global economy? One important conclusion emerges from our study of planning in MNCs: Strategic planning represents a discipline and a methodology for gaining consensus among a multiplicity of actors representing many different cultures and value systems, in a large number of businesses, in many countries. Moreover, there is a learning curve, with experience in managing and in planning representing a strong competitive advantage

over another company that does not have the same experience curve both qualitatively and quantitatively.

3.   To what extent is the process of decision making in planning part of the political process? There is no calculus for planning. The predilections, cognitive mind sets, personalities, and power bases, of the strategic planners are more significant in the formulation and implementation of strategy than any intrinsic substantive issues. Although we have no definitive data to answer this question, our impression would seem to affirm the findings of other studies cited earlier. There is clearly a need in this area for more empirical work which would attempt to examine the degree to which coalitions and negotiation serve to determine strategic direction in the MNC.

4.   Over the last decade, what have been the problems and issues facing top management in the two countries? There would appear to be a convergence in the strategic issues facing United States- and United Kingdom-based MNCs. In a manner that would have been difficult to predict in 1977, the two countries in the 1980s seem to have moved politically in the same direction in support of a business and market ethos. Similarly, in many respects, the United States appears to be following in the United Kingdom's steps, facing problems of productivity; increases in the national debt; expansion of the deficit in the balance of trade; decline of currency values; declines in manufacturing productivity, lower than all other Western societies; major global competition principally, but not exclusively, from Germany and Japan; and a decline in the shares of world gross national product and market shares on a global basis for major industries.

Debates that had focused national consciousness in the United Kingdom on declining industries and regions, have had their corresponding parallels on this side of the Atlantic. One major environmental difference between the two countries has been the growth of employment in the United States, attributed mostly to small business, and the growth of unemployment in the United Kingdom. The two societies do share some important cultural heritages, despite the many differences. The ideal of parliamentary democracy; the tolerance of pluralism; the strength of the free press; the commitment to individual rights protected by laws and free judicial systems; and many more common strands—language included—which make for hospitable environments for each country's MNCs and their subsidiaries. At different times, depending on the party in power, there are some strong ideological differences, but often these differences are not so apparent in practice.

5.   What has been the planning environment in these two countries, and has this environment affected the outlook of, and the strategy chosen by, top management? Certainly, so far as the planning process is concerned there is a high degree of similarity among the companies studied, regardless of where they are based. An overfocus on a corporation's planning process may very well substitute a mechanical and mundane view of what is, in fact, a complex

and subtle interrelationship between the planning, and the overall managerial, process. Moreover, a limited view would also obscure an unfettered understanding of the culture of a particular organization and of its relationships to the larger society in which it is principally based and of the political, ideological, and other cross-currents and issues prevalent in that society.

6. Have any influences in the headquarters' environments had an impact on the strategic issues and their formulation and diagnoses? The preliminary nature of the data in our study did not provide conclusive evidence of headquarters' influences on strategic issues, as much as demonstrate some degree of convergence between the strategic issues common to both countries. Certainly, MNC managers in the United States and the United Kingdom are apparently drawing on the same sources of intellectual capital in coping with their respective environments, and nowhere is this more true than in the global planning arena. No doubt, the intraindustry competitive forces and tendencies toward imitation are greater on a global basis than interindustry influences. Fewer, larger firms become more visible actors dominating a particular industry on the global stage. Our study would seem to point the way for further research on the interrelationships among these various factors so that decision making, as well as planning processes, in the MNCs can be more fully understood.

Our study could not fully substantiate the hypothesis that the immediate national environment of headquarters' staffs would have some measurable effects on the strategic planning process, as reflected in the strategic issues characteristic of each respective domestic environment. There is enough evidence to suggest that the hypothesis deserves further study of a larger population of MNCs, perhaps moving away from an English-speaking environment to include other European and Asian MNCs.

The hypothesis that there would be distinctive differences in the strategic issues affecting the strategic planning process in the two countries was not upheld. But there is some evidence to support the proposition that the headquarters' environments in both the United States and the United Kingdom are highly sensitive and responsive to the immediate political, economic, and cultural currents pervading the headquarters' society over a given period of time. There is no reason to believe that the period under study would affect any future results. Perhaps a study of the period 1987–1996 might find a degree of divergence in the strategic issues.

References

Aharoni, Y. 1966. *The foreign direct investment process.* Boston: Harvard Graduate School of Business.

Bower, J.L. 1970a. *Managing the resource allocation process: A study of planning and investment.* Boston: Harvard Business School.

———. 1970b. Planning within the firm. *American Economic Review* 60(2): 186–94.

Davidson, W.H. 1982. *Global strategic management.* New York: John Wiley & Sons.

———. 1984. Administrative orientation and international performance. *Journal of International Business Studies* 15(2): 11–23.

Dutton, J.A., and Duncan, R.B. 1987a. The influence of the strategic planning process on strategic change. *Strategic Management Journal* 8(2): 103–16.

——— and Duncan, R.B. 1987b. The creation of momentum for change through the process of strategic issue diagnosis. *Strategic Management Journal* 8(3): 279–95.

Dymsza, W.A. 1984. Global strategic planning: A model and recent developments. *Journal of International Business Studies* 15(2): 169–83.

Fayerweather, J. 1982. *International business strategy and administration,* 2d ed. Cambridge, Mass.: Ballinger.

Garland, J., and Farmer, R. 1986. *International dimensions of business policy and strategy.* Boston: Kent/Wadsworth.

Granick, E. 1972. *Managerial comparisons of four developed countries: France, Britain, United States, and Russia.* Cambridge, Mass.: MIT Press.

Henry, H.W. 1967. *Long-range planning practices in forty-five industrial companies.* Englewood Cliffs, N.J.: Prentice-Hall.

———. 1977. Formal planning in major U.S. corporations. *Long Range Planning* 10: 40–45.

Higgins, J.C., and Finn, R. 1977. The organization and practice of corporate planning in the United Kingdom: Some recent results. *Long Range Planning* (10): 88–92.

Hoffman, R.C. 1987. Political versus rational sources of decision power among country clusters. *Journal of International Business Studies* 18(3): 1–14.

Kennedy, Jr., C.R. 1984. The external environment-strategic planning interface: U.S. multinational corporate practices in the 1980s. *Journal of International Business Studies* 15(2): 99–108.

Kolde, E.J. 1985. *Environment of international business,* 2d ed. Boston: Kent/Wadsworth.

Lindsay, W.M., and Rue, L.W. 1980. Impact of the organization environment on the long-range planning process: A contingency view. *Academy of Management Journal* 23(3): 385–404.

Litschert, R.J. 1968. Some characteristics of long-range planning: An industry study. *Academy of Management Journal* 11(3): 315–28.

Negandhi, A.R. 1987. *International management.* Boston: Allyn & Bacon.

Pearce II, J.A.; Robbins, D.K.; and Robinson, Jr., R.B. 1987. The impact of grand strategy and planning formality on financial performance. *Strategic Management Journal* 8(2): 125–34.

Sim, A.R. 1977. Decentralized management of subsidiaries and their performance. *Management International Review* 2: 45–52.

Steiner, G., and Cannon, W.M. 1966. *Multinational corporate planning.* New York: Macmillan.

Zwick, J. 1966. Is top management really on top? *Columbia Journal of World Business* 1(1): 87–96.

8

The Cultural Components of Strategic Decision Making in the International Arena

Coral R. Snodgrass
Uma Sekaran

T he vast majority of managers of U.S. companies resort to strategic
planning as a means of enhancing their growth and profits. However,
the internationalization of business has forced managers to look at
the strategic planning process in a new light to achieve a competitive position
in the global marketplace. Many U.S. managers are surprised and frustrated
when they attempt to implement on an international scale strategies formulated according to traditional strategic planning models only to find that
they seem to be faring worse than some of their global competitors. They are
often dismayed that the United States has lost its primacy in certain markets
and now lags behind in the international marketplace. Has the strategy of
U.S. corporations somehow failed or is the success of the foreign competitors
due to favorable environmental factors, such as low capital costs and more
favorable industrial policies? Although it is difficult to come up with a
definitive answer to this question, this chapter draws attention to some of the
shortcomings found when attempting to apply a traditional strategic planning
model to the international arena. Such shortcomings might adversely affect a
firm's global competitive edge. The paper highlights the cultural components
of the strategic decision making process as they impact the competitive position of organizations in the international arena. Strategic planners will do well
to consider these before embarking on strategic planning designed to gain a
competitive edge in the global marketplace.

The Complexities in Strategic Planning

The globalization of the market has put an onerous burden on strategic planners who deal with the knotty issues of competitive advantage and long-term

viability of the organization by adding several dimensions of complexity to their decision making. Unlike the case of purely domestic operations, strategic management becomes ill-structured and frustrating in the face of diverse and poorly-understood political, economic, legal, and social factors that vary radically across the globe. Add to these the complexity of the differences in the cultural values of organizational members in different parts of the world and strategic planning in today's organization indeed becomes a formidable task. No wonder then that international business operations have continued to remain an enigma to those in business and has posed several dilemmas to strategic planners (Ghosal 1987).

Some of the complexity of strategic management in the international arena has already been successfully addressed by other researchers. As an example, the assessment of the political environment has been greatly enhanced by the development of systematic models for the evaluation of such factors as political risk (Vernon 1985). Further understanding of the business environment has also been enhanced by the development of many comparative management models such as those cataloging differences in accounting practices (Schweikart 1986). Management strategies for global operations have also been advocated (Negandhi 1985, 1987; Negandhi and Baliga 1979). However, the impact of cultural variations on the success of strategic management endeavors has not yet been systematically explored. Understanding these phenomena is essential to the development of useful models for assisting strategic planners in dealing with the dynamics of cultural complexity. The purpose of this chapter is the development of an understanding of the role of culture in strategic planning. The chapter first highlights the three stages of the strategic planning process identifying a specific strategy decision relevant to each stage. Next it defines and operationalizes culture. Finally, the cultural concepts are applied to each of the identified decisions to explore their impact on strategic decision making. The chapter thus develops a broader understanding of how the careful explication of the cultural components of the strategic planning process can lead to more effective strategic decision making in the international arena.

The Strategic Planning Process

The strategic planning process has as its goal the long-term viability of the organization within all of its environment (Jauch and Glueck, 1987). Toward the accomplishment of this goal, strategic decisionmakers must deal with issues regarding strategy formulation, implementation, and evaluation. Strategy formulation deals with determining the organization's domain and analyzing its internal and external environments and choosing a strategic direction. Strategy implementation deals with structuring the organization in such a way that the chosen strategy can be appropriately carried out. Strategy evaluation deals with assessing the effectiveness and efficiency of performance and identifying the need for change, if any.

Each of these three stages has a specific decision whose cultural components render the strategic decision making process more complex in the international arena. In the strategy formulation process, a vital factor or ingredient is the assessment of the competitive environment of the business and an understanding of how the organization can remain viable in that environment. An integral component of strategy implementation is the design or the structure of the organization. The size, shape, number of hierarchical levels, and management control systems that are incorporated in the organization are basic design decision issues that spell the difference between the success and failure of the system. An important aspect of the strategy evaluation phase is detecting deviations from planned goals and closing the gap between desired and actual performance results by incorporating the requisite changes. The competitive analysis at the strategy formulation phase of strategic management, the design of structural aspects at the strategy implementation phase, and the incorporation of changes to close the gap between desired and actual results in the evaluation phase are the three basic issues examined in the context of cultural complexities in this chapter.

The need for comprehending the impact of culture on these three decisions should not be underestimated. Managers in the United States are often perplexed about the dynamics of competition in other cultures for formulating their strategies. For instance, in some countries, governments subsidize companies on a long-term basis to compete in foreign markets. U.S. companies are puzzled and frustrated by this and consider such practices as unfair. However, if the U.S. managers can understand culture's role in such practices, they can then make informed choices and formulate appropriate and viable alternative strategies for successfully competing in the international market.

Likewise, in the strategy implementation phase, understanding the influence of culture on structural design is vital to a U.S. company having an office or subsidiary abroad employing local nationals. In such a case, understanding how to make strategic choices in structuring the organization and developing management control systems that facilitate the effective coordination of individuals' efforts within the organization becomes critical for the organization's success. If the organization simply tries to transplant the same structures, processes, and even goals that it has in the home office, without understanding the cultural differences and making appropriate modifications for the preferred modes of operation of the individuals in the foreign culture, it faces serious problems.

In the strategy evaluation plan, managers are often confused about how to bring about changes when the outcomes fall short of their goals. They must address the cultural dynamics of change processes when trying to close the gap between desired and actual performance, especially when the change involves the transfer of technology from one culture to another. Technology that is very useful and easily and successfully incorporated into a system in one country may produce just the opposite results when transferred to another country. For instance, strategic planners in the United States might try to transplant a technology which is very successfully applied in Japan and may be baffled that it does not work. A significant reason for this could be that the cultural predispositions of people may run counter to the demands that a particular technology imposes, and hence the technology may fail to work. Understanding the part that culture plays in assessing whether or not technology can be successfully transferred to close a performance gap helps managers make good strategic decisions regarding such attempts at transplantation at the strategy evaluation phase.

These three specific strategic decision situations can be examined from a cultural perspective by using Hofstede's (1980) four dimensions of culture. Such an examination produces an understanding of culture's role in formulating, implementing, and evaluating strategies to gain a competitive edge in the international arena.

Hofstede's Four Cultural Dimensions

The relevance for strategic decision making of the four dimensions of culture delineated by Hofstede becomes clear once these dimensions are explained. Hofstede did a questionnaire survey of nationals from over forty countries employed by a multinational corporation; he collected data from them at two different points in time. Analysis of his data applying ecological correlations suggested that the countries surveyed can be placed along four dimensions of culture. These four dimensions are useful for understanding organizations and their members' predispositions in the different countries. Hofstede called these dimensions power distance, uncertainty avoidance, individualism-collectivism, and masculinity-femininity.

Power Distance. Power distance basically refers to the nature of the distribution of power within the organizational system. Hofstede defines power distance as the difference between the influence that a superior feels comfortable in exerting over a subordinate and that which the subordinate feels comfortable in exerting over a superior in any particular system. Where subordinates are afraid or feel uncomfortable to say what they genuinely think and feel in the work setting, the power distance is greater. Usually too much centralization and a hierarchical structure creates greater power distance between the bosses and subordinates in the system. In some cultures, such a distance is desired by both the superiors and the subordinates; in others, it is not.

Uncertainty Avoidance. Uncertainty avoidance refers to a country's level of intolerance for ambiguity or uncertainty. That is, it indicates the extent to which members experience feelings of anxiety and stress because they have to face an uncertain future. Different cultures adapt to uncertainties in different ways—they either try to fiercely protect themselves against uncertainties through various mechanisms, or at the other extreme, simply accept them as a way of life. Organizations embedded in cultures with a high need to avoid uncertainty reduce anxiety levels by setting rules and regulations, planning, and forecasting. Organizations in cultures with a low need to avoid uncertainty take things as they come and avoid a lot of bureaucratic rules and procedures.

Individualism-Collectivism. Individualism-collectivism reflects how an individual perceives his or her relationship with the rest of the collectivity or other people in the environment. More collectivistic societies have a tendency to look for a good deal of emotional dependence among members within the system as well as to rely on the organizational system to take care of members' needs. In more individualistic societies, members have a tendency to feel that each is an active agent in the system pursuing his or her own goal and making an impact on the environment in which the individual operates. Members in such societies have a very low need for dependency on the organization or other members within the system, thus exhibiting an individualistic rather than a collectivistic orientation.

Masculinity-Femininity. Masculinity-femininity refers to the primary goals and objectives that societies have for their progress. Some cultures have a need to be machismo (exhibit ostentatious manly qualities) while others have a need to be marianismo (exhibit soft and near saintly qualities). The masculinity-femininity dimension is reflected in organizational systems in different cultures in the dominant job values and organizational goals that are set. In masculine cultures where the dominant values include showing off, performing, achieving, and becoming big, organizations' primary goals tend to be to make profits, increase market share, and compete aggressively. In feminine cultures, on the other hand, where the dominant values include being people oriented, being sensitive to the environment, and considering small as beautiful, organizations tend to emphasize the goals of dedication to service ideals and quality of life through cooperation and empathy.

These four dimensions are related to the three issues of interest discussed earlier and can be effectively explored with a view to enhancing the effectiveness of strategic decision making.

Strategy Formulation in the Context of Cultural Dynamics of Competition in the International Marketplace

To formulate effective strategies U.S. managers must obtain a grasp of the dynamics of competition and the underlying frame of reference from which people in different cultures operate in the international marketplace. This will help U.S. managers not to get perplexed or frustrated by what they encounter in international competition. For example, U.S. managers often deal with a Japanese competitor. Being in masculine countries, both compete on the basis of profits; even so, the way they compete in the international sphere is totally different and may often be confusing to the U.S. party. The Japanese, being high on collectivism, approach competition from a completely different perspective than Americans despite the fact that both countries are masculine and desire profits as a goal. A comparison of Japan and the United States on the two cultural dimensions of masculinity-femininity and individualism-collectivism is graphically displayed in table 8–1.

The competitive prices of Japanese goods in the international market are in good measure due to the collaborative collectivistic orientations of the Japanese. This is manifested in: (1) the high degree of cooperation between management and labor where both work toward mutual common good; (2) cooperation between government and business where the government sub-

Table 8–1
Comparison of Japanese and U.S. Cultural Dimensions Relevant for Competing in the International Marketplace

Cultural Dimension	Country	Characteristic	Goals and Plans to Become Competitive
Masculinity-Femininity	Japan	Masculine	Profits as the goal or end result
	United States	Masculine	Profits as the goal or end result
Individualism-Collectivism	Japan	Collectivistic	Cooperation among union, government, and other companies as the means for achieving the goal
	United States	Individualistic	Competing from one's own strength without entering into relationships with other entities in one's environment

sidizes the companies to gain a competitive edge in the international market; and (3) surprisingly, even cooperation among competing firms within Japan when it comes to international competition, taking a nationalistic collectivistic approach (Ronen 1986). The collectivistic orientation of the Japanese allows for the dynamics of a successfully operating competitive international strategy to come into play through internal collaboration. In contrast, it is more natural for individualistically oriented U.S. companies to fight the battles on an individual basis to maximize profits, and quite frequently, deliberately avoid the prospects of entering into collaborative relationships with other American companies. The U.S. government, as a matter of fact, does not encourage such cooperation with its antitrust laws. Thus, by looking at the two dimensions of masculinity-femininity and individualism-collectivism, U.S. managers can gain some insights into the nature of the competition they are up against. When perceived in this light, instead of getting frustrated with the Japanese for competing unfairly through government subsidies, U.S. managers can understand and make sense of highly confusing situations in the international marketplace. Obtaining a clearer understanding of how different organizations from different cultures formulate their own strategies to compete in the international arena helps the U.S. companies to formulate their own counter strategies to successfully compete—strategies that are in keeping with their own cultural orientations and preferred modes of behavior.

Dealing with International Competition

In the western tradition, competition is the lubricant of a free market. The operating belief is that all competitors have free and equal access to the market and the player with the best goods and services at the best prices gets the biggest share of the market. When this does not happen in the international arena because of government intervention, monopolistic power concentration, or some other "unnatural" intercession, the western manager cries "unfair." The fact is that in the international marketplace, many culturally legitimate interferences take place which are not in consonance with the western notion of the free market. Recognizing this is the first step in taking further steps to enhance our competitive advantage. As an illustration, let us consider how the United States can compete against Japan. U.S. managers cannot emulate the Japanese style of cooperation nor can they hope to establish such webs of interdependencies that the Japanese use to lower costs. Not only can the Americans not cooperate in this manner due to their individualism orientation, but many such forms of cooperation are also considered illegal in the United States. Thus, Americans have to find other culturally acceptable ways to enhance their competitive position. The key goal is cost containment and enhancing the quality of products to achieve a competitive edge. One way the United States can achieve this is by inspiring and encouraging innovation, technological breakthroughs, and creativity. Such a strategy is also congruent with the American cultural value of individualism because individuals who creatively contribute ideas to attain the goal are recognized and rewarded for their individual talents, skills, and contributions. Thus, it becomes clear that trying to enhance U.S. competitiveness through the adaptation of collectivistic Japanese techniques such as quality circles is just the opposite of what U.S. managers should do—unless these techniques are considerably modified to encourage and reward individual work. America achieved greatness through the entrepreneurial spirit of individuals working to creatively build their companies as is typical of "the American way." Likewise, American competitiveness can be enhanced through individual creativity by capitalizing on the American cultural values of individualism and growth.

Strategy Implementation in the Context of Culture and Strategic Choices Governing Structure

Generally, an organization chooses to design its various branches and subsidiaries modeled on one structural pattern—usually the same that it has developed at the head office. This is understandable in terms of efficiency because designing different structures and systems is highly resource consuming. However, quite frequently, the single design phenomenon does not work effectively across multiple cultural units with the result that the goals of the organization are often compromised. Thus, in the interests of efficiency, effectiveness is sacrificed in many cases. How then, can the manager know how to evolve different structures and design control mechanisms to attain effectiveness in different cultures? Hofstede's four dimensions of culture are very useful here.

Two main issues are of concern in the design of an organizational system in any culture: One is prescribing the appropriate roles to the individuals and placing them within the organization; the other is developing appropriate management control systems to ensure that the efforts of individuals are coordinated through proper monitoring, evaluation, and rewards. In effect, four factors attain importance in systems design: (1) the number of levels in the hierarchy (organizational structure); (2) information flows that are organized to ensure that proper directions and feedback mechanisms are available in the system for the employees to get the job done (monitoring systems); (3) evaluation of the performance of the employees in a way that will keep them motivated to perform their best (evaluation system); and (4) dispensing rewards that would be valent to those who performed well on the job (reward system).

The four cultural dimensions described earlier relate to the four aspects of structural and systems design mentioned earlier. The number of hierarchical levels is directly related to the power distance dimension, the monitoring system is related to the uncertainty avoidance dimension, the evaluation system is closely connected with the individualism-collectivism dimension, and the reward system is aligned with the masculinity-femininity dimension. For an organization to attain its goals, there should be a fit among the four cultural dimensions and the various aspects of structure. To put it differently, the way in which the organization is structured should mesh with the preferred modes of behavior of the employees in a particular culture.

Alignment between Structure and the Cultural Dimension of Power Distance

If the foreign country in which the organization is to be designed is high in power distance—that is, both the superiors and subordinates want to maintain a respectful distance between them—the larger the number of hierarchical levels embedded in the system, the better fitted the structure is to the predispositions of the people who interact within the system. In the low power distance culture, however, the fewer the number of hierarchical levels in the structure of the organization, the greater are the opportunities for constant two-way interactions and influence processes. Thus, the structure of the organization—that is, the number of levels in the hierarchy—has to fit the preferred modes of behavior of the superiors and subordinates in the culture so that there are no undue stresses and discomfort experienced by individuals operating in the system.

Alignment of the Monitoring System and the Cultural Dimension of Uncertainty Avoidance

In cultures where there is a high need to avoid uncertainty, organizations and their members feel comfortable when mechanisms that offer them a hedge against future uncertainties are evolved. These include plans, rules, building complex information systems, and instituting legal and institutional measures that act as safeguards against future uncertainties and offer security and relief from anxiety to organizations and their members who function effectively without experiencing dysfunctional stress. On the other hand, in cultures where uncertainty avoidance is very low, elaborate plans, rules, information systems, and legal documents would be considered a bureaucratic hindrance to effective performance. In such cultures, minimal control systems are needed and one plays it by ear rather than elaborately preparing for an unknown future. Such a strategy helps individuals within the system to operate freely without being constrained by "unnecessary bureaucratic red tape." The design of information and control systems should thus fit the level of need for uncertainty avoidance of organizational members in different cultures to allow them to perform their roles effectively.

Alignment of the Evaluation System with the Cultural Dimension of Individualism-Collectivism

Evaluation systems designed within organizations are closely related to Hofstede's cultural dimension of individualism-collectivism. That is, organizational members in a highly individualistic society need evaluation systems designed differently than those in a highly collectivistic society. In the former, evaluation of performance has to be on the basis of individual performance, effectiveness, and achievement. For instance, individual members operating within the system have to be held accountable for defect rates and dysfunctional alienated behaviors such as frequent absenteeism. Likewise, individual members have to be evaluated highly for their extraordinary unique contributions in the individualistic culture. In collectivistic cultures, on the other hand, the organization has to take responsibility for organizing work around interdependent group members and evolve group-based training and reward mechanisms. Such steps alone motivate members to perform effectively in the collectivistic culture. The members in such cultures do not see themselves as unique individuals in the organizational system, but as a cooperative group in which unlimited interdependence among members is desired, valued, and considered important for successful performance. Members in such groups like to be evaluated as a group and rewarded for the group efforts. Following an evaluation system that somehow does not acknowledge the group notion, results in dysfunctional consequences in such cultures. Hence, the evaluation system and the extent of individualism or collectivism of the members should be congruent.

Alignment of the Reward System with the Cultural Dimension of Masculinity-Femininity

Masculine societies have as their goals profits, growth, and bigness. When members have accomplished these goals, they expect to be compensated in monetary rewards, higher status, and recognition and promotion. If these are not forthcoming, most members cease to be motivated to work toward the goals of the organization. In feminine cultures, quality of life, service ideals, and social welfare are the primary goals toward which organizations gravitate. Employees in such cultures feel gratified when the organization creates a cooperative work climate, offers a good quality of working life for the members, and provides security and a sense of overall satisfaction with the workplace. In only monetary rewards are provided, to the exclusion of these other factors, organizational members in such cultures are not motivated to work toward accomplishing the goals of the organization. Thus, again, the reward systems should be congruent with what is considered valent by members in masculine and feminine societies. The most effective structural patterns for the different culture groups are portrayed in table 8–2.

Implications of Culture for Strategy Implementation through Organization Design

It follows from what has been discussed earlier that before designing the structure and the management control systems in foreign offices, managers must become knowledgeable about the cultural characteristics of the foreign land and try to make their design congruent with the preferences of the organizational members in that culture. For a detailed discussion and comparison between the United States and Japan/India, see Sekaran and Snodgrass (1986). If, for any reason, U.S. managers consider that having different structural and systems designs for their different offices abroad is not appealing to their managerial philosophy, they can then investigate the feasibility of conducting their international operations in countries culturally similar to their own. This enables them to have the same systems wherever they operate and to develop a uniform corporate culture irrespective of the location.

Strategy Evaluation in the Context of Cultural Variations to Be Considered in Making Strategic Decisions

At the strategy evaluation stage, when the actual performance of a system falls short of expectations or goals set, corrective measures are usually contem-

**Table 8–2
Dimensions of Culture and the Structure of the Organization**

Cultural Dimensions	Structural Dimensions
Power distance	Hierarchy
High	Many levels
Low	Few levels
Uncertainty avoidance	Monitoring/information system
High	Complex
Low	Minimal
Individualism/collectivism	Evaluation system
Individualistic	Based on individual performance
Collectivistic	Based on group performance
Masculinity/femininity	Reward system
Masculine	Money, power
Feminine	Quality of life

plated. It is not unusual for organizations going through this process to resort to the use of more sophisticated throughput processes, often in the form of new technology. For instance, just-in-time (JIT) inventory management so effective in Japan is frequently contemplated by U.S. manufacturing organizations as a profit enhancing mechanism. But before adopting technology transfers such as the JIT, managers have to examine the cultural setting of the organization that proposes to use it and compare it with the cultural conditions ideally suited for the success of such technology.

The JIT inventory system is designed to eliminate raw materials inventory, thus cutting down on the costs of advance ordering and storage. Because JIT technology eliminates the costs of inventory, its success is contingent on the reorder goods arriving on time so that the production is not held up for want of raw materials. For the JIT technique to be successful, at least two conditions should be met: One is a shared goal of profit maximization based on cost reductions; the second is adequate and reliable mechanisms built in to ensure supplies of raw materials at the critical time. The JIT technique is highly successful in Japan, a masculine country subscribing to the notion of profit maximization and cost reduction. If it were to be used in the United States, it should pose no ideological problem since the United States is also a masculine country. However, for the technology to function effectively, there must be a close interdependent relationship established between the organization and its supplier, with a high degree of trust and reliance operating between the two. In other words, both the supplier and the organization must see themselves as functioning together as a close-knit, interdependent, and mutually benefiting dyad who jointly operate smoothly and reliably. In Japan's collectivistic culture, a reliable, mutually dependent relationship between the supplier and the customer is smoothly worked out. As a matter of fact, Japanese organizations expend a lot of time identifying, establishing, and developing such long-term relationships with their suppliers (Bolwijn and Brinkman 1987). Such deals establish a direct link and partnership; they can also be successfully and reliably worked out because Japan is high on the uncertainty avoidance dimension. Because of their low tolerance for facing ambiguity or future uncertainty, the organization as well as the supplier derive a sense of security from such deals. The organization feels comfortable knowing that there is a definite source of supply from one reliable and trustworthy supplier and the supplier is secure in the thought that there is one organization that will surely guarantee business. Thus, the supplier and the organization see themselves functioning together as an integral unit.

Transferring JIT Technology to the United States

Can a U.S. organization embedded in a highly individualistic culture work out such a cooperative and highly interdependent form of relationship with specific suppliers so as to make the JIT technology work just as successfully as it does in Japan? The technology, though appealing to the U.S. managers because of the masculine profit orientation, may not be successfully transplanted to the United States. Being in a highly individualistic society, U.S. organizations perceive themselves as distinct from other units in their environment and are highly reluctant to share risks with an external organization. Also, being much lower in the uncertainty avoidance dimension compared to Japan (the U.S. score being 46 against 92 for Japan—a high score indicating a high need to avoid uncertainty), the U.S. approach would be to shop around and negotiate with several potential suppliers to obtain the best prices as and when supplies become necessary. This is a much easier process for a U.S. organization trying to cut down on inventory costs, than establishing long-term relationships with an outside system and being fully dependent on them to ensure just-in-time supplies. These considerations help to explain why firms in the United States have such trouble instituting JIT systems (Hutchins 1986).

This example illustrates that strategic decision making designed to close the gap between desired and actual outcomes is also culture bound. Understanding the uniqueness of each culture helps managers to make viable strategic decisions on whether, for instance, a technology that works well in one culture ought to be transferred to another or not.

Conclusion

This chapter presents three different situations from the three phases of the strategic planning process to illustrate the impact of culture on strategic decision making in the highly competitive international arena. Not understanding the dynamics of culture or ignoring the impact of culture on strategic planning only results in impairing an organization's competitive position. Before the globalization of the marketplace, strategic planners were simply concerned about domestic competition. Today, as goods produced in Korea from raw materials imported from India are marketed in the United States by Japanese or Taiwanese nationals, or as Japanese cars are manufactured in the United States, not only for the local market but for export to other countries, culture becomes a significant variable in international competition. Currently, there exists a growing body of knowledge concerning cultural variations among different nations and researchers are increasingly trying to delineate the organizationally relevant dimensions of culture. There is no longer any need to treat culture as a "black box" and ignore it. Since there is ample evidence that culture's consequences have a tremendous impact on international competitiveness, the dynamics of culture should be understood and incorporated into the strategic planning process by corporate planners to ensure that the

United States regains its competitive edge in international operations by not making strategic mistakes in the strategic planning process.

References

Bolwijn, P.T., and Brinkman, S. 1987. Japanese manufacturing: Strategy and practice. *Long Range Planning* 20(1): 25–34.

Ghosal, S. 1987. Global strategy: An organizing framework. *Strategic Management Journal* 8(5): 425–40.

Hofstede, G. 1980. *Culture's consequences: International differences in work-related values.* Beverly Hills, Calif.: Sage Publications.

Hutchins, D. 1986. Having a hard time with just-in-time. *Fortune* 113(12): 64–66.

Jauch, L.R., and Glueck, W.F. 1987. *Business policy and strategic management,* 5th ed. New York: McGraw-Hill.

Negandhi, A.R. 1985. *Management strategies and policies of American, German, and Japanese multinational corporations. Management Japan* 18(1): 12–20.

———. 1987. *International management.* Boston: Allyn & Bacon.

Negandhi, A.R., and Baliga, B.R. 1979. Quest for survival and growth: A comparative study of American, European, and Japanese multinationals. New York: Praeger.

Ronen, S. 1986. *Comparative and multinational management.* New York: John Wiley & Sons.

Schweikart, J. 1986. The environment and multinational accounting systems. In *Advances in international comparative management,* Vol. 2, ed. R.N. Farmer, 85–94. Greenwich, CT: JAI Press.

Sekaran, U. and Snodgrass, C.R. 1986. A model for examining organizational effectiveness cross-culturally. In *Advances in international comparative management,* Vol. 2, ed. R.N. Farmer, 211–32. Greenwich, CT: JAI Press.

Vernon, R. 1985. Organizational and institutional responses to international risk. In *Strategic management of multinational corporations* by H.V. Wortzel and L.H. Wortzel, 112–29. New York: John Wiley & Sons.

Part III
Functional Area Strategies in an International Setting

9

International Market Entry Strategies and Level of Involvement in Marketing Activities

Syed H. Akhter
Roberto Friedman

S ince the end of World War II, the international component of world gross national product (GNP) has been growing more rapidly than the world GNP itself. The economic consequences of this tremendous increase in global trade will have significant bearing not only on multinational corporations, but also on domestic companies finding themselves in secured positions in their local markets. As this growth in foreign trade provides opportunities to companies that have reached out of their home markets, it also threatens the market positions of companies that are geopolitically confined in their marketing operations.

For a long time the operating frontier of businesspeople has been their national home market, which they considered understandable and fairly predictable. Currently, faced with an array of new challenges and competitive pressures through burgeoning foreign competition, organizations are reshaping their marketing strategies and broadening their domain of operation. Executives are realizing that the future success or failure of their organizations in today's competitive marketplace depends on their ability to restructure business involvement and marketing strategies in response to changing global environments and markets.

This chapter pursues two major objectives: (1) the identification and analysis of factors affecting the strengths and weaknesses of foreign markets, and (2) the development of a conceptual framework for selecting foreign market entry strategies and programming marketing activities.

To achieve the first objective, a list of economic and political factors have been identified and examined for their contribution to economic opportunity and political risk, two composite variables having significant bearing on business potentials of foreign markets. To achieve the second objective, a matrix showing the interaction between economic opportunity and political risk has been developed for judging the appropriateness of different international marketing entry strategies, and examining the level of marketing activities involved with each entry strategy. To position the subject matter of this chapter in its proper perspective, the following section briefly explicates the international marketing implications of the emerging global competitive threats and opportunities.

The Great Wall Hypothesis

In this age of discontinuity characterized by rapid change in social, political, and economic fabrics, business executives are finding it necessary to define and redefine their respective markets. Thus, environmental scanning, the process of reading, understanding, and anticipating the environments that come together in a firm's market, is becoming an important managerial activity for gaining a competitive edge in today's marketplace.

As international competitors become increasingly sophisticated in developing and implementing effective marketing strategies, firms find it exceedingly difficult to protect their domestic markets. Many companies with well-established home markets have generally considered themselves invulnerable to threats coming from the outside. They think that they have built a *Great Wall* of customer and distributor loyalty around their markets; a wall that foreign competitors will find impregnable. The reasons for this attitude are twofold: First, these firms operate in their home base, and so consider themselves experts in fending off most international marketing encroachments. Second, even if they see any possibility of threats, they cannot envision that their marketing strategies and understanding of the market can be matched in the long run—let alone surpassed—by foreign competitors. This attitude, not surprisingly, has spelled many major casualties. For instance, American TV manufacturers, failing to realize that they were competing not only in their domestic market but also in the world market, found themselves defenseless against better quality and price competitive Japanese TVs (Davidson 1982). In contrast, however, through successful application of international marketing strategies, U.S. perfume companies managed to reduce France's exports of perfumes to the United States while increasing their own market share in France (*A U.S. Inversion,* Sep. 1).

Reduction in international trade barriers along with the increased participation of Eastern European countries in world trade have opened up new vistas of marketing opportunities (Naor 1986). Ideological and economic barriers, once considered inexterminable and hence a deterrent to international trade, are now being slowly removed by pragmatic approaches to politics and economics. Consequently, trade with China, Russia, and other communist countries is expected to increase in the future (Czinkota and Ronkainen 1988; Hisrich et al. 1981). In addition, and as a direct consequence of the state of the art in information and communication technologies, the economic and social aspirations of people around the world increasingly demand access to a better standard of living, achievable only through mutually beneficial exchange of goods, services, and ideas with citizens of other countries that may not necessarily share the same political and economic dogma.

As international marketing competition increases with increasing international trade, managers are faced with two critical tasks: (1) protect their home market, and (2) establish and/or strengthen their marketing presence internationally. Marketing executives confronting the emerging global competitive reality are encouraged to restructure their market and marketing strategies. For example, Gerber Baby Foods, recognizing the effect on its business of the falling U.S. birth rate, established operations in Costa Rica, where the birth rate was increasing (Norvell 1980). In the future, therefore, not only market boundaries but also relevant competitors will change due to changes in competitive milieu. As international competition increases, managers have to creatively select foreign market entry strategies and design appropriate international marketing involvement strategies.

International Market Entry Strategies

Within the parameters of a company's resources and objectives, foreign market entry decisions should be formulated in the context of economic opportunity and political risk present in different country markets. Broadly speaking, international market entry strategies can be grouped under exporting, licensing, contract manufacturing, management contracting, and investing (cf. Business International 1970; Root 1982; Terpstra 1987). A brief explanation of the different modes of entry follows:

Exporting. Direct and indirect exporting are two options available to a firm wishing to establish marketing presence in a foreign market. In direct exporting, a firm performs the activities necessary for selling products in a foreign market. A firm becomes an indirect exporter when it performs no special activity for the selling of a product in a foreign market. Indirect exporting is performed through an intermediary.

Licensing. Licensing involves payment of a specified fee or royalty by the licensee in exchange for the use of a patent, trademark, product formula, or anything of value. The licensor has little control over strategic and operational decision making and does not participate fully in the profits made by the licensee.

Contract Manufacturing. Under a contract manufacturing arrangement, the firm agrees to let a local manufacturer produce the product, but retains the marketing responsibilities. Entry into the market is obtained with little risk to investment.

Management Contracting. In management contracting the firm provides management expertise and technical know-how to a foreign company that is providing the capital. The management team acts as a consultant to the company, and faces the same problem inherent with staff positions.

Joint Ventures. In a joint venture the company shares in ownership, risk, profit, and control of the business with local businesspeople. It represents a higher level of business involvement than exporting, licensing, contract manufacturing, and management contracting.

Wholly Owned Subsidiary. Compared to the previously mentioned entry strategies, a wholly owned subsidiary provides greater control over strategic and operational decisions, greater economies of operation, and greater potential for identifying with local values and aspirations. With a wholly owned subsidiary, both investment commitment and exposure to risk are the highest.

The selection of a market entry strategy is facilitated by evaluating the following two conditions: those internal to the firm and those existing in foreign markets. In evaluating internal conditions, managers should answer the following: How much risk is the company willing to undertake? How much return does the company expect on its investment? How long is the designated payback period? How much cash flow does the company expect? How much control does it want on decision making related to manufacturing and marketing? How experienced is the company in international marketing? What are the short-term and long-term goals of the company? The answers to these questions help a company select an appropriate entry strategy developed in the context of economic opportunity and political risk present in different country markets.

Determinants of International Economic Opportunity and Political Risk

International markets provide a unique set of opportunities and threats. Primarily, due to lack of information and knowledge about foreign markets, many business executives shirk from committing their resources to international marketing and in the process forgo existing and incipient marketing opportunities.

While acknowledging the existence and importance of several other variables such as sociocultural, educational, legal, and religious, two factors that have significant bearings on determining foreign market attractiveness are economic conditions and political conditions. The significance of economic and political conditions in determining the strengths and weaknesses as well as the opportunities and threats of a particular market is well accepted in international business literature (Doz 1980; Chakravarthy and Perlmutter 1985). This chapter suggests that the interaction between these two variables generates various viable options for entering a foreign market.

Economic conditions in a foreign market can be dichotomized as representing high opportunity or low opportunity, whereas politcal conditions can be characterized as representing high-risk or low-risk situations. In this chapter, we relate economic and political conditions to provide a pragmatic framework for developing international market entry strategies and deciding on the level of involvement in marketing activities in a given foreign market. As international marketing becomes more complex, the development of a formal and pragmatic framework to aid practitioners in their decision making process becomes imperative. In the absence of a conceptual framework, decision making proceeds heuristically, generally with adverse consequences.

The matrix in figure 9.1 reflects the interaction between economic and political conditions, and delineates the level of investments that can be thought of as baseline measures from which to derive market entry and marketing involvement strategies for foreign markets. This matrix extends the product portfolio (Henderson 1979) and market portfolio (Harrell and Kiefer 1981) matrices—two decision-making tools that have proved useful for strategic business and marketing decisions. Building on these generally accepted tools, the proposed matrix provides a structured approach for using economic opportunity and political risk in the delineation of international market entry and marketing involvement strategies.

Economic Opportunity

Economic opportunity exists when the conditions required for conducting business activities are present or can be developed, and also when adequate effective demand exists or can be developed to satisfy the organizational objectives of the firm. High economic opportunity or low economic opportunity, thus, is determined by the relative presence or absence of factors conducive to the production and marketing of a firm's goods and services. Depending on the business, the factors necessary for the production and/or marketing of goods and services vary and so do each factor's importance. The first step, therefore, in assessing economic opportunities in a host country is to identify the major factors that determine economic opportunities. These are infrastructure, competition, financial climate, population, and other related variables.

Government's role
Type of government
Internal and external strife
Regional alliance
Special interest groups
Political objectives
Nationalism
Human rights

POLITICAL RISK

			High	Low
Infrastructure	E	O		
Competition	C	P	High	Joint venture / Management contracting / Contract manufacturing / Exporting	Joint venture / Wholly owned subsidiary
Exchange rate	O	P		
Inflation rate	N	O		
Population	O	R		
PCI	M	T		
GNP	I	U		
Culture	C	N	Low	Management contracting / Contract manufacturing / Exporting	Exporting / Licensing
Language		I		
Religion		T		
Legal constraints		Y		

(Left vertical label: ECONOMIC OPPORTUNITY)

Matrix cells:

	POLITICAL RISK High	POLITICAL RISK Low
High	Joint venture Management contracting Contract manufacturing Exporting	Joint venture Wholly owned subsidiary
Low	Management contracting Contract manufacturing Exporting	Exporting Licensing

Figure 9–1. Foreign Market Entry Strategies

Infrastructure. Infrastructure includes items such as the number of different modes of transportation and their relative conditions, availability of communication media, availability of energy and power, and the level of technological development. The infrastructure of a given nation can be categorized as developed, developing, or underdeveloped, depending on the needs and requirements of production and/or marketing activities of the firm.

A developed infrastructure exists when factors comprising infrastructure are adequately and reliably available to meet the needs and requirements of a company's production and/or marketing activities. An infrastructure is developing when substantial public and private investment has been made to improve the existing market relevant conditions. Infrastructure is underdeveloped when infrastructural conditions do not exist for efficient business operations, nor has any substantial investment been made to change the existing conditions.

Whereas a developed infrastructure represents high economic opportunity and an underdeveloped infrastructure indicates low economic opportunity, a developing infrastructure can be categorized in terms of economic opportunity, only when viewed in its potential for future developments. Analysis of each of the relevant factors of an economy's infrastructure helps determine its effects on market potential. For instance, in summarizing the effect of only one of the infrastructure variables, Sarma and Rao (1972) have shown that deficiency in communications can limit the extent of the market.

Competition. For the purpose of the framework proposed in this chapter, competition can be characterized as either weak or strong. The level of economic opportunity in a market is influenced by the degree of competitive activities challenging the firm. High economic opportunity is present in industries where the degree of competitive activity (indigenous and/or international) is negligible and weak, and low economic opportunity exists in industries that have strongly entrenched indigenous and/or international competitors. However, in some cases, even in the presence of fierce competition, a firm can compete effectively by capitalizing on economic opportunity present in certain untapped market niches.

Financial Climate. Four important variables can be studied under this heading: gross national product (GNP), per capita income (PCI), exchange rate, and inflation rate. GNP provides a general picture of the strength of the economy. PCI, on the other hand, is a good indicator of purchasing power of the people. In general, the higher the PCI, the more discretionary income consumers have, and hence more demand for luxury goods and services. The exchange rate provides a measure of the value of the currency. By affecting exports and imports, repatriation of earnings, and costs of conducting business, varying exchange rates influence the business potential of a market, and thus, should be carefully examined. On the other hand, the inflation rate provides a measure of loss in the value of the local currency. A high inflation rate, therefore, means a decline in the real purchasing power of consumers, and thus a reduced discretionary spending power. The influence of the inflation rate on demand for a product or brand should be evaluated to determine economic opportunity.

Population. The number of people in a given geopolitical area represents the size of the market, but not the strength and potential. Strength and potential of a market are determined by effective demand (demand backed by purchasing power). A large number of people with insufficient incomes creates a low overall economic opportunity, whereas a small number of people with large incomes may represent a profitable market. To illustrate the point, we can take two extremes, Bangladesh and Kuwait. Bangladesh has a population of 100 million people but low PCI of $130, whereas Kuwait has a small population of 1.5 million but very high PCI, around $21,000. However, care should be taken not to apply the above generalization indiscriminately in different situations and for different product categories. For example, although the PCI of Bangladesh is less than $200, it is not sufficient evidence for concluding that there is no market for expensive goods. In this case, the distribution of income provides better information about market potential for specific product categories.

Related Variables. Because of their significant impact on people's consumption behaviors, cultures, languages, value systems, religions, legal constraints, and other factors play an important part in determining economic opportunity. As evidenced by the discussions of just about every international marketing textbook currently on the market, these factors should be studied carefully. For instance, in Saudi Arabia and in some other Islamic countries one should not think of producing and marketing liquor and pork products because Islam, the religion practiced in these countries, forbids Muslims from drinking liquor and eating pork (Luqmani et al. 1980). Likewise, there are cultural and social constraints that by very strongly affecting attitudes, preferences, beliefs, and the societal role of individuals, can hinder the marketing of certain goods and services (Terpstra and David 1985).

The determination of economic opportunity is a complex task. A country can have a high economic opportunity for one product and a very low economic opportunity for another. Economic opportunity in international markets should, therefore, be evaluated in relation to each individual product. Each product demands a unique set of conditions to be successful; and complicating matters even further, the success of a product in one country does not assure its success in another.

Political Risk

Given that, by definition, international marketers generally operate in several nations simultaneously, the political realities of the nations represent an inescapable uncontrollable business variable that must be considered. An integral component of the political environments affecting a multinational firm is the degree of political risk present in such environments. Political risk exists when as a result of governmental or societal actions, operations and investments of foreign firms are adversely affected (Simon 1982).

Political risk is not a country-specific, product-specific, brand-specific, or even, a firm-specific phenomenon. It is present in industrialized countries such as France and Canada, as well as in the less developed countries (LDCs) (Robock et al. 1977). Therefore, a systematic analysis of political risk should be conducted involving its identification, likely incidence, and consequences on a company's operations (Root 1968). For a multinational marketer trying to develop or maintain a competitive advantage, an awareness of political risk is not enough. This awareness must be incorporated into the operating procedures and strategic plans of the corporation. A lack of awareness, or the failure to act on such awareness of political risk can negate the best laid international marketing plans. Variables influencing political risk should, therefore, be identified, analyzed, and interpreted. Variables relevant to political risk are discussed next.

Government's Role. Governments are increasingly playing an important role in regulating the business climate of their countries. Just as a business enterprise programs its business and marketing activities to achieve its organizational goals, governments, likewise, through decrees and legislative enactments, attempt to achieve societal goals.

At a macro level the societal goals of a government are generally concerned with broad social, economic, and political issues, such as monetary stability, inflation, trade deficit, productivity, balance of payment position, and employment of indigenous resources. On the other hand, the corporate goals of both indigenous and foreign businesses are at a micro level, generally concerned with issues such as market share, return on investment, and growth of the firm. To achieve their explicit and implicit societal goals, governments may therefore attempt to restructure different elements of the economy which may adversely affect some firms while benefitting others. The socioeconomic and political agenda of a government, therefore, considerably influences the actions that are taken to restructure the national business climate, thus determining the type of political risk that evolves (Akhter and Lusch 1988).

Type of Government. Trying to determine the degree of political risk in a nation by classifying countries based on the type of government (democracy, autocracy, socialist, communist, and military rule) rather than considering the stated and implied agenda of the political party only brings about sweeping generalizations about political risk present in that country. It cannot be said that democratic countries are politically more stable than communist countries and, therefore, have less of the various types of political risk. To gain a proper perspective of the political risk associated with the government of a nation, that government must be evaluated with respect to its stated and implied agenda reflecting the problems and potentials within the existing socioeconomic and political environment.

Internal and External Strife. A country with a high frequency of lockouts, strikes, riots, social disorder, and armed conflicts can be characterized as going through a severe adjustment process. Internal strife shows basic discontent among the populace, and occasionally this discontent may be diverted against international corporations within the country. External strife, on the other hand, is depicted by war with neighboring countries which may create uncertainties in the business climate.

Related Variables. Related variables like regional alliances, special interest groups, political freedom, nationalism, and human rights issues should be studied when determining the degree of political risk. The nature and composition of these variables influence the severity of risk. For instance, IBM Corporation was asked to terminate its business in India because of the political objectives of the Indian government. Likewise, a trend toward nationalism can create a situation of high risk. If the citizens of a particular country decide to boycott certain foreign products and services, this can create a precarious situation for international operations.

The assessment of political risk is an ongoing process. Environmental situations may change rapidly and drastically, necessitating a change in societal goals, and thus in the probability of occurrence of different political risks. The social, economic, and political environment should, therefore, be regularly monitored for emerging threats from political risk.

Drawing Up the Matrix

The task before the international marketing manager is to find a way to determine whether a country's economic opportunity and level of political risk are high or low. A grading system can be developed to reduce the complexity of the problem. We can take the example of a hypothetical company X to illustrate the system using, first, economic opportunity.

Company X divides all the factors that determine economic opportunity into three broad categories: critically relevant, moderately relevant, and marginally relevant. Next a weight is assigned to these categories on a scale of 1 to 9. Marginally relevant factors have a range of 1 to 3; moderately relevant factors fall within 4 to 6; and critically relevant factors are assigned weights from 7 to 9. The weight assigned to each factor is called its relevance weight.

1 2 3	4 5 6	7 8 9
Marginally	Moderately	Critically
Relevant	Relevant	Relevant

Critically relevant factors are those factors without which the company cannot produce and/or market its goods and services in a foreign country. For instance, widespread availability of electricity is critical for marketing TVs, but not for transistor radios. Moderately relevant factors are those factors whose presence or absence affects the company's operations, but not critically. Marginally relevant factors are those factors whose absence or presence have little significant bearing on the company's operations.

The next step is to evaluate the extent to which these three categories of factors are present in a particular country. The extent to which they are present can be divided into three categories: satisfactory, moderately satisfactory, and unsatisfactory. A weight can also be assigned to these categories on a scale from 1 to 9, with unsatisfactory from 1 to 3, moderately satisfactory from 4 to 6, and satisfactory from 7 to 9. The weight assigned to the degree of factor availability is called presence weight.

1	*2*	*3*		*4*	*5*	*6*		*7*	*8*	*9*
Unsatisfactory				Moderately Satisfactory				Satisfactory		

We can determine:

$$\sum_{i=1}^{n} x_{e,i} \cdot j_{e,i} > o_e^*,$$

where $x_{e,i}$ is the relevance weight assigned to each factor taken to determine the economic opportunity of a country.

$j_{e,i}$ is the presence weight assigned to each factor taken to determine the economic opportunity of a country.

o_e^*, is the cut-off point chosen to categorize economic opportunity into high and low categories.

Next, the same method is applied to the analysis of political risk, and we thus obtain:

$$\sum_{i=1}^{n} x_{p,i} \cdot j_{p,i} > o_p^*,$$

where $x_{p,i}$ is the relevance weight assigned to each factor taken to determine the degree of political risk of a country.

$j_{p,i}$ is the presence weight assigned to each factor taken to determine the degree of political risk of a country.

p_p^*, is the cut-off point chosen to categorize political risk into high and low categories.

Both the relevance and presence weights of different factors comprising economic opportunity and political risk vary from business to business and from country to country. For instance, a company planning to establish a manufacturing plant for digital watches evaluates the market related factors differently than a company planning to build a paper factory.

We acknowledge that in the procedure just described the determination of factor and presence relevancy, and the assignment of weights require considerable analysis, insight, and a priori managerial judgments. However, we suggest that the framework presented here systematically provides directions for appropriately examining market relevant factors and making international market entry decisions. Different entry strategies for each cell have been proposed so that firms can select the most appropriate one based on their objectives, resources, and experiences. (See figure 9–1 for entry strategies.)

When both political risk and economic opportunity are high, the managers are faced with an interesting dilemma of how to tap the market opportunities and also reduce exposure to political risks. The four recommended strategies for this cell, joint-venture, management contracting, contract manufacturing, and exporting, are motivated by the idea of reducing exposure to risk. Joint venture, in comparison to the other three strategies, involves the highest level of resource involvement and the most exposure to risk. However, by allowing local participation in equity and by increasing the stake of indigenous people in the business, the firm not only establishes its marketing presence but also may reduce the adverse consequences of political risk in the event of governmental intervention. Joint venture is therefore a viable option, although political risk is high for this cell.

When political risk is high and economic opportunity is low, contract manufacturing, management contracting, and exporting are recommended. Given that political risk is high and economic opportunity is low, a firm should reduce its financial commitment in the market, which can only be achieved by following the strategies recommended for this cell.

When political risk is low and economic opportunity is high, a firm should consider a joint venture or a wholly owned subsidiary. These two strategies are motivated by the idea of establishing a strong presence in the market. As the economic opportunity is high in these markets, it would encourage competitors to expedite their entry into these markets. Therefore, by establishing a subsidiary, a firm would not only preempt some competitors from entering the market but also improve its competitive performance by a better understanding of the market.

When both political risk and economic opportunity are low, firms should export or license to establish marketing presence in the market. These two strategies are recommended because they provide the company with the necessary experience for higher levels of business involvement in the future when the business climate improves.

Level of Involvement in Marketing Activities

The matrix developed by the interaction of economic opportunity and political risk serves as an indicator of business opportunities and threats. Placement in the respective quadrants of the matrix serves as the general basis from which appropriate international marketing involvement strategies can be developed.

Multinationals' operations in different countries' markets provide them with significant competitive advantages accruing from their global network (Kogut 1984). Therefore, the level of business involvement in each country's market should be determined by the overall contributions of each market. This suggests that, if in a given country conditions for establishing a joint venture are not present, the firm can examine other relevant possibilities. Effective international business and marketing decisions are generally multidimensional involving not only numerous countries, but also numerous resources and strategies (Naylor 1985).

For each market entry strategy proposed earlier, the delineation of levels of involvement in marketing activities is important. The important question for a multinational is to decide how many of the foreign marketing activities should be performed by the firm in a given market. In each market, however, the firm should attempt to attain success through a differential advantage in one or several business and marketing variables (Porter 1986). The level of involvement in marketing activities and the entry strategy selected are closely interlinked. For instance, the level of involvement desired in marketing activities may determine entry strategy, and vice versa. The latitude in the level of involvement in marketing activities associated with each alternative is discussed later.

In the case of exporting, the company does not have much choice when it chooses indirect exporting as a mode of entry. In direct exporting, however, the firm has a choice about performing and controlling marketing activities in foreign markets. Under this scenario, the firm may decide to open its own distribution network in foreign markets, and thereby control marketing mix decisions.

Licensing as a form of entry does not provide much leeway in deciding about the level of involvement in marketing activities in foreign markets. The licensee, in most cases, is not only responsible for the manufacturing of the product, but also for marketing-related tasks.

In contract manufacturing it is the company's responsibility to market the product. Contract manufacturing is becoming an important way of establishing marketing presence in foreign markets. This arrangement capitalizes on the expertise of the firm in marketing products, while it delegates manufacturing problems and responsibilities to the contractual partner in the host country.

Management contracting provides an excellent opportunity for gaining firsthand marketing knowledge about a given country's market. The multinational can be responsible for day-to-day management of the foreign firm, and thus, in the process, may acquire information and expertise that can be most useful for subsequent business involvement. Management contracting, by itself, does not result in a permanent market presence for the multinational.

Foreign direct investment can take two forms, joint ventures and wholly owned subsidiaries. In a joint venture, the performance of marketing tasks can be shared with the local owners, or alternatively, the firm may contractually agree to fully control the marketing activities. On the other hand, in a wholly-owned subsidiary it is the responsibility of the multinational to market the product.

Determining the level of involvement in marketing activities is not equivalent to determining international marketing strategies. Whereas the former can be derived through the matrix discussed earlier, attempting to prescribe specifics about the latter would be unrealistic and naive. The idiosyncratic elements of marketing mix strategies to follow in given markets are directly dependent on factors such as the product or service being marketed, the number of markets currently being served, the experience of the organization, economies of scale and critical mass, and the life cycle of the product or service in both the host and home markets. The specific marketing strategies to follow, therefore, depend on the specific circumstances and realities of the market in question. We contend though, that in the process of arriving at these appropriate strategies, our framework simplifies managerial decision making, and is thus a useful tool.

By delineating the basic entry strategies to follow in the internationalization of the firm, we are de facto setting up the parameters to the number and possible alternative strategies one may utilize. One may think of the different market entry alternatives as a continuum ranging from exporting to wholly owned subsidiaries. Moving from the exporting stage to the wholly owned subsidiary stage takes the firm to progressively higher levels of commitment, risk, income, control, challenges, and complexity, and to progressively lower levels of convenience, uniformity in decision making, and homogeneity of operating procedures.

Conclusion

International marketing is becoming important not only for the survival of companies but also for the growth and development of host countries' economies. The intricate mixture of economic and political environments determine economic opportunity and political risk. The grid developed by the interactions of these two variables suggests appropriate market entry strategies and levels of involvement in marketing activities for different countries' markets.

The trend toward internationalization of business will continually force companies to reorient their strategic thinking. The development of marketing involvement and market entry strategies in today's competitive international environment require considering not only the local competitive milieu but also all relevant country markets. Business executives have to consider foreign competitors' expertise in encroaching their established markets, both domestic and foreign. As we increasingly become a part of the global village, today's firms need to philosophically declare, as Socrates did centuries ago, "I am not an Athenian or a Greek, but a citizen of the world."

References

Akhter, H., and Lusch, R.F. 1988. Political risk and the evolution of the control of foreign business: Equity, earnings, and marketing mix. *Journal of Global Marketing.* 1 (Spring): 109–28.

Business International. 1970. Alternative ways to penetrate a foreign market, in *100 Checklists: Decision Making in International Operations,* pp. 6–8.

Chakravarthy, B.S., and Perlmutter, H.V. 1985. Strategic planning for a global business. *Columbia Journal of World Business,* Summer 20, 3–10.

Czinkota, M.R., and Ronkainen, I.A. 1988. *International marketing.* Hinsdale, Ill.: Dryden Press.

Davidson, W.H. 1982. *Global strategic management.* New York: John Wiley & Sons.

Doz, Y.L. 1980. Strategic management in multinational companies, *Sloan Management Review* 21 (2): 27–46.

Harrell, G.D., and Kiefer, R.O. 1981. Multinational strategic market portfolios. *MSU Business Topics,* (Winter), 20, 5–15.

Henderson, B.D. 1979. *Henderson on corporate strategy.* Cambridge, Mass.: ABT Books.

Hisrich, R.D.; Peters, M.P.; and Weinstein, A.K. 1981. East-west trade: The view from the United States. *Journal of International Business Studies,* Winter, 12, 109–21.

Kogut, B. 1984. Foreign direct investment as a sequential process. In *The Multinational corporation in the 1980s,* eds. Charles P. Kindleberger and David B. Audretsch, 38–56. Cambridge, Mass.: MIT Press.

Luqmani, M.; Quraeshi, Z.A.; and Delene, L. 1980. Marketing in Islamic countries: A viewpoint. *MSU Business Topics* 28(3): 17–25.

Naor, J. 1986. Toward a socialist marketing concept—The case of Romania, *Journal of Marketing* 50 (January): 28–39.

Naylor, T.H. 1985. The international strategy matrix. *Columbia Journal of World Business* 20 (Summer): 11–19.

Norvell, D.G. 1980. Eleven reasons for firms to go international. *Marketing News,* 17 October, pp. 1–2.

Porter, M.E. 1986. Changing patterns of international competition, *California Management Review* 28 (Winter): 9–40.

Robock, S.H.: Simmonds, K.; and Zwick, J. 1977. *International business and multinational enterprises.* Homewood, Ill.: Richard D. Irwin.

Root, F.R. 1968. U.S. business abroad and the political risks, *MSU Business Topics* (Winter): 73–80.

———. 1982. *Foreign market entry strategies.* New York: AMACOM.

Sarma, M.T.R., and Rao, T.R. 1972. Problems of rural marketing in India. *New*

Perspectives in Marketing. Indian National Council of Applied Economic Research. 1–15.

Simon, J.D. 1982. Political risk assessment: Past trends and future prospects, *Columbia Journal of World Business* 17 (Fall): 62–71.

Terpstra, V. 1987. *International marketing,* 4th ed. Hinsdale, Ill.: Dryden Press.

——— and David K. 1985. *The cultural environment of international business,* 2d ed. Cincinnati: South-Western Publishing.

A U.S. inversion in high cost perfumes. 1980. *Business Week.* 1 Sept., pp. 31–32.

10
A Model for Designing Global Financing Strategy under Conflicting Goals

Hyun B. Eom
Sang M. Lee

T he number of companies or industries that are globalizing, as well as competition in global industries, is increasing. Gaining a competitive advantage over domestic and foreign competitors requires an integrating and coordinating strategy that encompasses many functional areas. Because of the nature of international competition in the past two decades, traditional management techniques, as well as research based on earlier periods, are no longer sufficient for designing and implementing global strategies (Porter 1986). To compete globally, multinational corporations (MNCs) must adopt integration-oriented planning and control systems. Managing a business as an international entity could be a crucial factor in gaining a comparative advantage over purely domestic firms and a competitive advantage over competing MNCs. This chapter presents a model for designing global financing strategy under conflicting goals to lower the consolidated firm's cost of capital and thereby increase the financial competitiveness. Complex financing decisions are made in a dynamic, uncertain environment and thus must often satisfy these conflicting goals simultaneously: minimizing the cost of external funds after adjusting for the foreign exchange risk; maintaining the consolidated worldwide debt ratio within an acceptable range; choosing internal sources to minimize worldwide taxes and political risks; and ensuring that foreign affiliates are geared toward minimizing the firm's consolidated worldwide cost of capital rather than their own cost of capital (Eiteman and Stonehill 1986).

Using a linear programming (LP) model, Ness (1972) provided a framework for the financing and capital structure decisions that MNCs must make. The Ness model, however, assumed that the optimal debt-equity (D/E) ratio is a single point and did not deal with foreign exchange risk management. Vinso (1982) and Kornbluth and Vinso (1982) extended Ness's LP model by using stochastic GP and multiobjective fractional LP, respectively. Their models have contributed to solving financing problems by showing that the best financial planning minimizes the consolidated firm's financing cost. But these models ignore a critical dimension of global financing decision—the analysis of trade-offs among multiple and potentially conflicting financing objectives. In other words, many financing strategies generate the same expected financing cost but different risks. Lessard and Shapiro (1984:68) point out that "the corporate financing decision reduces to a trade-off between two objectives: minimizing the expected after-tax cost of financing and keeping risks within acceptable levels." Thus, trade-offs among various financing objectives can be crucial and, according to many international finance theoreticians, a key to devising an effective global financing strategy formulation (Eiteman and Stonehill 1986; Shapiro 1986). The model presented here extends previous models to resolve a critical issue that has not been dealt with in prior literature.

Model-Assisted Financing Strategy Formulation

In an attempt to anticipate and adapt to future environmental uncertainty, many MNCs have developed more integrative strategic planning systems to rationalize resources more effectively on a global basis in an effort to respond to rapid environmental changes (Dymsza 1984). Although there may be neither a universal pattern of global competition nor one global strategy, a prime source of competitive advantage is the global integration and coordination of a parent company and its own subsidiaries with coalition partners (Porter 1986). The strategic planning process begins with the reevaluation of a company's philosophy, mission, and definition of business. The next step is a realistic and subjective evaluation of the firm's present strength and weakness, and an assessment of the strength and weakness of major competitors. Analyzing major opportunities and risks and specifying strategic issues for entire corporate units are essential in formulating objectives and goals for each unit of the MNC. The primary objective is to increase the firm's return on investment by expanding investment in profitable product lines and divesting countries and product lines that do not meet the firm's mission and definition of business (for a detailed discussion of this topic, see Dymsza 1984).

The financing strategy formulation, a subset of comprehensive strategic planning and control system, is concerned with choosing an appropriate financial structure for a consolidated firm and its foreign affiliates and selecting a set of best sources for funds from global and local debt/equity markets to finance the entire corporation's financial needs. In general, the strategy formulation process has four stages: defining problems, defining objectives, establish goals, and generating strategies, as shown in figure 10–1. Figure

10–1 depicts the several steps required to transform the specific objectives of global financial planning to a specific global financing strategy.

Defining Objectives of Global Financing

Due to the different value systems and a variety of political, cultural, legal, and economic factors in many countries, there may be no single financial objective, such as stockholder wealth maximization, that is universally applicable. In this chapter, we adopt a compromise viewpoint suggested by Eiteman and Stonehill (1986) to minimize sensitive conflicts of interests among the parent company and its subsidiaries in many foreign countries. Thus, financial strategy should be formulated, implemented, and evaluated to maximize the firm's long-run consolidated earnings per share (EPS), cash flow, and market value.

Establish Goals of Global Financing Decision

The next step in developing a worldwide financing strategy is to translate the qualitative corporate objectives of financial management into several potentially conflicting quantitative financing goals to be achieved during the next strategic financial planning period. The goal programming model requires that a proper level of goals, specified by numbers, be set through repetitive cycles. The iterative process begins with the initial setting of each goal based on the information generated by the forecasting and simulation models in figure 10–2. Setting each financing goal requires basically the same process.

The forecasting model predicts the political stability of each operating country and the changes in average annual exchange rates of the currencies involved in the firm's financial planning. The simulation model attempts to anticipate future cash flows within the MNC, the future foreign exchange exposure position by currency or by affiliate, and the effects of exchange exposure on the company's consolidated and subsidiary operations. The statistical analysis system (SAS) aims at deriving a variance and covariance matrix between the parent company's functional currency, each subsidiary's, and any third currencies. Using variance and covariance analysis to manage global cash and foreign exchange risk has attracted increasing attention since Makin (1978) suggested using the portfolio theory in reducing foreign exchange risks (see, also Madura and Nosari 1984; Soenen 1985). Because the currency of each operating country may not move exactly in the same direction due to appreciation or depreciation, the multinational financial manager can identify the portfolio of a group of currencies that has proved to be less vulnerable to foreign exchange gains or losses through the variance and covariance analysis.

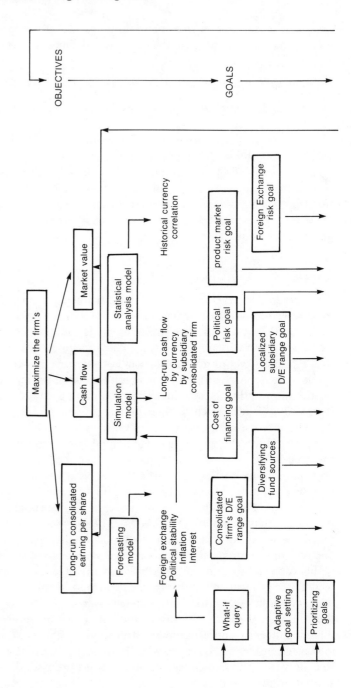

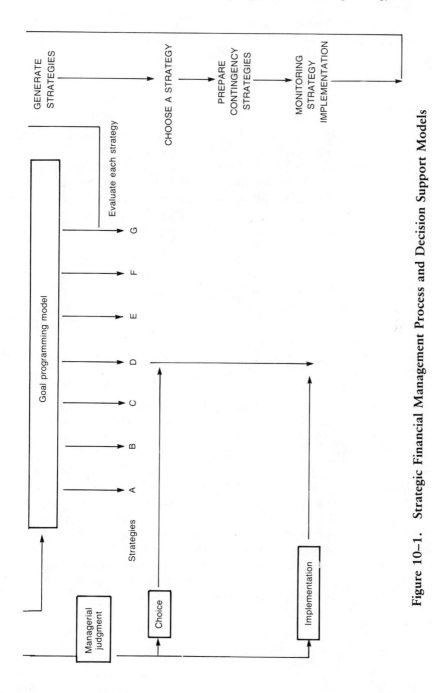

Figure 10–1. Strategic Financial Management Process and Decision Support Models

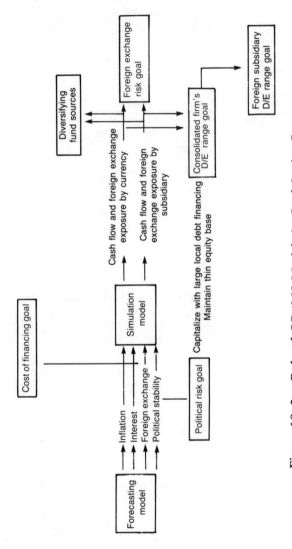

Figure 10–2. Role of OR/MS Models in Goal Setting Process

Goal Programming Model Formulation

Decision Variables

An MNC must provide each of its units with an estimate of the funds needed for the next financial planning period by making decisions as to the sources of financing (i), destination of financing (j), type of financing (k), and currency denomination (m). The GP model, as the key to integrating all three model components, is designed to effectively allocate limited resources (internally generated funds) and to select the most desirable sources of financing from those available, that is, local debt, local equity, internally generated funds, and international equity and debt markets. Decision variables are defined as follows:

X_{ijkm} = Amount of funds to be financed from the capital market (or company unit) in country i, for use in company unit in country j, in form k, denominated in currency m.

where N number of operating countries (or company units) including parent country;

i index for financing source ($i = 1, 2, ..., N, N + 1$) indicating capital market or company unit in parent country, host countries ($i = 2, ..., N$), international capital market ($i = N + 1$);

j index for receiving company units ($j = 1, 2, ..., N$) representing a parent company and foreign subsidiaries ($j = 2, ..., N$);

k index for different forms of fund ($k = 1, 2, 3$ indicating debt, internally generated fund, or equity respectively);

M number of currencies used in the financing decision for all company units;

m index for currencies used in the financing decision for all company units ($m = 1, 2, ..., M$).

Assumptions for the Model

1. Internally generated funds are assumed as equity if they are used in the country where they are generated. If those funds are transferred to other subsidiaries, they are assumed to be debt except to the parent. External funds raised as equity are transferred as equity, those raised as debt are transferred as debt.

2. Financing costs are assumed to be a constant proportion of the amounts raised.

3. All loans are creditor currency denominated. The transaction risk is borne by the final receiving company unit, and each payment of principal and interest is adjusted by the exchange rates at the time of payment.

4. Debt raised in the capital markets is transferred to the receiving company unit at the same cost of debt as in the source capital market, and the effective incremental tax rate is assumed to be the stated tax rate.

5. The target capital structures for the consolidated firm and each foreign affiliate are known.

System Constraints

A GP model consists of an objective function and two types of constraints: system and goal. Table 10–1 presents the complete list of notation used in the formulation. System constraints represent absolute restrictions imposed on the model by the decision environment.

Internally Generated Funds Constraints. Internally generated funds consists of net income, depreciation and noncash expenses, and excess liquid assets. According to Zenoff's (1967) and Robbins and Stobaugh's (1972) studies on remittance policies, the foreign affiliate's dividend policy is determined by at least six factors—tax, political risks, foreign exchange risk, age and size of affiliates, availability of funds, and presence of joint-venture partners. Constant, minimum, and maximum payout policies were examined in their studies (Robbins and Stobaugh 1972; Zenoff 1967). The current model we present treats dividend payments as parameters rather than decision variables.

$$\sum_{jm}\sum X_{ij2m} = NI_i + DEP_i + EL_i - \sum_j DIV_{ij}(i = 1 \ldots N) \qquad (10\text{–}1)$$

Investment Budget Constraints. Budget constraints must distinguish between dividends paid by the parent to the shareholder of the parent company and dividends paid to the parent company by each subsidiary. Parent dividends are lost from the financial system of a MNC, but subsidiary dividends flow to the parent and out of the system in proportion to the factor given for the portion of local ownership. Thus, subsidiary dividends to the parent company become revenue of the parent company.

For the parent:

$$\sum_{ikm}\sum\sum X_{i1km}(1 - TL_{i1km}) = IB_1 + LTD_1 + DIV_{11} - \sum_{i=2}^{N} DIV_{i1}(1 - TLD_{i1})$$
$$(10\text{–}2a)$$

where DIV_{11} = Dividend paid by the parent company to the shareholders of the parent company.

Table 10–1
Notation Summary

C_{ijkm}	=	After tax, foreign exchange risk adjusted cost of financing channel X_{ijkm}, expressed in the parent company's functional currency.
DEP_i	=	Depreciation generated funds and noncash charge for subsidiary i.
DIV_{ij}	=	Dividend paid to subsidiary j, by subsidiary i.
DLB_i	=	Desirable amounts of local borrowing to minimize the agency costs for subsidiary i.
$DRMAX_i$	=	Maximum allowable debt-equity ratio for each subsidiary i.
$DRMIN_i$	=	Minimum allowable debt-equity ratio for each subsidiary i.
EL_i	=	Excess liquid assets from subsidiary i.
$EPRMAX_i$	=	Maximum equity participation ratio by local joint venture partner in subsidiary i.
IB_j	=	Investment budget for subsidiary j.
ID_j	=	Initial debt for subsidiary j.
IE_j	=	Initial equity for subsidiary j.
IFD_j	=	The funding needs of subsidiary j for repayment of intrafirm loan scheduled.
IGF_i	=	Internally generated funds for subsidiary i.
LTD_j	=	Long-term debt repayments scheduled for subsidiary j.
$MAXD_i$	=	Maximum available debt capital for subsidiary i.
$MAXE_i$	=	Maximum available equity capital for subsidiary i.
$MINE_j$	=	Minimum external equity investment for subsidiary j from outside source of the host country before local borrowing.
NI_i	=	Net income generated by subsidiary i.
$TCF\$$	=	Target cost of financing for a consolidated firm ($\$$).
TL_{ijkm}	=	Coefficients to reflect capital transfer leakage associated with decision variable X_{ijkm}.
TLD_{ij}	=	Coefficient to reflect capital transfer leakage associated with parameter DIV_{ij}.
$IMIX_{im'}$	=	Initial mix percent of borrowing currency m' for subsidiary i, as defined as total debt denominated in each of the set of currency m'/total debt. Currency m' is a subset of currency m, used in the initial currency mix.

For each subsidiary:

$$\sum_{ikm}\sum\sum X_{ijkm}(1 - TL_{ijkm}) = IB_j + LTD_j + \sum_i DIV_{ji}$$

$$(\text{for } j = 2 \dots, N) \qquad\qquad (10\text{--}2b)$$

Prohibitions on transferring international capital raised in one country to subsidiaries in other countries.

$$\sum_{jkm}\sum\sum X_{ijkm} = 0 \ (i \neq j, \ k \neq 2) \ (\text{for some } i) \qquad (10\text{--}3)$$

Limit on issue size based on capital availability.

$$\sum_{jm}\sum X_{ij3m} \leqq MAXE_i \ (i = 1 \ldots N + 1) \tag{10-4}$$

$$\sum_{jm}\sum X_{ij1m} \leqq MAXD_i \ (i = 1 \ldots N + 1) \tag{10-5}$$

Host government's restriction on minimum external equity investments in some countries.

$$\sum_{im}\sum X_{ij3m} \leqq MINE_j \ (i \neq j) \ (\text{for some } j) \tag{10-6}$$

Local joint venture partners' maximum limit on equity participation in foreign subsidiaries that are more than 50 percent owned by the parent company.

The D/E financing decisions for foreign affiliates have been strongly influenced by legal factors in various host countries and the ownership strategy of the parent company (Dufey 1982). These decisions should, therefore, be made within the system constraints of ownership strategies that regulate equity participation by local investors, the host government agency, and other third-party investors.

$$\sum_{jm}\sum X_{ij3m} < \left[IE_i + \sum_{jm}\sum X_{ij3m} + \sum_{jm}\sum X_{ji3m} + NI_i - \sum_j DIV_{ij} \right]$$
$$(i \neq j)$$

$$* \ EPRMAX_i - IE_i \ (\text{for some } i) \tag{10-7}$$

Goal Constraints

Debt-Equity Ratios. A majority of today's financial theorists accept the existence of an optimal financial structure for a firm (Eiteman and Stonehill 1986; Shapiro 1986), based on taxes, bankruptcy costs, and the cost of the agency relationships between stockholders (as principal) and management (as agents). The optimal capital structure is not a single low point but a broad flat area over a wide range of debt/equity ratios on the U-shaped weighted average cost of capital curve. MNCs, unlike pure domestic corporations, are concerned with three different financial structures: the consolidated firm's worldwide debt ratio, the debt ratio of joint-venture subsidiary, and the debt ratio of wholly owned individual foreign affiliates. The consensus among a majority of finance theorists is that a MNC's primary concern should be the consolidated firm's financial structure; therefore, the financial structure of each wholly owned affiliate is relevant only as it affects the MNC's overall goals, because creditors ultimately look to the profitability and cash flow of the consolidated firm for satisfaction of their claim (Eiteman and Stonehill 1986; Lessard and Shapiro 1984; Shapiro 1986).

Consolidated Firm's D/E Range Goal.

$$\sum_{ijm}\sum\sum X_{ij1m} - DRMIN_1 \sum_{ijm}\sum\sum X_{ij3m} + d_{pi}^- - d_{pi}^+$$

$$= - ID_1 + LTD_1 - IFD_1 + DRMIN_1[IE_1 + NI_1 - DIV_{11}]$$
(10–8)

$$\sum_{ijm}\sum\sum X_{ij1m} - DRMAX_1 \sum_{ijm}\sum\sum_{ij3m} + d_{p(i+1)}^- - d_{p(i+1)}^+$$

$$= -ID_1 + LTD_1 + IFD_1 + DRMAX_1[IF_1 + NI_1 - DIV_{11}]$$
(10–9)

where DIV_{11} = Dividend declared to stockholders of parent company.

The presence of noncorporate stakeholders, such as governments and joint-venture partners, may require an additional goal constraint. The interests of a joint-venture partner in equity financing are especially likely to conflict with a MNC's. But, the joint-venture partner may enable a MNC to lower its local cost of capital by reflecting the capitalization norms in each foreign country, without a proportional increase in risk. For example, a Japanese joint-venture subsidiary of a U.S.-based MNC may lower its local cost of capital by conforming to local Japanese debt norms.

Joint-Venture Subsidiary's D/E Goal.

$$\sum_{jm}\sum[X_{ij1m} + X_{ji1m}(1 - TL_{ji1m})] + \sum_{jm}\sum X_{ji2m}(1 - TL_{ji2m})$$
$$(i \neq j) \qquad\qquad (i \neq j)$$

$$- DRMIN_j\left[\sum_{jm}\sum X_{ij3m} + X_{ji3m}(1 - TL_{ji3m})\right] + d_{pi}^- - d_{pi}^+$$
$$(i \neq j)$$

$$= - ID_j + LTD_j + DRMIN_j\left[IE_j + NI_j - \sum_i DIV_{ji}\right]$$

(for j = joint-venture subsidiary) (10–10)

$$\sum_{jm}\sum[X_{ij1m} + X_{ji1m}(1 - TL_{ji1m})] + \sum_{jm}\sum X_{ji2m}(1 - TL_{ji2m})$$
$$(i \neq j) \qquad\qquad (i \neq j)$$

$$- DRMAX_j\left[\sum_{jm}\sum X_{ij3m} + X_{ji3m}(1 - TL_{ji3m})\right] + d^-_{p(i+1)} - d^+_{p(i+1)}$$
$$(i \neq j)$$

$$= - ID_j + LTD_j + DRMAX_j\left[IE_j + NI_j - \sum_i DIV_{ji}\right]$$

(for j = joint-venture subsidiary) $\qquad$ (10–11)

After selecting a proper financial structure of the consolidated worldwide firm, the financial structure of each wholly owned foreign subsidiary should be established. Conflicting view have been suggested as to whether subsidiary financial structure should:

1. conform to the debt ratio norms established in each operating country (Stonehill and Stitzel 1969); or

2. vary, to take a comparative advantage (over local firms) of imperfections in national capital markets (Lessard and Shapiro 1984; Shapiro 1986); or

3. localize the foreign affiliates' financial structure if debt is available to a foreign affiliate at equal cost to that which could be raised elsewhere (Eiteman and Stonehill 1986).

The financial structure goal of the wholly owned foreign subsidiary allows financial managers to analyze the trade-offs between the cost of localizing financial structure and minimizing other risks, for example, political risk or foreign exchange risk.

$$\sum_{jm}\sum[X_{ij1m} + X_{ji1m}(1 - TL_{ji1m})] + \sum_{jm}\sum X_{ji2m}(1 - TL_{ji2m})$$
$$(i \neq j) \qquad\qquad (i \neq j)$$

$$- DRMIN_i\left[\sum_{jm}\sum X_{ij3m} + X_{ji3m}(1 - TL_{ji3m})\right] + d^-_{vi} - d^+_{vi}$$
$$(i \neq j)$$

$$= - ID_i + LTD_i + DRMIN_i[IE_i + NI_i - DIV_i]$$

(for i = wholly owned subsidiary) $\qquad$ (10–12)

$$\sum_{jm}\sum [X_{ij1m} + X_{ji1m} (1 - TL_{ji1m})] + \sum_{jm}\sum X_{ji2m} (1 - TL_{ji2m})$$
$$(i \neq j) \qquad\qquad (i \neq j)$$

$$- DRMAX_i \left[\sum_{jm}\sum X_{ij3m} + X_{ji3m} (1 - TL_{ji3m}) \right] + d_{vi}^- - d_{vi}^+$$
$$(i \neq j)$$

$$= - ID_i + LTD_i + DRMIN_i [IE_i + NI_i - DIV_i]$$

$$\text{(for } i = \text{wholly owned subsidiary)} \qquad (10\text{--}13)$$

Maintenance of the Average Weighted Cost of Capital for a Consolidated Firm. Within the single-objective financing decision framework (Ness 1972), the sole objective is to minimize the sum of the cost of financing a consolidated firm. But the MODM approaches limit the sum of the consolidated firm's expected cost of financing (after-tax foreign exchange risk adjusted) not to exceed the TCF$. The TCF$ can be obtained by the following computation:

$$TCF\$ = \text{Total amounts of funds required (\$)} * AWCC;$$

where AWCC is the consolidated firm's average weighted cost of capital over time (used as the basis of project selection).

Determination of the TCF$ depends on the hurdle rate used to select projects. Projects can be selected on the base of the cost of financing available in that year (Rodrigues and Eugene 1976) or the consolidated firm's average weighted cost of capital over time (for an estimate of the cost of each financing channel, see Shapiro 1986).

$$\sum_{ijkm}\sum\sum\sum [X_{ijkm} C_{ijkm}] + d_q^- - d_q^+ = TCF\$ \qquad (10\text{--}14)$$

By minimizing the positive deviational variable d_q^+, the model attempts to limit the consolidated firm's after-tax foreign exchange risk adjusted cost of financing to less than or equal to the TCF$.

Maintaining an Acceptable Level of Foreign Exchange Risks. Managing a MNC's economic exposure to exchange risk, not its balance sheet exposure, is the key to formulating a global financing strategy. Here, the economic exposure includes both real inflation-adjusted operating exposure and transaction exposure. The international diversification of both operations and financing has been suggested as the fundamental approach to managing economic exposure (Eiteman and Stonehill 1986; Makin 1978), because that approach does not require the superhuman ability to forecast a disequilibrium condition such as foreign exchange rates.

Diversifying a MNC's financing base consists of constructing an optimal currency cocktail for each unit of the MNC by choosing sources of funds in more than one capital market and/or by using more than one currency. The optimal currency mix or cocktail can be constructed by using matching (hedging) and/or exposure netting (or the portfolio approach) in which two decision variables are used—the number of currencies and the proportion of each currency in the mix. The matching approach may be used to hedge a firm's long-term operating exposure at no cost to the value of the firm by structuring dept financing so that the decrease or increase in asset earnings is matched by a corresponding increase of decrease in the cost of servicing these liabilities (Eiteman and Stonehill 1986; Lessard and Shapiro 1984). Exposure netting is used to construct a Markowitz efficient portfolio of a group of currencies that has proved to be less vulnerable to foreign exchange gains or losses (through variance and covariance analysis) (Madura and Nosari 1984; Makin 1978; Soenen 1985).

Figure 10–3 shows the construction of an initial mix (percent) of borrowing currencies (*IMIX*) and optimal currency mix (*OMIX*). The determinants of the *IMIX* are sales revenue configurations based on noncontractual operating cash flows and contractual items (Eiteman and Stonehill 1986; Lessard and Shapiro 1984) currency correlations information (Madura and Nosari 1984; Makin 1978; Soenen 1985), and the firm's financing base diversification policy. The *OMIX* in global financing is determined by considering other long-term financing objectives in addition to the determinants of *IMIX*. The set of currency m includes currencies in the parent country, host countries, other third countries, and Eurocurrencies. The set of currency m' is the subset of currency m that is selected to construct the *IMIX*. The selection of m' depends on the firm's sales revenue stream by currency, the degree of correlations among the currencies in the current set m. For the parent company:

$$\sum_i X_{i11m'} - IMIX_{1m'} \sum_{im'}\sum X_{i11m'} + d_{r1}^- - d_{r1}^+ = 0 \ (\text{for } m' = 1 \ ..., M)$$

(10–15)

For each subsidiary:

$$\sum_i X_{ij1m'} + \sum_i X_{ij2m'} - IMIX_{im'}\left[\sum_{jm'}\sum(X_{ij1m'} + X_{ij2m'})\right] + d_{ri}^- - d_{ri}^+ = 0$$

$$(i \neq j) \qquad\qquad (i \neq j) \qquad\qquad (i \neq 1)$$

$$(\text{for } m' = 1 \ . \ . \ . , M')$$

(10–16)

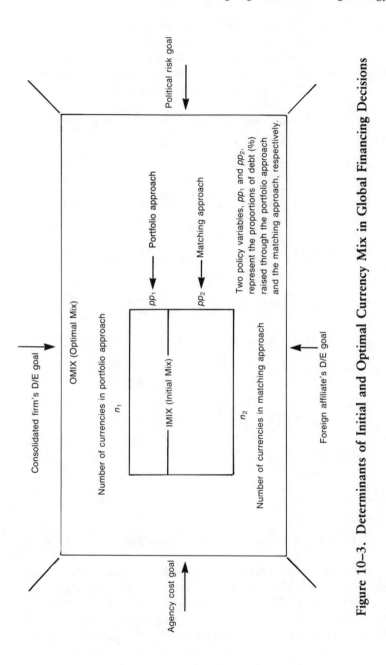

Figure 10–3. Determinants of Initial and Optimal Currency Mix in Global Financing Decisions

Political Risk. Relevant political risks in financing decisions of an MNC include currency inconvertibility and repatriation risk. Dividend payments and reductions in committed equity are characteristically more closely controlled by government regulations than are principal and interest payments (Robbins and Stobaugh 1972). Minimizing losses from political interference in a high-risk host country include maintaining a thin equity base, using a maximum allowable D/E ratio, and capitalization with a large portion of local debt financing.

Thin Equity Base Goal.

$$\sum_{jm}\sum [X_{ij1m} + X_{ji1m}(1 - TL_{ji1m})] + \sum_{jm}\sum X_{ji2m}(1 - TL_{ji2m})$$
$$(i \neq j) \qquad\qquad (i \neq j)$$

$$- DRMAX_i\left[\sum_{jm}\sum(X_{ij3m} + X_{ji3m}(1 - TL_{ji3m}))\right] + d_{si}^- - d_{si}^+$$
$$(i \neq j)$$

$$= -ID_i + LTD_i + DRMAX_i\left[IE_i + NI_i - \sum_j DIV_{ij}\right]$$

(for i = subsidiary with high political risk)   (10–17)

Local Debt Maximization Goal.

$$\sum_{jm}\sum [X_{ij1m} + X_{ji1m}(1 - TL_{ji1m})]$$
$$(i = j) \qquad\qquad (i \neq j)$$

$$- DRMAX_i\left[\sum_{jm}\sum(X_{ij1m} + X_{ji1m}(1 - TL_{ji1m}))\right.$$

$$\left. + \sum_{jm}\sum X_{ij2m}(1 - TL_{ji2m}) - ID_i - LTD_i\right] + d_{ti}^- - d_{ti}^+ = 0$$
$$(i \neq j) \qquad\qquad\qquad (i \neq j)$$

(for i = subsidiary with high political risk)   (10–18)

Minimizing the Cost of Maintaining an Agency Relationship. The recent finance literature (Anthony 1960; Donaldson 1963; Findlay and Whitmore 1974; Jensen and Meckling 1976; Jensen and Smith 1985; Ross 1973) has recognized the conflict of interests between the participants in an organization that is pursuing its own self-interest. Jensen and Meckling (1976) recommended minimizing the costs of agency relationships between the principals (stockholders) and the agents (managers) by investing in bonding or monitoring arrangements only to the point that the benefits from enforcement outweigh the costs.

According to a survey (Robbins and Stobaugh 1972), some parent companies still follow a policy of not providing financing beyond their initial investment, and managers of foreign affiliates may often be forced to borrow locally, regardless of the cost of financing, to foster good relations with local financial institutions. For the parent company, there is a trade-off between the decreased agency/monitoring cost and the increased financing cost. In other words, the parent company may decrease its cost of monitoring the management activities of foreign affiliates by turning over some of its monitoring responsibilities to local financial institutions. Relinquishing their monitoring responsibilities may, in turn, increase their after-tax foreign exchange risk adjusted cost of financing for the foreign affiliate assuming high local borrowing cost. Whether the parent will guarantee the debt of the foreign affiliate may be another important factor in the analysis of the trade-offs (see Shapiro 1986 for the detailed discussions on the relationships between the agency costs and corporate policy regarding parent guarantees of the debt of foreign affiliates).

$$\sum_m X_{ij1m} + d_{ui}^- - d_{ui}^+ = DLB_i \text{ (for some } i) \tag{10-19}$$

$$(i = j)$$

The Objective Function

$$\text{Minimize } Z = p_1\left[\sum_i d_{pi}^- + d_p(i+1)^+\right] + p_2(d_q^+) + p_3\left[\sum_i (d_{qi}^- + d_{qi}^+)\right]$$

$$+ p_4\left(\sum_i d_{si}^- + d_s(i+1) + d_{ti}^+\right) + p_5(d_{ui}^-)$$

$$+ p_6\left(\sum_i [d_{vi}^- + d_v(i+1)^+]\right)]$$

Subject to equations 10–1 through 10–19 and nonnegativity constraints for all deviational and decision variables.

Developing Alternative Financing Strategies

A crucial contribution of the GP model is to provide MNC financial managers with the most powerful multicriteria decision-making tool for generating large sets of financing strategies and for estimating the consequences of each of those financing strategies on a global scale. As shown in figure 10–4, the model utilizes two avenues for generating strategies: first, it allows the pri-

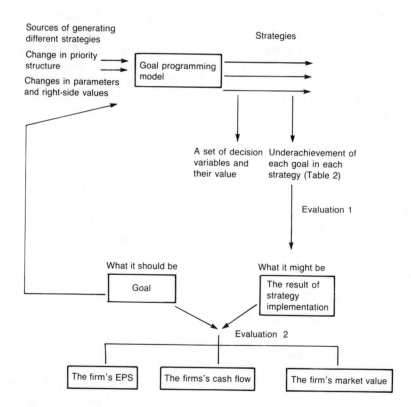

Figure 10–4. Generation and Evaluation of Alternative Strategies

ority structure of the established goals to be altered; second, it allows managerial judgment about environmental uncertainty to be incorporated into the analysis (changes in parameters and right-hand side values).

Select a Best Financing Strategy

In this stage, decisionmakers should select only one alternative from those available by evaluating the possible impact of specific alternatives on corporate goals and objectives. The model produces two different sets of information for decisionmakers: A set of decision variables and their values as a strategy and the impact of each decision alternative on the financing goals in the form of underachievement of each goal in each strategy. Table 10–2 illustrates only the impact of each alternative on the attainment of various financ-

Table 10–2
Nonachievement of Each Priority/Goal

Priority/Goal	Nonachievent				
	I	II	III	IV	V
6 Foreign subsidiary's D/E goal	63.62	9.55	0.0	69.33	63.03
5 Agency cost goal	0.0	0.0	0.0	0.0	0.0
4 Political risk goal	48.92	66.37	94.95	71.28	38.03
3 Foreign exchange risk goal	5.41	0.0	0.0	1.95	3.32
2 Financial cost goal	0.0	0.0	0.0	0.0	0.0
1 Consolidated D/E goal	0.0	0.0	0.0	25.56	0.0

ing goals without showing decision alternatives (for a detailed discussion, see Eom and Lee 1987; Eom et al. 1987). Two steps of evaluation are required to interpret table 10–2, as indicated by evaluation 1 and evaluation 2 in figure 10–4. The first evaluation process is simple mathematical interpretation of deviational variables (d^-, d^+) in table 10–2, without use of managerial judgment. Thus, the zero in each priority row indicates that the financing alternative will completely attain that specific priority goal. On the other hand, the size of underattainment of each priority goal indicates that potential factors exist that may increase the effective cost of financing with some unknown probability. For example, the sixth goal of localizing the financial structures of a wholly owned subsidiary was not completely achieved as indicated by 63.62 ($ million), under the Strategy I. Through the computational analysis, the deviations from the right-hand-side stated goals in GP outputs, the decisionmaker can identify the sources of deviations from the stated goals and the extent (degree) of the deviations. In this example, the user of the DSS identified that localized financial structure goals of all foreign subsidiaries, except a certain foreign subsidiary, can be maintained within the specified range. Therefore, this deviated amount from the right-hand-side stated sixth goal, 63.63, indicates that the D/E ratio of a subsidiary will be pushed out of the discretionary range of acceptable local financial structure norms previously set.

The next step of evaluation (indicated by evaluation 2 in figure 10–4) must heavily depend on the management's judgment. Based on the preceding evaluation, how will the nonlocalized financial structure of the subsidiary in that country affect the consolidated firm's cash flow, earnings per share (EPS), and market value? To answer that question, the decisionmaker should estimate environmental uncertainty, taking into account the host government's policy toward the financial structure of the MNC, and evaluate the outcome accordingly (for the details, see Eom and Lee 1987; Eom et al. 1987).

Conclusions

Because of the semistructured nature of the financing decisions (numerous and conflicting goals, uncertain decision environments, and complex decision variables), neither OR/MS models nor managerial judgment alone may be adequate to provide satisfactory solutions. Therefore, the simultaneous use of managerial judgment (qualitative) and computer-based information systems (quantitative) significantly increases organizational abilities to cope with future uncertainty by extending the manager's limited information processing ability and by correcting the manager's tunnel/myopic vision.

Gaining a competitive advantage over domestic and foreign competitors requires an integrating and coordinating strategy. Theoretically, previous research (Eom and Lee 1987; Kornbluth and Vinso 1982; Vinso 1982) suggests that the cost of financing can be minimized by the simultaneous consideration of all potential financing sources on a global scale. In practice, financing decisions of large MNCs have been based only on the consideration of a subset of all financing sources, primarily because of lack of information and extreme complexity. The larger the number of financing alternatives a firm considers simultaneously, the lower the financing cost it can achieve with reduced risks. With fully intergrated financial planning, a MNC can increase its financial competitiveness by lowering the consolidated firm's cost of capital and maintaining an optimal range of financial structures for the consolidated firm and its foreign subsidiaries.

References

Anthony, R. 1960. The trouble with profit maximization. *Harvard Business Review,* Nov./ Dec., 126–34.

Bennett, J.L. 1983. *Building decision support systems.* Reading, Mass.: Addison-Wesley.

Donaldson, G. 1963. Financial goals: Management vs. stockholders. *Harvard Business Review,* May/June, 116–29.

Dufey, G. 1982. Funding decisions in international companies. In *International financing management,* ed. G. Bergendahl, 29–51. Stockholm: P.A. Norstedt & Soners Forlag.

Dymsza, W.A. 1984. Global strategic planning: A model and recent developments. *Journal of International Business Studies* 15(2): 169–84.

Eiteman, D.K. and Stonehill, A.I. 1986. *Multinational business finance,* 4th ed. Reading, Mass.: Addison-Wesley.

Eom, H.B., and Lee, S.M. 1987. A large scale goal programming model-based decision support for global financing strategy formulation. *Information & Management* 12(1): 33–44.

Eom, H.B.; Lee, S.M.: Snyder, C.A.; and Ford, F.N. 1987. A multiple criteria decision support system for global financial planning. *Journal of Management Information Systems* 4(3): 94–113.

Findlay III, M.C., and Whitmore, G.A. 1974. Beyond shareholder wealth maximization. *Financial Management,* Winter, 25–35.

Jensen, M.C., and Meckling, W.H. 1976. Theory of the firm: management behavior, agency costs, and ownership structure. *Journal of Financial Economics,* October, 305–60.

Jensen, M.C., and Smith, Jr., C.W. 1985. Stockholder, manager, and creditor interests: applications of agency theory. In *Recent advances in corporate finance,* eds. E.I. Altman and M.G. Subrahmanyam, 93–131. Homewood, Ill.: Richard D. Irwin.

Kornbluth, J.S.H., and Vinso, J.D. 1982. Capital structure and the financing of the multinational corporation: A fractional multiobjective approach. *Journal of Financial and Quantitative Analysis* 17(2): 147–76.

Lee, S.M. 1972. *Goal programming for decision analysis.* Philadelphia: Auerbach.

Lessard, D.R., and Shapiro, A.C. 1984. Guidelines for global financing choices. *Midland Corporate Finance Journal,* Spring, 68–80.

Madura, J., and Nosari, E.J. 1984. Utilizing currency portfolios to mitigate exchange rate risk. *Columbia Journal of World Business,* Spring, 96–99.

Makin, J.H. 1978. Portfolio theory and the problem of foreign exchange risk. *Journal of Finance,* May, 517–34.

Ness, W.N. 1972. A linear programming approach to financing the multinational corporation. *Financial Management* 1(3): 99–100.

Porter, M.E. 1986. Introduction and summary. In *Competition in global industry,* ed. M.E. Porter, 1–11. Boston: Harvard Business School.

Robbins, S.M., and Stobaugh, R.S. 1972. Financing foreign affiliates. *Financial Management* 1(3): 56–65.

Rodrigues, R.M., and Eugene, C.E. 1976. *International financial management.* Englewood Cliffs, N.J.: Prentice-Hall.

Ross, S.A. 1973. The economic theory of agency: the principal problem. *American Economic Review,* May, 134–39.

Shapiro, A.C. 1986. *Multinational financial management,* 2d ed. Boston: Allyn & Bacon.

Soenen, L.A. 1985. The optimal currency cocktail: A tool for strategic foreign exchange management. *Management International Review* 25(2): 12–22.

Stonehill, A.I., and Stitzel, T. 1969. Financial structure and multinational corporations. *California Management Review,* Fall, 91–6.

Vinso, J.D. 1982. Financial planning for the multinational corporation with multiple goals. *Journal of International Business Studies,* Winter, 43–58.

Zenoff, D.B. 1967. Remittance policies of U.S. subsidiaries in Europe. *Banker,* May, 418–27.

11
Global Financing for MNCs: The Quest for Geocentric Advantage

Laurent L. Jacque
Howard V. Perlmutter

T he fundamental challenge of strategic management in multinational corporations (MNCs) is to balance the economic imperative of global production and marketing rationalization with the political imperative as brought about by host countries' demands and host markets' idiosyncrasies. This process, more often than not, has to be carried out in the context of two-tier oligopolistic industries comprised of an upper multinational tier (other MNCs based in the same or other home countries) competing in distinct national markets with domestic firms (lower tier) nurtured by their respective governments (see figure 11–1).

When understood primarily as a factor sourcing constrained optimization problem financial strategy has a crucial role to play in satisficing the economic imperative. However, the advent of floating exchange rates and prolonged periods of dollar overshooting coupled with continued mild segmentation of capital markets is blurring the true cost of alternative financial strategies while offering yet an uncharted comparative advantage to the truly global firm. It is the purpose of this chapter to unravel this puzzle.

Specifically, we posit three goals for the financial strategy of a MNC:[1]

1. Ensure that a MNC's financial costs are no higher than its major multinational competitors' (the competitive motive).

2. Enhance the management of foreign exchange risk and political risk (the hedge motive).

3. Create value in its own right by jointly exploiting currency overshooting with arbitrage opportunities among financial markets through the multinational enterprise system (opportunistic motive).

The thesis of this chapter is that achieving these goals rests on the pursuit of a geocentric financial strategy—the so-called quest for geocentric advan-

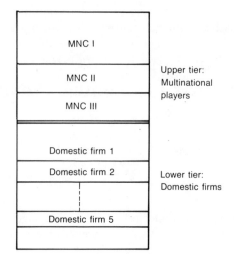

Figure 11–1. Two-Tier Oligopolistic Industries

tage—whose design has to be firmly grounded in the overall strategic setting of the firm in so far as it relates to its industry and contextual environments.

This chapter is organized in three sections: First, we map the changing profile of the international monetary system stressing the strategic concepts of capital market segmentation and currency overshooting. Second, we profile the global financing conundrum in the context of the ethnocentric/polycentric/geocentric (EPG) conceptual framework. And last, with the help of unorthodox corporate illustrations we show how the satisficing of the competitive, hedge, and opportunistic motives can be enhanced by a geocentric financial strategy.

The International Monetary Environment: The Ascent of Structural Turbulence

The breakdown of the Bretton-Woods world of quasi-fixed exchange rates has been followed by major structural changes in the international monetary system including an increasing degree of financial market integration and a substantial increase in the level of systemic turbulence as characterized by a higher exchange rate, interest rate, and relative price volatility, coupled with prolonged exchange rate overshooting.

The Financial Markets Segmentation/ Integration Continuum

There is no denying the increasing degree of financial market integration among the most advanced industrial economies spurred by the dismantling of exchange controls and other financial border restrictions, as well as the accelerating scope of deregulation within national banking and financial jurisdictions.[2] However, third world countries as well as newly industrialized countries continue to be marred by a sprawling web of credit and exchange controls unlikely to be dismantled anytime soon because of overwhelming foreign debt servicing burdens—a problem compounded by excessive reliance on undiversified staple commodity exports portfolios.

Even among closely integrated financial markets a tiering of credit markets between onshore or domestic and offshore or Eurocurrency segments continue to exhibit subtle but nonnegligible differences in degrees of financial market integration both within and across currency space. By and large, asymmetry in tax treatment and banking reserve requirements almost always imply a greater degree of financial market integration in the offshore component than in the onshore component of given credit market and explain small discrepancies from interest rate parity equilibriums.[3]

Because of differing investors' perceptions and expectations—perhaps fostered by discrepant disclosure requirements—national equity markets continue to suffer from mild degrees of capital market segmentation with far-ranging competitive implications as the last three sections of this chapter illustrate.

The ongoing controversy about the presumably lower cost of capital enjoyed by Japanese firms vis-a-vis U.S. firms is a direct consequence of the continued, albeit steadily eroding, mild capital market segmentation between the two countries. Because of close relationships with their industrial group's bank and the very limited reliance on profit-based incentive compensation schemes, Japanese firms are generally able to maximize their long-term international competitiveness rather than be constricted by the delivery of a smooth stream of earnings and dividends so cherished by financial analysts on Wall Street.[4]

Clearly, Japanese executive compensation systems based on seniority more than any other criteria tend to foster long-term growth. Unlike their American counterparts, typical Japanese executives rarely receive stock options; Japanese CEOs own little or none of their company's common stock, and executive salaries, which are modest by American standards, are not closely tied to profits. The psychic and social rewards Japanese managers reap from successful growth outweigh those they receive from maximizing short-term shareholder wealth or achieving a given return on investment (Abegglenn and Stalk 1986).

This emphasis on long-term growth, competitive viability, and stable employment can only be pursued because of financial policies acceptable to the Japanese capital market. The symbiotic relationship between Japanese firms and their banks has allowed highly leveraged capital structures; this has in turn reduced the after-tax cost of capital for Japanese firms and allowed them to invest in projects with very distant payoffs.[5] Indeed, access to patient capital may allow a company to intensify R&D, or marketing efforts to win a technology race or outlast its opponents in a price war. As Baldwin (1986: 186) puts it

> The belief among competitors that one's cost of capital is low and one's staying power unlimited is worth cultivating purely for its effect on competitors' behavior . . . . Companies with access to low cost capital can thus outspend, undersell and outlast their competition and by these methods may come to dominate their product markets.

Furthermore, the miniscule yearly dividend based on the historical par value—typically 50 yens—rather than the market value of the company's stock, as in the case of U.S. stocks, has nurtured aggressive self-financed growth. Thus, these qualitative differences in management philosophies and capital market conventions, unlike obvious quantitative differentials in capital costs, continue to buttress mild degrees of capital market segmentation in the long term.

Exchange Rate Volatility and Currency Overshooting

In the thirteen-year history of the current exchange rate system, bilateral exchange rates have fluctuated over a wide range. Many exchange rates have appreciated and then depreciated by 25 percent or more in a single year. The dollar itself has depreciated by as much as 50 percent in a single year against the Japanese currency. It is not uncommon for the price of a currency to vary by as much as 5 percent within a single day but when foreign exchange is recognized as a financial asset its price volatility is not abnormal with what is commonly observed on other speculative markets.

Perhaps more perplexing than intrinsic exchange rates volatility itself is the increasing evidence of prolonged periods of exchange rate overshooting that has played havoc with the best-laid plans of offshore sourcing or global production rationalization schemes to mention only a few. Currency overshooting for the purpose of this chapter is defined as long-term deviations of nominal exchange rates from their intrinsic equilibrium levels. Although there is considerable controversy among economists as to what constitutes equilibrium exchange rates we rely on a bilateral purchasing power parity definition of equilibrium rates illustrated graphically by figures 11–2 and 11–3 in the case of the U.S. dollar overshooting against the Japanese currency.[6] Empirically, overshooting has been most dramatic in the case of the U.S. dollar versus foreign currency exchange rate relationships; from a strategic point of view, the key questions center on the amplitude in the exchange rate oscillation—from a peak to a trough—as well as the period elapsing from one extreme to the other.

The Global Financing Conundrum

We now turn to the unique problems of financial strategy in the context of increasingly global competition given mild capital market segmentation and prolonged currency overshooting. We do not dwell on the well-documented techniques of global financing strategy (see for example Eiteman and Stonehill 1986 or Shapiro 1986) which can be characterized within the framework of the EPG paradigm (Perlmutter 1969 and Heenan and Perlmutter 1978).

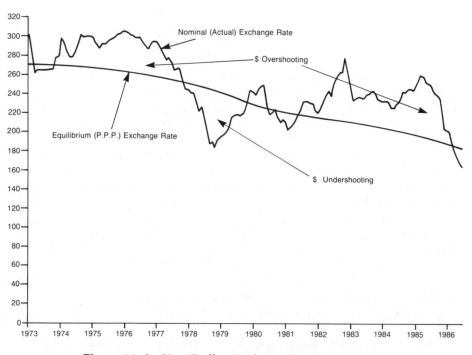

Figure 11–2. Yen/Dollar Exchange Rate Overshooting

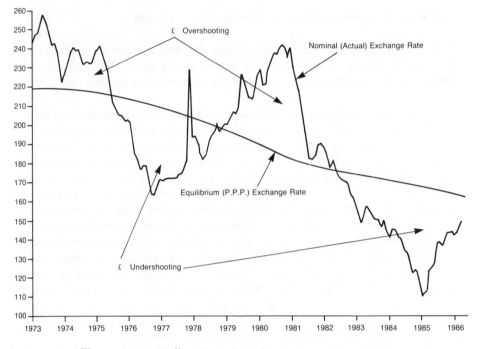

Figure 11–3. Dollar/Pound Exchange Rate Overshooting

According to this paradigm, *ethnocentric* (*E*) firms—well ensconced in their home-country mental set—pursue myopic financial policies. *Polycentric* (*P*) firms suffer from the disaggregation syndrome (often warranted under multidomestic competition) and pursue strictly local financial strategies thereby forfeiting any competitive advantage that *geocentric* (*G*) firms reap from the uniqueness conferred on them by their multinationality by adopting a truly global view of their system's potential. Table 11–1 further elaborates these three concepts in the context of specific financial decisions while the balance of this chapter focuses on the nurturing of a geocentric financial competence which should guide MNCs in resolving the issue of wherefrom to source equity and debt financing given the constraint of satisficing the competitive, hedge, and opportunistic motives.

Geofinancing and the Competitive Motive: Exploiting Capital Market Segmentation in Equity Funding

Assume that national capital markets are insulated from one another (hypothesis of capital market segmentation) but that MNCs compete freely

Table 11–1
The EPG Profile for Financing Decisions

	Ethnocentric	Polycentric	Geocentric
Equity financing	Source from home country market exclusively.	Will consider host country equity issue.	Multiple stock listing in several national markets. Widespread share holding stabilizes stock price, enhances global strategic management, and reduces cost of capital.
Long-term debt financing	Rely on parent company or home country financial market.	Rely on host country financial markets.	Minimize systematically cost of funding by worldwide scanning of onshore and offshore credit markets. Use international finance subsidiary to reduce taxes.
Short-term financing	Use local currency funding. Locus of decision making rests with parent company.	Use local currency funding. Decision decentralized at local subsidiary level.	Minimize cost of short-term financing by exploiting mild degree of money market segmentation through covered or uncovered arbi-loan.
Foreign exchange risk management	Protect reference currency value of earnings through systematic hedging of both transaction and translation exposure to foreign exchange risk.	MNC perceives itself as a diversified portfolio of foreign currency position. Foreign exchange risk management is decentralized at host country level.	Aggressive worldwide port-hedging of translation/transaction and economic exposure. Use reinvoicing centers, transfer price adjustment, and lead/lags manipulation to reduce systematic exposure to exchange rate movements.

in the world product market (hypothesis of product market integration). It follows that the returns required to adequately reward capital need not be the same across countries (see figure 11–4).

Each firm must compete against investment decisions based on return criteria that vary among national capital markets. Clearly the MNCs with the lowest standards for acceptable returns and access to capital—at least equivalent if not better than its competitors—can pursue a broader array of investments, lower prices, or increase service to achieve a competitive advantage. In this light it is helpful to think of financing as a sourcing decision.

U.S.-based or other MNCs have traditionally pursued ethnocentric policies in sourcing equity and long-term debt from their home capital markets, even though it may not have been the least cost sourcing decision. When capital market segmentation is a reality—and there is good evidence that it persists in a mild form sense—multiple stock listing or simultaneous equity funding in several national capital markets becomes an aggressive way of surmounting such sourcing cost disadvantage. Furthermore simultaneous equity funding (dubbed Euro-equity financing) can free foreign multinationals from the small and somewhat segmented domestic equity market: witness the recent flurry of Euro-equity funding by MNCs such as Nestlé, Volvo, Fiat, Allianz, and KLM (see table 11–2). Indeed, a wider geographical spread of

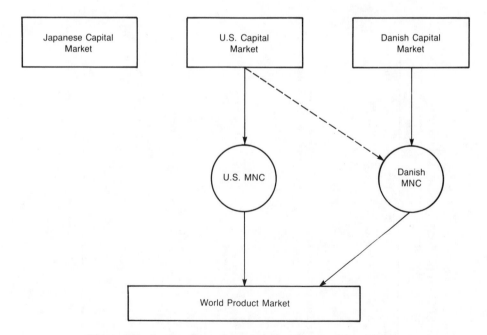

Figure 11–4. Geofinancing and the Competitive Motive

Table 11–2

Some of the Firms Issuing International Equities, 1983–85

July 1983	Bell Canada Enterprises 2 million shares ($43.4 million) international offering
September 1983	Alcan Aluminum Ltd. 7 million shares ($40 million) European offering
September 1984	Esselte Business Systems 1.9 million shares ($26 million) international offering
October 1984	Swiss Bank Corporation 160,000 bearer participation certificates (Swiss franc 46 million) private placement in Japan
November 1984	British Telecom 90 million shares (£117 million) Swiss tranche of initial public offering
March 1985	Nederlandsche Middenstandsbank NV 500,000 shares (Dfl83 million) secondary offering in Switzerland
April 1985	Buhrman Tetterode NV 201,370 shares (Dfl17 million) secondary offering in Switzerland
May 1985	Thomassen & Drijver-Verblifa NV 197,323 shares (Dfl12 million) Swiss tranche of IPO
May 1985	Nestlé SA 300,000 BPC (Swiss franc 373 million) international offering
June 1985	Banca del Gottardo 65,000 bearer shares (Swiss franc 40.3 million) international secondary offering
July 1985	Student Loan Marketing Association (Sallie Mae) 1.5 million shares ($50 million) international offering
July 1985	Britoil PLC 25 million shares (£45 million) international offering
August 1985	Banca Commerciale Italiana 5 million shares L111.5 billion ($59 million) international secondary offering

Source: Khoury and Ghosh, *Recent Developments in International Banking and Finance,* Vol. 1. Lexington, Mass.: Lexington Books, p. 5.

shareholders is inherently good as it makes the company's share more liquid and presumably its stock prices less volatile thereby reducing its cost of capital and freeing its strategic management from the myopia of individual capital markets.

As hinted earlier capital market segmentation implies that the same firm raising debt or equity funds in different national capital markets may face a different cost of capital as a result of diverging investor perceptions between domestic and foreign shareholders or of asymmetry in tax policies, exchange controls, and political risks. Indeed, a firm based in a fully segmented capital market is likely to have a higher cost of capital due to a relatively depressed price for its stock than if it had access to fully integrated capital markets. A good illustration of how a company can overcome such segmentation barriers to effectively reduce its cost of capital is provided by NOVO, a Danish multinational firm recognized as an industry leader in the manufacturing of industrial enzymes and pharmaceuticals (mostly insulin) in Western Europe (Stonehill and Dullums 1983).

Internationalizing NOVO's Cost of Capital

In 1977 NOVO embarked on an ambitious strategy to internationalize its cost of capital to be in a position to better compete with its major multinational rivals such as Eli Lilly & Company (United States), Miles Laboratory (United States-based but a subsidiary of the giant chemical conglomerate Bayer head-quartered in West Germany), and Gist Brocades (the Netherlands). All had access to considerably cheaper equity funding as measured by their respective lower P/E ratios than NOVO did.

The first step was for NOVO to float a $20 million convertible Eurobond issue while listing its shares on the stock exchange in London (1979). Shortly thereafter, NOVO decided to capitalize on the newly emerging interest among capital venture investors for biotechnology companies. NOVO sponsored an "American Depository Receipts" system in the United States while listing its shares on the over-the-counter market.

Having gained significant visibility on both the London and New York stock exchanges, NOVO was ready to take the final and admittedly most difficult step, that is, to float an equity issue on the New York Stock Exchange. Under the guidance of Goldman Sachs, a prospectus was prepared for SEC registration of a U.S. stock offering and eventual listing on the New York Stock Exchange. On July 8, 1981, NOVO became the first Scandinavian firm to successfully sell equity through a public issue in the United States.

Figure 11–5 illustrates how the price of NOVO's shares increased dramatically between the issue of the convertible Eurobond issue (1979) and the equity issue on the New York Stock Exchange (1981). This gain in share price correlates highly with, and presumably partly as a result of, steady foreign buying. Indeed, by July 1981 Danish ownership of NOVO's B shares had fallen to 25 percent as Danish investors were more than willing to sell a stock that they considered to be either grossly overvalued or a nonsuitable vehicle for international diversification. As its P/E ratio had more than roughly tripled from 9 to 31, NOVO was successful in sourcing much needed capital to better compete with its oligopolist rivals. A bold geocentric equity funding strategy had paid off.[7]

Geofinancing and the Hedge Motive: Coping with Currency Overshooting and Political Risk

The management of international risk can be facilitated through astute geofinancing. This section argues that hedging exchange risk and political risk

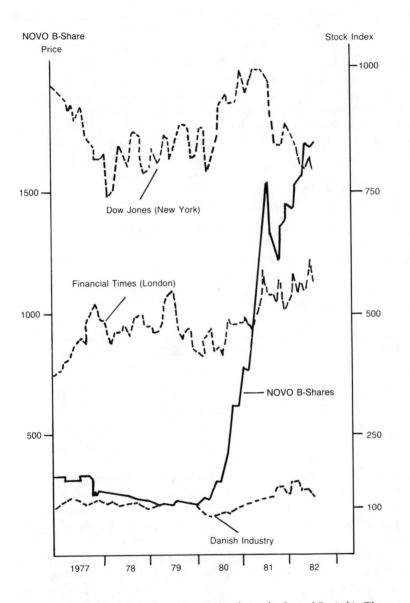

NOVO B-Share Price

Stock Index

Dow Jones (New York)

Financial Times (London)

NOVO B-Shares

Danish Industry

Source: A. Stonehill and K. Dullums, *Internationalizing the Cost of Capital in Theory and Practice: The NOVO Experience and National Policy Implications* (New York: John Wiley & Sons, 1982) p. 73. ©Copyright 1982. Reprinted by permission of John Wiley & Sons, Ltd.

Figure 11–5. NOVO's Geocentric Equity Funding

should be carefully woven into global financing decisions. Indeed, satisficing the hedge motive may result in a suboptimal financing package (when viewed from a strictly cost-of-capital-minimization point of view). In this case the premium paid above the least cost financing option should be construed as an insurance premium for hedging exchange risk and political risk. A good illustration of how the impact of currency overshooting on the profitability of ongoing export sales can be neutralized through appropriate currency denomination in long-term debt financing is provided by the vicissitudes experienced by Rolls-Royce Limited in the U.S. market (Srinivasulu 1983).

Hedging Exchange Risk through Geofinancing

Rolls-Royce Limited, the British aeroengine manufacturer, suffered a loss of £58 million in 1979 on worldwide sales of £848 million pounds. The company's annual report for 1979 blamed the loss on the dramatic revaluation (overshooting) of the pound sterling against the dollar, from £1 = $1.71 in early 1977 to £1 = $2.12 by the end of 1979:

> The most important was the effect of the continued weakness of the U.S. dollar against sterling. The large civil engines which Rolls-Royce produces are supplied to American air frames. Because of U.S. dominance in civil aviation, both as producer and customer, these engines are usually priced in U.S. dollars and escalated accordingly to U.S. indices.[8]

A closer look at Rolls-Royce's competitive position in the global market for jet engines reveals the sources of its dollar exposure. For the previous several years Rolls-Royce export sales had accounted for a stable 40 percent of total sales and had been directed at the U.S. market. This market is dominated by two U.S. competitors, Pratt and Whitney Aircraft Group (United Technologies) and General Electric Company's aerospace division. As the clients of its mainstay engine, the RB 211, were U.S. aircraft manufacturers (Boeing's 747SP and 747,200 and Lockheed's L1011), Rolls-Royce had little choice in the currency denomination of its export sales but to use the dollar.

Indeed, Rolls-Royce won some huge engine contracts in 1978 and 1979 that were fixed in dollar terms (see figure 11–6). Rolls-Royce's operating costs (wages, components, and debt servicing) on the other hand, were almost exclusively incurred in sterling unlike General Electric and Pratt-Whitney which enjoyed perfectly matched (currency-wise, that is, dollar-denominated) cash inflows and cash outflows. Rolls-Royce exports contracts were mostly pegged to an exchange rate of about $1.80 for the pound, and Rolls-Royce officials, in fact, expected the pound to fall further to $1.65. Hence, they didn't cover their dollar exposures. If the officials were correct, and the dollar strength-

Source: S. Srinivasulu, "Currency Denomination of Debt: Lessons from Rolls-Royce and Laker Airways," *Business Horizons,* Sept./Oct. 1983, p. 20.
Note: Not to scale. Cash inflows and outflows in all other currencies, being very small, are ignored (or they can be considered to have been included in one of these currencies).
A: Excess of $ cash inflow over $ cash outflow.

Figure 11–6. Currency Mismatch in Cash Inflows and Outflows (Rolls-Royce)

ened, Rolls-Royce would enjoy windfall profits. When the dollar weakened instead, the combined effect of fixed dollar revenues and sterling costs resulted in foreign exchange losses in 1979 on its U.S. engine contracts that were estimated by the *Wall Street Journal* to be equivalent to $200 million.[8]

Moreover, according to that same *Wall Street Journal* article, "The more engines produced and sold under the previously negotiated contracts, the greater Rolls-Royce's losses will be." Had Rolls-Royce matched the funding strategy of its U.S. competitors in currency denomination terms, it would have effectively neutralized the effect of exchange rate overshooting (hedge motive) and preserved its competitiveness in its key exports market. As the pound was appreciating against the dollar, the effective cost of funding export operations would have provided Rolls-Royce with a windfall gain offsetting its transaction exposure losses due to dollar invoicing (higher nominal interest cost but significant capital gains due to a lower sterling cost of repaying a dollar liability). Conversely, as the pound sterling depreciated against the U.S.

dollar, windfall exports profits would have been partly neutralized by a higher cost of servicing/repaying a dollar debt. Clearly subordinated to satisficing the exchange risk hedge motive, such geofinancing could have been combined with a currency swap when the pound sterling reached its high point against the dollar. (See the last section of this chapter for a discussion of this approach.)

More generally, such geofinancing could be critical to strictly domestic firms facing the onslaught of imports boosted by an overvalued dollar as a number of U.S. manufacturing companies experienced in 1980–1985. By funding their domestic operations in yen and/or DM, U.S. firms could have buffeted the punishing impact of foreign imports—literally subsidized by an overvalued dollar—by smoothing their domestic sales, that is, matching import dollar prices with foreign financing cost savings.

Hedging Political Risk through Geocentric Financial Entrapment: Kennecott vs. Anaconda

Most raw material seekers active in the third world have found themselves under considerable pressure to either divest or enter into minority-joint ventures to avoid outright nationalization/expropriation by host governments submerged by the tidal wave of economic nationalism. The tale of two U.S. copper MNCs' involvement in Chile (Moran 1974) is illustrative of how political risk can be managed "ex-ante" through a policy of multilateral entrapment based on a geocentric view of the multinational financial and trade system.

Both Kennecott Corporation and Anaconda Company had long held and operated substantial copper mines in Chile but had a radically different outlook on its future. Kennecott relied on the giant mine of El Teniente reinvesting minimally above depreciation to keep production slightly increasing: no efforts at developing new mining sites were initiated over 1945–1965. In 1964 however, under pressure from Christian Democrat President Eduardo Frei Montalva to expand and modernize its operation at El Teniente, Kennecott initiated an ambitious capital expenditures plan to increase copper production from 180,000 to 280,000 metric tons per year. The expansion plan was to be financed by the sale of a 51 percent interest in the mine for $80 million to the Chilean government in exchange for a ten-year management contract. In addition, further financing came from the Exim Bank ($110 million to be paid back over a ten-to-fifteen-year period) and the Chilean Copper Corporation ($24 million). In exchange for agreeing to a minority position in the newly created joint venture, Kennecott demanded and obtained a special reassessment of the book value of the El Teniente property (from $69 million to $286 million) and a dramatic reduction in taxes from 80 to 44 percent on its share of the profits.

Not only did Kennecott not commit one cent to the new mine, but it also developed a multinational web of stakeholders in the project. Kennecott began by insuring its equity sale to the Chilean government (reinvested in the mine) with the Agency for International Development (AID) and saw to it that the Exim Bank loan be unconditionally guaranteed by the Chilean government and submitted to the law of the State of New York. Kennecott also raised $45 million for the new joint venture by writing long-term contracts for the future output (literally mortgaging copper still in the ground) with European and Asian customers. Finally, collection rights on these contracts were sold to a consortium of European Banks ($30 million) and Mitsui & Co. ($15 million), the Japanese trading company.

Anaconda, by contrast, had been bullish on Chile all along and continued to rely on its traditional ethnocentric approach to financing foreign direct investment showing insensitivity to potentially explosive political risk and uncertainty. Having invested heavily in new mines and the modernization of old ones in its own name throughout 1945–1965, Anaconda refused voluntary divestiture and was eventually forced to sell 51 percent of its Chilean holdings to the state in 1969. Although it had partial coverage of its holdings with AID prior to its forced divestiture, Anaconda had allowed the policy to lapse after 1969.

With the defiant new Marxist government of President Salvador Allende Gossens assuming power in 1971 came the real test. Fulfilling his lifelong pledge to expropriate foreign interests in Chilean copper without compensation, Kennecott and Anaconda shortly fell prey to the Allende's vengeance. Kennecott received compensation from OPIC (which had taken over from AID) of $80 million plus interest, an amount surpassing the book value of its pre-1964 holdings and which was eventually reimbursed to the U.S. government by Chile as a condition for rolling over the Chilean debt. Kennecott, on its own, was using the unconditional guarantee initially extracted from the Frei government for the original sale amount to obtain a writ of attachment in the U.S. federal courts against all Chilean property within the courts' jurisdiction including the jets to Lanchile, when they landed in New York. This ensured that the Allende government would assume all debt obligations the joint venture had contracted with Exim Bank and the European consortium of banks together with Mitsui; this it did in October 1971. Kennecott had, in effect, been freed from any further international obligations (financial and otherwise) thanks to a systematic geocentric strategy in funding its operations in Chile.

Anaconda was expropriated without compensation from either the Chilean government because it had no leverage being the sole investor, nor OPIC because it had failed to insure against political risk. The only recourse left to Anaconda's board of directors was to fire its entire management as it did; but this was a poor recourse to its ethnocentric financial myopia.

Geofinancing and the Opportunistic Motive; Capitalizing on Capital Market Segmentation with Currency Overshooting; and Exploiting the MNE's Financial System's Potential

Capital market segmentation and prolonged currency overshooting generally avail MNCs of unique opportunities ranging from risk-free skillful arbitrage operations to more speculative financing endeavors. Here the firm acts as an unconstrained decisionmaker in pursuit of its geocentric potential—unhampered by competitive or the hedge motives. This section reviews successful arbitrage between the onshore and offshore capital market components in the same currency space, aggressive capitalization on foreign debt funding denominated in an overpriced currency, and arbitrage of exchange market distortions through the multinational enterprise system.

Arbitraging Capital Market Segmentation through Long-Term Debt Financing

Small but recurring differences in the cost of capital between the onshore and offshore component of the same currency credit market can be a lucrative source of arbitrage profit and result in significant savings in financing costs. Thus, in 1982 the Coca-Cola Company with a triple A rating and better-than-global name recognition was able to issue $100 million of five-year Eurobonds at 10.5 percent or 40 basis points (.4 percent) below the then prevailing rate on U.S. domestic Treasury bonds of similar maturity.

In a similar vein, in 1985 Exxon Corporation purchased $175 million of U.S. Treasury thirty-year, zero coupon bonds yielding 8 percent and simultaneously sold $200 million of thirty-year, zero coupon Eurobonds priced to yield 7.6 percent. The future proceeds from the Treasury bonds exactly offset Exxon's liability on its own issue. This interest rate differential and Exxon's ability to span the onshore and offshore components of the same credit market yielded a $25 million profit to the arbitraging firm (Finnerty 1985). Obviously, such international arbitrage opportunities tend to be self-destructive in so far as profit opportunities for MNCs are incentives to bid up underpriced securities and bid down overpriced ones until the interest rate differential disappears. Time and again, however, such arbitrage windows of opportunity have been skillfully exploited by geocentric MNCs.

Capitalizing on Currency Overshooting in Long-Term Financing: The IBM/World Bank Swap

In a world of mildly segmented capital markets where exchange rate overshooting, credit rationing with interest rate ceilings, and crowding out effect by public or quasi-public borrowers is generally the norm rather than the exception, the issue of optimal currency denomination in global financing assumes real operational significance.

Through the use of new financing techniques such as currency swaps it is possible to reduce the cost of long-term debt funding by exploiting what may be perceived as temporary aberrations in the pricing of foreign-currency-denominated, long-term debt instruments (currency overshooting hypothesis). Once a lower-interest-rate debt instrument has been secured, it is possible to lock in an exchange gain (which further reduces the effective cost of foreign currency financing) by entering into a fixed-interest-rate-to-fixed-interest-rate currency swap. Indeed, by exchanging interest payment and principal repayment obligations at a fixed (once-and-for-all) exchange rate, borrowers can free themselves from a foreign debt obligation without incurring the additional cost of prepayment penalty and floatation cost on a new debt issue as evidenced by the IBM/World Bank currency swap summarized in table 11–3. Thus a bold geocentric funding strategy (opportunistic motive) could substantially reduce the effective cost of long-term debt above and beyond IBM's major competitors.

Exploiting the Multinational Enterprise System Potential

In competing with local firms, MNCs are typically able to arbitrage financial market distortions (perhaps due to currency overvaluation/undervaluation, or multiple exchange rate systems that subsidize certain categories of transactions), provided that they adroitly exploit their multinational financial sys-

Table 11–3
**Capitalizing on Currency Overshooting through Currency Swaps
of Debt Payments**

- In previous years IBM had borrowed fixed-interest-rate DM and SF.

- As the dollar appreciated sharply against these two currencies (the DM fell from DM1.93 in March to DM2.52 per dollar in August 1981), IBM enjoyed a capital gain from the reduced dollar value of its foreign debt liabilities.

- IBM realized its capital gains immediately by swapping its foreign debt for a dollar debt; it also saved any prepayment penalties typically associated with early principal retirement.

- The World Bank issued two dollar Eurobonds, one which matched the maturity of IBM's DM debt, and the other which matched the maturity of IBM's SF debt.

- The World Bank agreed to pay all future interest and principal payments of IBM's DM and SF debt, while IBM in turn agreed to pay future interest and principal payments on the World Bank's dollar debt. By swapping dollar debt for SF and DM debt, the World Bank gained instantaneous access to the Swiss and West German capital markets—markets which are otherwise characterized by queues for nonresident borrowers.

tem's potential. Specifically, the MNCs possess a unique characteristic—the ability to shift funds among various foreign subsidiaries and the parent company through internal transfer mechanisms. Indeed, this highly coordinated intracorporate flow of goods (material parts, subassemblies, and finished products), services (technology, management skills, trademark) and money (debt and equity) is the hallmark of the modern MNC (figure 11–7). This in itself allows the firm to create value above and beyond what its arm's length activities would earn provided that arbitrage opportunities do exist which are not readily available to strictly domestic firms (Lessard 1979). Figure 11–7 unbundles the total flow of funds between each pair of affiliates into separate components associated with resources transferred in the form of products, financial services, and technology. This should allow the truly geocentric firm to arbitrage:

1. Tax distortions.
2. Financial market distortions.
3. Regulatory system distortions.

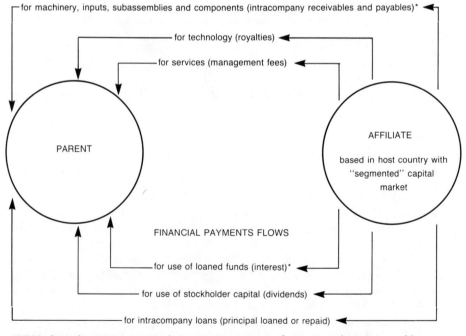

*MNCs have discretion to manipulate maturity structure of account and interest payables or receivables (leading or lagging) and adjust the magnitude of payment flow (overinvoicing or underinvoicing).

Figure 11–7. The Multinational Enterprise System

Consider the case of one U.S. automotive manufacturer contemplating the expansion of its production capacity in Mexico in early 1986. The investment could have been financed in at least two ways; both partially capitalized on distortions in the foreign exchange market through fine-tuning of the multinational enterprise system. These financing techniques are described next.

Intracorporate Debt Financing. Intracorporate debt financing in U.S. dollars at the rate of 10 percent per annum was one option. The loan would be denominated in U.S. dollars with debt servicing allowed at the controlled rate of 335 Mexican peso/$; eventual principal repayment would be fully incurred at the free rate (then at 410 Mexican peso/$) which would increase considerably the effective cost of financing as the free rate was widely expected to depreciate further.[9] Given the two-tier nature of the Mexican foreign exchange market, however, the U.S. investor could mitigate or lessen the foreign exchange loss by underinvoicing exports from its Mexican subsidiary to its U.S. parent or overinvoicing exports to its Mexican subsidiary.[10] Because trade-related transactions enjoy a favorable (overvalued) controlled exchange rate, the U.S. firm would be able to lessen its cost of capital courtesy of the Mexican Central Bank (clearly, a subsidy not available to domestic Mexican firms). Thus, by jointly arbitraging the two tiers of the Mexican exchange market and exploiting its system potential, the MNC is able to reduce its cost of capital.

Debt-Equity Swap. A debt-equity swap—the second option—allowed the U.S. investor to buy Mexico's hard currency debt on the secondary U.S. capital market at a discount of 58 percent and to swap it for local equity with the Mexican government at a buy-back price of 88 percent of the debt face value (see figure 11–8 for a flowchart of the technique). Thus, the investor gained access to local currency at an exchange rate considerably more favorable than the controlled one thereby reducing its upfront dollar investment by approximately one-third (as compared to intracorporate debt financing) and lowering its cost of capital commensurately. Dividends remittance restrictions may limit the return on the equity injection to the historical interest rate on the original hard currency debt but the investor may arbitrage the two tiers of the Mexican foreign exchange market by exploiting its system potential (disguise dividends remittances as overinvoiced imports of components or subassemblies).

Conclusion

In a world of mildly segmented capital markets and misaligned exchange rates, MNCs and domestic firms alike should nurture a global financing

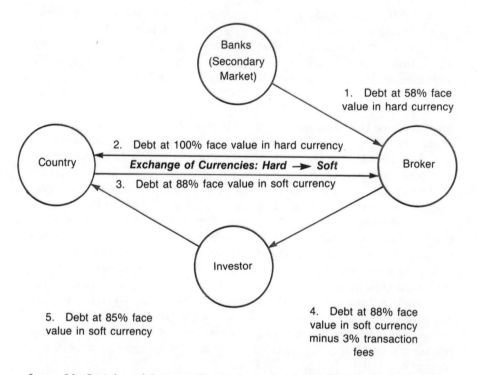

Source: J.L. Ganitsky and G. Lema, "Foreign Investment through Debt-Equity Swaps," *Sloan Management Review* 29, no. 2, pp. 23. By permission of the publisher. Copyright © 1988 by the Sloan Management Review Association. All rights reserved.
Note: Percent values are for illustrative purposes only.

Figure 11–8. Participants and Their Relationships in Transnational Debt-Equity Swaps

competence that can enhance their competitive advantage by turning the finance function into a value-adding activity.

This article decomposed this geocentric boundary scanning capability as purporting to (1) ensure that a firm's financial costs are no higher than its major competitors' (the competitive motive illustrated by NOVO's international equity funding); (2) enhance the management of exchange and political risk (the hedge motive illustrated by Rolls-Royce's vicissitudes in its key exports market and the tale of Anaconda versus Kennecott in Chile); and (3) create value in its own right by exploiting the scope of the multinational enterprise system or currency overshooting as demonstrated by the IBM/World Bank swap.

Indeed, a mechanistic approach to minimizing the cost of financing too often ignores industry and contextual environment threats and opportunities which should be carefully woven in a truly geocentric financial strategy. Specifically, geocentric financing that satisfices the hedge motive may turn out to be more costly than financing strictly predicated on a cost of capital minimization argument: the premium paid is simply the cost of hedging exchange risk or political risk as illustrated earlier in the cases of Rolls-Royce or Kennecott.

Notes

1. This decomposition of the firm's financial objectives is intuitively consistent with the theory of shareholder wealth maximization; for a similar approach see Lessard's (1986) seminal work on "Finance and Global Competition."

2. For an overview of recent trends in banking and financial deregulation, see Khoury and Ghosh (1986), pages 1–33.

3. Interest rate parity (IRPT) refers to the convergence across money markets in the cost of short-term financing; see Dufey and Giddy (1978) for an extensive discussion of the IRPT concept for both onshore and offshore components of paired money markets.

4. This is further exacerbated by the considerably higher turnover rate on the New York Stock Exchange than the Tokyo or European stock exchanges; this point is illustrated in a comparative mode in Ellsworth (1985).

5. Although recent studies of cost of capital differences between the United States and Japan concluded that there is a significant gap, some questions can be raised as to the soundness of their methodological approach; see Baldwin (1986) for discussion and a critique of the latter.

6. The purchasing power parity (PPP) hypothesis refers to the long-run tendency for change in exchange rates to offset cumulative differences in rates of inflation in between countries; in the short term, however exchange rates deviate markedly from their PPP equilibrium values; that is, overshoot or undershoot. See Levich (1981) for alternative definitions of what should be construed as equilibrium exchange rates under overshooting conditions.

7. This is, of course, an illustration rather than a proof of how through skillful multiple listing of its stock a firm may be able to reduce its cost of capital.

8. *Wall Street Journal*, 11 March 1980.

9. Since the early eighties Mexico has relied on a two-tier exchange market allegedly to cope with a severe balance of payments deficit and domestic hyperinflation. Under this scheme the Mexican Central Bank channels preferential exchange transactions (e.g. imports of goods deemed essential to the Mexican economy and interest payments on hard currency debt) through a controlled tier at a favorable (overvalued) exchange rate whereas all other transactions are channeled through a freely-floating rate.

10. By disguising principal repayment or dividend remittances as import components or subassemblies through intracorporate transfer price adjustments, the US investor can take advantage of the controlled exchange rate. When done incrementally over a period of time over (under) invoicing is difficult to monitor by Central Bank

authorities; although this practice is in theory illegal, it is still widely used by foreign and domestic firms as a means of circumventing exchange controls or capitalizing on subsidized exchange rates.

11. Helpful comments from F.R. Root are gratefully acknowledged.

References

Abegglen, J.C. and Stalk, G.K. 1986. *The Japanese corporation.* New York: Basic Books.

Baldwin, C. 1986. The capital factor: Competing for capital in a global environment. In *Competition in global industries,* edited by M. Porter, 185–224 Boston: Harvard Business School Press.

Beidleman, C.R. 1985. *Financial swaps: New strategies in currency and coupon risk management.* Homewood, Ill.: Dow Jones-Irwin.

Dufey, G., and Giddy, I. 1978. *The international money market.* Englewood Cliffs, N.J.: Prentice-Hall.

———. 1981. Innovations in the international financial markets. *Journal of International Business Studies,* 12 (Fall): 35–51.

Dufey, G., and Srinivasulu, S. 1984. The case for corporate management of foreign exchange risk. *Financial Management,* 12(4): 54–62.

Eiteman, D.K., and Stonehill, A. 1986. *Multinational business finance,* 5th ed. Reading, Mass.: Addison-Wesley.

Ellsworth, R. 1985. Capital markets and competitive decline. *Harvard Business Review,* Sept.–Oct., 171–83.

Finnerty, J.D. 1985. Zero coupon bond arbitrage: An illustration of the regulatory dialectic at work. *Financial Management* 14(4): 13–17.

Frankel, J.A. 1985. Six possible meanings of 'overvaluation': The 1981–1985 dollar. Essays in International Finance, No. 159, Princeton, N.J.: Princeton University.

Ganitsky, J.L., and Lema, G. 1988. Foreign investment through debt-equity swaps. *Sloan Management Review* 29(2): 21–30.

Goldfinger, C. 1986. *La geofinance: Pour comprendre la mutation financiere.* Paris: Seuil.

Hatsopoulos, G.N. 1983. High cost of capital: Handicap of American industry. Report sponsored by the American Business Conference and Thermoelectron Corporation, April.

Heenan, D.A., and Perlmutter, H.V. 1978. *Multinational organization development: A social perspective.* Reading, Mass.: Addison-Wesley.

Hodder, J.E., and Tschoegl, A.E. 1985. Some aspects of Japanese corporate finance. *Journal of Financial and Quantitative Analysis* 20(2): 173–91.

Jacque, L., and Lang, P. 1987. Currency denomination in long-term debt financing and refinancing: A cross hedging paradigm. *Journal of the Operational Research Society* 38(2).

Khoury, S.J., and Gosh, A. 1986. *Recent developments in international banking and finance,* Lexington, Mass.: D.C. Heath.

Lessard, D.R. 1979. Transfer prices, taxes and financial markets: implications of international financial transfer within the multinational firm. In *The economic effects of multinational corporations,* ed. R.G. Hawking. Greenwich, Conn.: JAI Press.

————. 1986. Finance and global competition: Exploiting financial scope and coping with volatile exchange rates. *Midland Corporate Finance Journal* 4(3): 6–29.

Levich, R.M. 1981. *Overshooting in the foreign exchange market,* Occasional Papers No. 5. New York: Group of Thirty.

Moran, T.M. 1974. *The politics of dependence: Copper in Chile,* Princeton, N.J.: Princeton University Press.

Park, Y.S. 1984. Currency swaps as long-term international financing techniques. *Journal of International Business Studies,* 15 (Winter): 47–54.

Perlmutter, H.V. 1969. The tortuous evolution of the multinational corporation. *Columbia Journal of World Business* 4: 9–18.

Robbins, S.M., and Stobaugh, R.B. 1973. *Money in the Multinational Enterprise.* New York: Basic Books.

Shapiro, A.C. 1986. *Multinational financial management,* 2d ed. Boston: Allyn & Bacon.

Srinivasulu, S. 1983. Currency denomination of debt: Lessons from Rolls-Royce and Laker Airways. *Business Horizons,* Sept./Oct. pp. 19–23.

Stonehill, A., and Dullums, K. 1982. *Internationalizing the cost of capital in theory and practice: The NOVO experience and national policy implications.* New York: John Wiley & Sons.

Part IV
Empirical Studies of Global Strategy and Performance

12
Unrelated Product Diversification and Global Corporate Performance

Lawrence G. Franko

T his chapter examines the relationship between corporate strategies of unrelated product diversification and firms' subsequent growth and financial performance. It surveys the strategies and performance since 1975 of 105 of the largest American, European, and Japanese firms in five industries: computers and office equipment, electrical equipment and electronics, pharmaceuticals, chemicals, and tires and rubber. It also examines the volatility of firms' share prices, comparing the riskiness of returns of the predominantly American firms pursuing unrelated diversification strategies to that of more focused competitors.

The conclusion is clear: corporate diversification into products whose technologies and markets are unrelated to firms' principal, core businesses have typically been followed by growth rates below main-industry averages, and therefore, by losses in world market shares, by below-average accounting returns on assets, and by above-average volatility of stock prices. The statistical analysis presented in this chapter thus confirms what clinical case collection suggests. The International Competitive Analysis (ICA) data base from which our company sample is drawn (see exhibit 12–1) contains a large number of unrelated diversifiers and conglomerates of the 1960s and 1970s; they have ended up among the world's industrial also-rans in the 1980s. Many have been in the news of late, as their diversifications of yesteryear have given way to restructurings and deconglomeration, or to the outright disappearance of corporate identity.

The role of failed, doubtful or merely low-growth-and-profitability diversifiers is a long one. In the context of the declines in competitiveness and losses of world market share of many American and British enterprises, it is also noteworthy that among the world's largest industrial firms, the unrelated diversifiers and conglomerators have primarily been firms based in the United States and the United Kingdom. Any collection of cautionary tales would include the dubious histories of the moves of ITT Corporation and now-deceased RCA Corporation out of electronics; W.R. Grace and Company and Olin Corporation out of chemicals; Warner-Lambert Company out of phar-

Exhibit 12–1
The International Competitive Analysis Data Base

The mission of the International Competitive Analysis (ICA) research is to examine which firms are winning and which are losing world market share, and why.

The data base at the core of the analytical effort includes quantitative and qualitative information for the period 1960–1986 on more than three-hundred corporations in fifteen broadly-defined industries headquartered in the United States, Japan, Germany, France, Switzerland, the Netherlands, and other European and Asian countries.

The units of analysis in this work are firms. This is due to the fact that firms based in the same industry and country frequently have widely differing levels of growth and financial performance. Generalizations about nations' competitiveness should be treated with caution: one of the most striking facts to emerge from the data base is its demonstration that gross generalizations about U.S., or German, or Japanese industry are excessively simplistic.

The data base focuses on measures and determinants of strategic performance, that is, success over three-to-ten-year periods. The data base includes information on companies' worldwide growth and financial performance, R&D spending, product portfolios, geographical location profile, organization structures, and capital investment per employee during the period 1970–1986. A special emphasis is placed on compiling data on non-U.S. firms.

---

maceuticals; Xerox Corporation and Control Data Corporation (CDC) into financial services; B.F. Goodrich & Company, Uniroyal, Inc., and Britain's Dunlop away from tires and rubber; Exxon Corporation into office equipment and electric motors (Beman 1981); several oil companies into copper just as metal prices peaked; and of many conglomerates such as Gulf + Western Industries, Inc. (Davis 1985).

On the less frequent occasions when Continental European firms succumbed to the temptation of moving from their core industry into, as Monty Python might say, "something completely different," the results were often equally poor. Volkswagen's flirt with electronic trendiness in 1979 led it to acquire what turned out to be a bankrupt typewriter company. After several years of losses, the subsidiary, Triumph-Adler, was sold off to Olivetti in 1986 (Can VW 1984; Carr 1986). Volvo, following in the footsteps of a large number of acquisitive firms who buy into unfamiliar industries, just as a cycle (and acquisition cost) peaks, bought an oil-trading company just before the energy crisis turned to an energy glut.

Japanese firms, especially those so vigorously gaining shares of world markets in electrical equipment and electronics, autos, and tires were among the enterprises in the ICA data base *least* prone to venture far from their main, core business. (See also Franko 1983 especially chap. 5. This statement may not appear self-evident to readers who have seen Japanese *Keiretsu* business-groups referred to as conglomerates in the English-language financial press. Notwithstanding the often numerous cross-shareholdings allying many Japanese industrial corporations to other firms and banks, these linkages quite specifically exclude the overarching, central direction, corporate administration, and organizational structure characteristic of Western unrelated diversifiers or conglomerates.)

Previous Studies

The high risk of diversification and acquisition into unrelated businesses and industries has hardly gone unnoticed in the business strategy literature. The works of Kitching (1973), Rumelt (1974, 1982), Biggadike (1979), Montgomery (1979), Bettis and Hall (1982), Hill (1983), Palepu (1985) and Capon (1988) are especially noteworthy.

Kitching showed that U.S. companies acquiring European firms in unrelated businesses in the 1960s and early 1970s were far more likely to fail than were those making acquisitions in their main business or related lines. Kitching did not, however, make the direct link between firms' overall corporate diversification thrust and corporate performance.

Rumelt's initial work (1974) did test the link between corporate diversification strategies, corporate growth, and financial performance in U.S. firms during 1949–1969. Rumelt's rather complex taxonomy of corporate diversification strategies categorized firms as ranging from single business to dominant vertical, dominant linked, and dominant unrelated, through related, unrelated-passive, and acquisitive conglomerate categories. His findings concerning unrelated diversification strategies included the observations that firms pursuing unrelated-passive strategies did indeed have below-average sales growth rates and financial returns. He also found that acquisitive conglomerates, while often showing somewhat higher than average profitability as measured by return on equity (ROE), tended to produce such results by having a higher degree of financially risky leverage, while actually having a lower than average return on total capital employed in the business. Rumelt noted that acquisitive conglomerates were a relatively new phenomenon at the time of his investigation, whose long-term performance viability remained to be seen.

Using a very different data base—that of the PIMS group on managers' perceptions of financial returns to individual business activities within corporate groups—Biggadike (1979) concluded that there was a high risk of low financial returns for a long time in virtually any diversification into a new business—defined as products not previously marketed, and requiring new investments in equipment, people, or knowledge. As in the case of Kitching's investigation, however, the impact of such diversification decisions on total corporate performance over time was not examined.

Rumelt's 1982 article, as well as the work of Montgomery (1979), Palepu (1985), and Capon, et al. (1988) update Rumelt's analysis of the relationship between U.S. companies' diversification strategies and financial performance through the 1970s. Firms pursuing unrelated diversification strategies were once again found to have below-average returns to capital employed. These studies did not, however, examine performance in the context of intraindustry competition, nor did they control for possible industry effects on performance that might result from nonrandom choices within industries of firms' diversification strategies. Nor did they examine the possible trade-off of lowered risk as compensation for the lower returns of unrelated diversification strategies. This last issue was, however, addressed in the work of Hill (1983) and Bettis and Hall (1982).

It has often been pointed out in the finance literature that, where efficient capital markets exist, risk-reduction through corporate diversification cannot provide net benefits to shareholders, because on their own they can achieve a desired level of risk through portfolio diversification (Alberts 1966; Levy and Sarnat 1970). Notwithstanding, managers have often justified unrelated diversification strategies by asserting the desirability of reducing earnings volatility by means of packaging countercyclical businesses under one corporate administrative roof (Davis 1985; Lauenstein 1985; Amihud and Lev 1981). The available evidence, however, suggests that such hopes have typically not materialized. Bettis and Hall (1982) found that there was no significant difference in risk (measured by the volatility of return on assets) among firms pursuing different diversification strategies in their sample of eighty U.S. firms. In addition, they found that the higher average returns of focused corporations typically found in earlier studies have been due to industry effects, and in particular to the tendency of high-return pharmaceutical firms to avoid unrelated diversification. On the basis of a sample of sixty British firms covering the early 1970s, the Hill (1983) study found no significant differences between the return and growth performance of firms categorized as single business, concentric diversifiers, and conglomerates, but it did find that the earnings volatility of conglomerate diversifiers was considerably greater than that of firms eschewing unrelated diversification. (Further clinical evidence for the proposition that unrelated diversification is associated with an increase in earnings and return volatility, rather than with the decrease so often associated with management justifications of such strategies is found in Lauenstein 1985.)

In spite of the richness of the existing studies on corporate diversification and performance, each has been based on samples in a single nation. They have not considered the issue in the context either of intraindustry or international competition.

Evidence

The following investigation of the relationship between firms' degree of unrelated diversification in the mid-1970s and their subsequent growth and financial performance attempts to provide a view of corporate strategy and performance of firms based in five industries having global scope and competition: computers and office equipment, electrical equipment and electronics, pharmaceuticals, chemicals, and tires and rubber.

The overall statistical results based on data for the period 1975–1980 can be summarized briefly. In all five of these sectors there were striking, statistically verifiable negative relationships between unrelated diversification strategies and subsequent sales growth and financial results. These statistical results are presented in the accompanying tables.

Moreover, the lower growth performance and accounting returns of the unrelated diversifiers in each industry were not accompanied by reduced risk to shareholders, as measured by one widely employed measure of the volatility of returns to shareholders. As a general rule, the average five-year trailing "beta," or coefficient of covariation with the overall U.S. stock market of individual firms' stock prices as calculated by Value Line, was greater in 1980 for U.S. firms pursuing unrelated diversification strategies during the latter half of the 1970s than it was for these firms' more focused industry brethren. (See table 12–1.) This conclusion and the data reported in table 12–1 pertain only to the subset of U.S. firms in our sample universe. Value Line betas are calculated with respect to an index of the U.S. equities market only, and not a world market. Value Line does, in fact, calculate betas with respect to the U.S. market index for a limited number of non-U.S. firms' equity securities quoted on the major U.S. exchanges. The few betas available for non-U.S. firms were uniformly considerably below U.S. industry averages. This result may have been due, however, to the fact that the covariation measured was with the U.S. market, not with some world index, and could thence have resulted from limited covariation among national securities markets as whole, rather than from divergences among firm-specific characteristics and strategies.

Thus, not only does one oft-used management justification for the pursuit of unrelated diversification—the reduction of volatility in returns to shareholders—receive no support from these data, but patterns in these five industries also confirm the finding of Hill (1983) that unrelated diversification may simultaneously increase risk and diminish return. The companies surveyed in each industry are listed in the appendix.

As the hypothesis under test was that poor corporate growth and financial performance would follow when large portions of a firm's activity were unrelated to its core business either by market or technology, the simplest possible definition of unrelated business was used. Activities outside of a

Table 12–1
Unrelated Diversification and Shareholder Risk

Share price volatility relative to the U.S. equities market of U.S. firms in five industries, classified by pursuit of unrelated diversification strategies versus focused strategies between 1975 and 1980. Average 1980 five-year trailing betas, as calculated by Value Line, for firms in each category. Value Line betas are the coefficient of the covariation of the weekly movement of the price of a firm's common stock with movements in the New York Stock Exchange Composite Index over the preceding five-year period. (Value Line, *Subscriber's Guide,* undated, p. 55) A beta greater than one indicates that the stock price was more volatile than the market; a beta less than one indicates below-market volatility.

	Average 1980 Betas (Number of Firms)	
Industry	Unrelated Diversifiers	Focused Firms
Computers and office equipment	1.35 (3)	1.24 (8)
Pharmaceuticals	.99 (4)	.94 (10)
Electrical equipment and electronics	1.15 (4)	1.08 (6)
Chemicals	1.07 (3)	1.01 (4)
	1.13 (5)[a]	
Tires and rubber	1.03 (3)	.85 (3)

Note: Firms were classified as unrelated diversifiers if more than 10 percent of their sales came from unrelated activities in 1975, and such a strategy was maintained through 1980 inclusive.

[a]Includes two firms that adopted an unrelated diversification strategy during the period 1975–1980 and whose equities' betas substantially increased from their 1975 levels. In contrast, the other chemical firms' betas generally decreased between 1975 and 1980.

firm's main two-digit Standard Industrial Classification (SIC) code were considered unrelated, with one exception. Electronic equipment, such as components and telecommunication equipment (SIC 367 and 366) were considered related activities for computer and office equipment firms (SIC 357) and vice versa.

Computers and Office Equipment

The dangers of unrelated diversification might arguably be thought to be greatest to firms whose core businesses are technologically dynamic. Diversion of management time and attention from competitive challenge and technical change could lead to particularly high opportunity costs of unrelated diversification moves away from such businesses.

The negative relationship between unrelated diversification and performance is particularly salient in the computer and office equipment industry, one of the high-technology dynamism par excellence. (See table 12–2.) The high performing firms were all clearly focused on their main business. None of the firms that were attempting to manage businesses unrelated to computers and office machinery were among the growth and financial leaders.

Table 12-2
Computer and Office Equipment Firms Classified by Sales Growth,
Return on Assets (ROA), and Unrelated Diversification

Growth and Unrelated Diversification
(Sales Growth, 1975–1980 versus Unrelated Diversification, 1975, 18 Companies)

		Percent of Sales Unrelated to Main Industry, 1975		
		Low *(0–10%)*	*High* *(11–45%)*	
Annual Average Compound Growth Rate, 1975–1980	High (18 to 90%)	9	0	9
	Low (8 to 18%)	5	4	9
		14	4	18

(Fisher's Exact Test: One Tail: .041[a], Two Tail: .082. r = .53, significance: .011[a])

Financial Return (ROA) and Unrelated Diversification
(ROA, 1979–1980 Average versus Unrelated Diversification, 1975, 16 Companies)

		Percent of Sales Unrelated to Main Industry, 1975		
		Low *(0–10%)*	*High* *(11–45%)*	
Average Return on Assets 1979–1980	High (12 to 17%)	5	0	5
	Low (4 to 11.9%)	8	3	11
		13	3	16

(Fisher's Exact Test: One Tail: .295, Two Tail: .509. r = −.32, significance = .11.)

[a]Statistically significant at or above the 95 percent level of confidence.

A number of attributes were common to the computer and office equipment firms that had diversified operations well outside of that industry. Three of the four, low performing, unrelated diversifiers were U.S. firms. All were average to below average for the industry in R&D intensity in the mid-1970s. Two of the three American firms were the least internationally oriented in 1975 (as measured by the percentage of company sales outside of the United States) of the nine top U.S. firms in the industry.

Of the four firms, only Italy's Olivetti radically changed strategy during the late 1970s. It phased down its machine tool and other machinery activities (which had put it among 1975s unrelated diversifiers in our categorization), substantially upgraded its R&D effort, and adopted a far more international orientation. By 1980 Olivetti almost doubled the percentage of its sales outside of its home market.

The three American firms—Sperry Corporation, CDC, and Honeywell, Inc.—not only maintained their multi-industry posture during the late 1970s and early 1980s, but they were also joined in 1982 by Xerox Corporation which came into the ranks of the unrelated diversifiers by purchasing an insurance company. This move, coinciding as it did with the onslaught of a ferocious price war in the insurance industry and intensification of Japanese (and some U.S.) competition directed toward Xerox's traditional copier activities, led Xerox's growth rate, margins, and financial returns to plummet in the early 1980s. Although the company appeared by the mid-1980s to have made something of a turnaround, both in stopping the erosion of its copier market share by the Japanese and in improving the financial results of its insurance activities, corporate financial and growth performance measures bear little comparison to 1970s levels. (On the recent history of Xerox see: Jacobson and Hillkirk 1985; Harris 1986; and Value Line various issues, p. 1137.)

By the mid-1980s, the strategic consequences of CDC's dispersion of activities saw it in a near brush with bankruptcy. Its once commanding position in very large mainframe computers was eroded by the distractions of financial services and the competitive success and greater R&D commitment of former employee, Seymour Cray, in developing the modern supercomputer.

The Honeywell saga reached its dénouement in September 1986 when, after years of continued customer defections and losses in computer market share to IBM and Japanese producers, the firm announced that it would spin off its computer activities to a new entity in which Japan's NEC and France's Groupe Bull would have a dominant position. (Honeywell Retreats 1986.)

Only Sperry drew the logical conclusion from its and other firms' experience with unfocused operations: During the early 1980s it sold off its consumer, farm equipment, and hydraulics operations, and once again became a company primarily focused on the product it—not IBM—had pioneered: computers and their applications. In the process, it became an attractive prospect for what became, much to the benefit of shareholders who had wagered on the firm's refocusing, a successful acquisition bid in mid-1986 by industry colleague, Burroughs Corporation.

Pharmaceuticals

A strong negative relationship between unrelated diversification and corporate performance has also characterized the pharmaceutical industry. (See table 12–3.) During the period 1975–1980, the nine highest growth firms among the twenty-one largest firms in the world industry were focused on their pharmaceuticals businesses. (Activities of these high performing firms also sometimes included related fine chemicals and health care products, but rarely, if ever ranged much further afield.)

Table 12–3
Pharmaceutical Firms Classified by Sales Growth, Return on Assets (ROA), and Unrelated Diversification

Growth and Unrelated Diversification

(Sales Growth, 1975–1980 versus Unrelated Diversification, 1975, 21 Companies)

		Percent of Sales Unrelated to Main Industry, 1975		
		Low (0–10%)	*High 11–50%)*	
Annual Average Compound Growth Sales, 1975–1980	High (15 to 26%)	9	0	9
	Low (9.9 to 14.9%)	5	7	12
		14	7	21

Financial Returns and Unrelated Diversification

(1979–1980 Average Returns on Assets (ROA) and Stockholders' Equity (ROE) versus 1975 Unrelated Diversification.)

		Percent of Sales Unrelated to Main Industry, 1975		
		Low (0–14%)	*High (15–50%)*	
Return on Assets 1979–1980 Average	High (9 to 19%)	10	1	11
	Low (1.9 to 8%)	6[b]	5	11
		16	6	22
Return on Equity 1979–1980 Average	High (16 to 32%)	12	1	13
	Low (3 to 15.9%)	4[b]	5	9
		16	6	22

(Fisher's Exact Test: One Tail: .044[a]; Two Tail: .05[a])

[a]Statistically significant at or above the 95 percent level of confidence.
[b]Includes one German and two Swiss companies whose reported profits are considerably understated in their accounts, compared to results that would be reported were those firms to use U.S. Generally Accepted Accounting Principles (GAAP) methods.

Pharmaceutical firms with significant proportions of their sales (15 percent or more) unrelated to their main line of business were also among the poor financial performers, whether measured by return on assets (ROA) or equity (ROE) in the late 1980s. Although (then) unrelated diversifiers such as Squibb Corporation or Warner-Lambert Company may have maintained or via acquisition added to their foods businesses in the hopes that such activities might be high financial return cash cows to feed pharmaceutical activities, the ultimate effect appeared to be to pull down the growth and financial performance of the whole.

In a syndrome of corporate characteristics similar to that observed in the case of the computer and office equipment industry, the four of seven unrelated diversifiers were American and with one Swiss exception were at the very bottom of the industry league in R&D intensity. Two of the four American unrelated diversifiers appeared also to be trading off international expansion for domestic diversification: They had the lowest proportion of their sales coming from non-U.S. operations of the fourteen leading U.S. firms.

Although the firms that were unrelated diversifiers in 1975 retained that posture through the end of the decade, two notable changes occurred early in the 1980s. Recognizing its underperformance in the pharmaceutical industry, Squibb adopted a strategy of shedding its nonpharmaceutical operations—for example selling Life Savers, Inc., to Nabisco in 1981—boosting its R&D from 4.4 percent of sales in 1975 and 4.6 percent in 1980 to 8.1 percent by 1985, and substantially increasing the proportion of its total activity in markets outside the United States. Indeed, a considerable part of the expansion in R&D has taken place in laboratories located outside the United States. The results of this strategic change begun in the early 1980s have thus far included a major boost to financial returns by the mid-1980s and a growth in sales well above the U.S. industry mean in 1984–85. Investors have seen the firm's stock price quadruple between the end of 1981 and mid-1986. (On Squibb's change in strategic direction and the results thereof see: *Value Line*, various issues, and company annual reports.)

American Home Products (AHP) was the other firm to refocus during the early 1980s—although to a much lesser degree than Squibb. Interestingly enough, AHP had been the only major pharmaceutical firm to have combined a portfolio of unrelated products with superior financial returns, if not superior growth during the 1970s. Although the firm continued to report strong ROA and ROE financial results during the early 1980s, it continued as a low growth firm and one of the least international companies in the industry. One can infer that some of its nonpharmaceutical operations were no longer fulfilling their cash cow, high financial return role from AHP's sale of its housewares division in 1984. (On AHP's recent history, see *Value Line*, various issues.)

Electrical Equipment and Electronics

Firms based in the electrical equipment and electronics industries and heavily involved in unrelated diversification moves during the 1970s also subsequently performed poorly in both growth and financial results. (See table 12–4.)

Three of the low-growth, eventually low-return, high unrelated diversifiers were American. One—ITT Corporation—had become synonymous with the very notion of the conglomerate strategy. However successful Harold Geneen had been in augmenting ITT's sales revenue and earnings per share during the late 1960s and early 1970s, the late 1970s already saw ITT among the growth and financial return also-rans in the electrical and electronics industry. Indeed, it was a comparatively low-growth company during the 1970s even without adjusting for increments in sales due to acquisitions.

In further evidence of a strategy syndrome all-too-common among American firms at the time, ITT's unrelated diversification strategy was accompanied by a relative de-emphasis not only of its core product line, telecommunications equipment, but also of international markets and R&D. ITT was one of the two or three least R&D intensive (own-funded R&D expenditure as a percentage of sales revenues) firms among the top twenty-five in the world electrical equipment industry in the mid-1970s.

If the ITT story in the late 1970s was one of low performance, by the mid-1980s it was of deconglomeration as his successors sold off pieces of what Geneen had assembled. It was also a story of the ignominious failure of the telecommunications system on which ITT had belatedly staked an attempt at a comeback in its once core business. The telecommunications core was sold to France's Compagnie Générale d'Electricité in mid-1986. Years of playing "me too" in a too wide range of industries had taken a toll. So had neglect of a core business that, after years of relative competitive tranquility and seeming technological maturity, was facing deregulation of user markets and integration with computer technologies. (On the fall of the house that Geneen built, see *Behind the ITT Deal* 1986; Taylor 1984; Wayne 1986; *ITT: Groping* 1980.)

The 1986 conclusion of the tale of RCA Corporation—ITT's fellow U.S. unrelated diversifier in the electronics industry—was perhaps even more dramatic, ending in that firm's takeover by General Electric. In the 1950s and 1960s RCA had been the industry leader in consumer electronics, especially color television. Succumbing to the late 1960s siren song of "the coming service economy," and a 1970s too-literal application of strategic portfolio management, during the 1970s the firm "reduced its research efforts and used its capital to diversify into car rentals, publishing, food processing, real estate brokerage and home furnishings." (DeSaint Phalle 1980: 59.) The International Competitive Analysis Data Base shows that not only did RCA reduce its

Table 12–4

Electrical Equipment and Electronics Firms Classified by Sales Growth, Return on Assets (ROA), and Unrelated Diversification

Growth and Unrelated Diversification
(Sales Growth 1975–1980 versus Unrelated Diversification, 1975, 30 Companies)

		Percent of Sales Unrelated to Main Industry, 1975		
		Low (0 – 9%)	High (10 – 45%)	
Annual Average Compound Growth Rate, 1975–1980	High (15 to 28.4%)	14	1	15
	Low (5.4 to 14.99%)	9	6	15
		23	7	30

Chi-Square	D.F.	Significance	Min E.F.	Cells with E.F. 5
2.98137	1	.0842	3.500	2 of 4 (50.0%)
4.65839	1	.0309[a]		(Before Yates Correction)

Return on Assets (ROA) and Unrelated Diversification
(Average 1979–1980 ROA versus Unrelated Diversification, 1975, 26 Companies)

		Percent of Sales Unrelated to Main Industry		
		Low (0 – 9%)	High (10 – 45%)	
Average 1979–1980 ROA	High (4.6 to 12%)	10	0	10
	Low (−6.5 to 4.59%)	1	5	16
		21	5	26

Chi-Square	D.F.	Significance	Min E.F.	Cells with E.F. 5
2.11869	1	.1455	1.923	2 of 4 (50.0%)
3.86905	1	.0492[a]		(Before Yates Correction)

[a]Statistically significant at or above the 95 percent level of confidence.

R&D during this period, but it also actually somewhat decreased its net fixed capital per employee (even in current, noninflation-adjusted dollars) at a time when Japanese and some European competitors were embarked on massive capital spending and plant modernization programs. Astoundingly, rather than noting any connection between RCA's allocation of resources far from its technological core and its increasing defeats at the hands of the rising Japanese consumer-electronics dynamos, in 1980 company management went on a splurge of expensive, debt-financed acquisitions in financial services and greeting cards—right on the eve of the early 1980s spectacular surge in interest rates. Divestitures, management changes, and refocusing all followed plummeting financial results.

In RCA's case, the record is also clear that international position, as well as technological leadership at home, was traded off for the growing stream of dubious diversifications. RCA was the very archetype of "The Great American U-Turn." Rather than building on its once towering R&D strengths to dominate global consumer electronics markets as Sony Corporation, Matsushita, and Hitachi were about to do, RCA remained one of the least internationally involved U.S. electronics firms, with mid-1970s foreign sales as a percentage of total sales of less than 20 percent. Indeed, although the company remained one of the United States' leading firms in numbers of patents and inventions registered even into the 1980s, RCA had typically licensed off its technologies to eventual foreign competitors, to raise cash to keep the R&D labs functioning on a self-financing basis, rather than globally commercializing its many innovations itself. (On the decline of RCA as a force in world comsumer electronics, see *RCA: Will It* 1984; *RCA Trades* 1983.)

Chemicals

Chemicals was yet another industry in which diversification outside closely related sectors resulted in subsequent poor performance. Table 12–4 shows that during the 1975–1980 period, out of twenty-three leading firms in the worldwide industry, below-average growth characterized seven of the eight companies which had more than 15 percent of their sales coming from unrelated businesses. (Pharmaceuticals were counted as a related business.) Only one firm with a high degree of unrelated diversification was in the high-growth group—Allied Corporation of the United States. The bulk of the firm's growth between 1975 and 1980 was accounted for by the effect of the 1979–1980 oil-price hike on Allied's oil producing activities. (Oil production, exploration, and refining were classified as unrelated businesses.)

Although a strong negative relationship between unrelated diversification and measures of financial results based on reported net profits (ROA or ROE) was not immediately observable among firms based in the chemical industry, a very clear result appeared once adjustments were made for the different accounting and reporting practices, principally the much higher depreciation charges, characteristic of many non-U.S. firms in the industry. Table 12–5 shows that if the ratio of cash flow, or net-profits plus depreciation charges, to shareholders' equity at the end of the 1970s is taken as the criterion of financial performance, a sharp distinction emerges between the high-performing firms, all focused on the chemicals and related businesses, and the low performance characteristics of unrelated diversifiers.

Table 12–5
Chemical Firms Classified by Sales Growth, Return on Assets (ROA), and Unrelated Diversification

Sales Growth, 1975–1980 versus Unrelated Diversification

		Percent of Sales Unrelated to Main Industry, 1975		
		Low (0 – 15%)	High (15 – 45%)	
Annual Average Compound Growth Rate, 1975–1980	High (12 to 20%)	12	1	13
	Low (2 to 11.99%)	3	7	10
		15	8	23

Chi-Square	D.F.	Significance	Min E.F.	Cells with E.F. 5
7.12152	1	.0076[a]	3.478	2 of 4 (50.0%)
9.67327	1	.0019[a]		(Before Yates Correction)

Financial Results and Unrelated Diversification
("Cash Earnings" Average 1979–1980 versus Unrelated Diversification, 1975)

		Percent of Sales Unrelated to Main Industry		
		Low (0 – 24%)	High (25 – 45%)	
"Cash Earnings" (= Net Profit and Depreciation Charges)	High (26–53%)	9	0	9
as a percent of Shareholders' Equity, Average 1979–1980	Low (7.3–25.99%)	4	6	10
		13	6	19

(Fisher's Exact Test: One tail .023[a]; Two tail .033[a])

[a]Statistically significant at or above the 95 percent level of confidence.

As in other industries, the majority of the unrelated diversifiers were American firms: Olin—already a low performer in Rumelt's earlier sample, W.R. Grace, Union Carbide Corporation, and Allied. In further apparent demonstration of a trade-off between energies and capital applied to diversification versus internationalization, Grace and Olin evidenced a sharp drop in the proportion of their sales coming from foreign markets between 1975 and 1980.

The low-performing, chemicals-based unrelated diversifiers of the 1970s have remained low-performing firms during the first half of the 1980s. Although the whole chemical industry has been buffeted by recession and maturity in many product lines, Grace, Allied, and Olin continued to underperform a troubled sector. (See, e.g., *Fortune*'s US chemical industry return rankings for 1985 in its May 1986 "500" issue.) Allied compounded its management challenges and problems by continuing on its unrelated diversification path with the acquisition of Bendix in 1981 and merger with the Signal Companies in 1985. Neither of these moves appear to have durably improved financial returns, as large losses due to restructurings were reported in 1983 and again in 1985. And the boost given to Allied's growth and earnings by its oil and gas activities turned to bust in the oil glut 1980s. (*Value Line,* various issues.) W.R. Grace, too, continued its unrelated-acquisitive ways, at a declining rate of profitability, and also suffered from oil boom turned sour. (Inside the troubled empire 1986.) Only Olin showed signs of a more focused future—at the costs of major write-offs and reported losses from restructurings—as it conducted what *Business Week* called its "long-running garage sale." (October 28, 1985.)

One further questionable development of the U.S. industry during the 1980s deserves mention: the acquisition by E.I. duPont de Nemours & Company of oil-producer Conoco, Inc., in 1981 as oil-prices were about to peak, a decision that appears more than somewhat responsible for a drop of some 30 to 50 percent in DuPont's ROE and ROA levels from 1970s levels. (*Value Line,* various issues.) Not only were such ventures not characteristic of European and Japanese firms during the 1980s, but if anything a refocusing on chemicals, with a strong orientation toward specialties, fine chemicals, and pharmaceuticals, characterized the once more widely spread activities of the few non-U.S. firms that had once trodden the unrelated diversification path.

Tires and Rubber

A priori, an industry such as tires and rubber might be thought to be mature and, therefore, to be less technologically dynamic and less demanding of focused management attention than the other sectors covered earlier. As a mature, low-growth industry, it could also be thought to be a good candidate for portfolio harvesting, with cash flows ideally invested in higher-growth businesses. Such rationales for unrelated diversification strategies, whether explicitly derived from Boston Consulting Group product-portfolio, strategic-management principles or not, could be and were applied by three American firms and one British-Italian group during the 1970s. (On the BCG portfolio management approach, see *A Vote* 1974.)

Partly because France's Michelin, Japan's Bridgestone and Germany's Continental Gummi-Werke did not treat the tire industry in the age of conversion to radials as a mature business unworthy of investment in equipment and R&D, the U.S. companies were outcompeted on quality, technology, and price. Therefore they were unable to harvest much cash flow to redeploy to "high growth" businesses. Other than defensively allied and conglomerated Dunlop and Pirelli, the non-U.S. firms invested in tires; several U.S. firms did not. And what diversification out of the tire and rubber industry took place almost never produced the hoped for growth or financial returns and stability. The story of the failure of such strategies during the late 1970s is summarized in table 12–6.

As in other sectors, once set in motion the trends of the 1970s continued into the 1980s. In the United Kingdom Dunlop disappeared as a corporate entity, selling off the majority of its unsuccessful non-British tire production to Sumitomo Rubber of Japan in 1984 prior to having its remaining, largely nontire assets and debts taken over by the British conglomerate BTR. (Stopford and Turner 1985.) Just before the oil crisis turned to an oil glut Goodrich invested heavily in polyvinyl chloride chemical resins, a product whose total energy cost of production was lower than that of competing wood, steel, and copper products, but whose success depended on continued oil shortage, (Cuff 1985; *Behind the Revolving* 1984) Goodrich took a $365 million writeoff to income in 1985 as part of the continuing aftermath of the failure of its strategy adopted in 1979, a strategy *Forbes* described as: "The strategy is simple: Make Goodrich the most diversified of the big tiremakers." (Byrne 1983: 78.)

Uniroyal, a company that "had been in businesses from golf balls to protective clothing," started divesting activities with combined sales of over $1 billion in 1977; its divestments included all tire operations outside of North America. In 1986 after a leveraged buyout followed continued low growth and profitability, Uniroyal's remaining tire activities were hived off into a joint venture with those remaining of Goodrich—under, Goodrich's management. (*Value Line,* various issues, esp. June 27, 1986.) Of the unrelated tire and rubber diversifiers of the 1970s, only General Tire (later Gencorp) remained in reasonable health during the early 1980s while retaining multi-industry form: perhaps because one of those multi-industry branches was a supplier to the U.S. military during its massive buildup of the early 1980s, and thus essentially sheltered from the winds of global competition. (*Value Line,* various issues.) Gencorp's de-emphasis of the tire business culminated in the sale of what had been General Tire to Continental of Germany in 1987. (Fisher 1987.)

Conclusions

Apart from the rarest of exceptions, it is clear that unrelated diversification as a strategy has not worked, either for firms diversifying out of or into the technologically dynamic industries surveyed in this study.

Table 12–6
Tire and Rubber Firms Classified by Sales Growth, Return on Assets (ROA), and Unrelated Diversification

Sales Growth, 1975–1980 versus Unrelated Diversification, 1975

		Percent of Sales Unrelated to Main Industry, 1975		
		Low *(0 – 15%)*	*High* *(6 – 48%)*	
Annual Average Compound Growth Rate, 1975–1980	High (14 to 22%)	5	0	5
	Low (1 to 13%)	3	4	7
		8	4	12

Financial Returns and Unrelated Diversification

		Percent of Sales Unrelated to Main Industry, 1975		
		Low *(0 – 5%)*	*High* *(6 – 48)*	
Cash Flow[a] as a percentage of Shareholders' Equity, 1980	High (18 to 40%)	4	0	4
	Low (5 to 17%)	1	4	5
		5	4	9

[a]Cash Flow = Net Income (reported profits) plus depreciation.

Unrelated diversification has not worked either for firms starting from high market share or low market share positions. Indeed, the relative failure even of firms pursuing such a strategy from a core position of seeming high market share in their main activity is perhaps one of the most striking findings of all. The one-time regional or even worldwide dominance of an RCA in consumer electronics or an ITT in non-US telecommunications provided no better base for long-term success in moving into unrelated business areas than did the low-market-share positions from which some of the second-rank firms in the tire industry, for example, were tryingn to escape. Harvesting a dominant position—or in Boston Consulting Group jargon, "milking" of a cash cow—and steering resources to (often acquired) low market share question marks in businesses with no market or technological commonality left firms with such initially strong positions open. Not only were they open to battle on the front they expected in their new industry, but also to competitors, usually Japanese or German, whose strategies centered on rejuvenating mature sectors, not harvesting them. (For a prescient analysis of some of the non-U.S. sources of the failure of U.S. companies' harvest-and replant strategies, see Vernon 1980.) For firms seeking to leave weak, low-share competitive positions in one industry, acquiring yet another weak, low-share position in a different one was an even surer path into two-front battle.

Still, notwithstanding the weight of negative evidence against unrelated diversification moves, the normative recommendation to management is surely more subtle than any simplistic exhortation for "shoemakers to stick to their lasts." As seen both here and in other ICA research papers, performance came from more than this. (See Franko 1987a and b.) The more successful firms did not just stick to old model shoes made on obsolete lasts. They focused on a coherent set of technologies and markets. They also developed their products and processes, invested capital in boosting productivity and quality, and scanned the world for the most rapid growth markets and lowest-cost production sites.

Appendix: Companies Included in Statistical Tests

Computers and Office Equipment

Control Data Corporation (CDC)	Wang Laboratories Inc.	
IBM Corporation	Prime Computer, Inc.	
Digital Equipment Corporation	Xerox Corporation	
Sperry Corporation	Canon	Japan
Honewell, Inc.	Fujitsu	Japan
Hewlett-Packard Company	Oki	Japan
Burroughs Corporation	Ricoh	Japan
Data General Corporation	Olivetti	Italy
NCR Corporation	Bull	France
	ICL	United Kingdom

Electrical Equipment and Electronics

Emerson Electric Company	Sony	Japan
General Electric Company	Toshiba	Japan
GTE Corporation	Siemens	Germany
RCA Corporation	AEG	Germany
ITT Corporation	CGE	France
Western Electric (ATT)	Thomson-Brandt	France
Motorola, Inc.	Philips	Netherlands
Raytheon Company	GEC	United Kingdom
Texas Instruments, Inc.	Plessey	United Kingdom
Westinghouse Electric Corporation	Thorn-EMI	United Kingdom
Zenith Electronics Corporation	Asea	Sweden
Hitachi	Japan	Electrolux	Sweden
Matsushita	Japan	L.M. Ericsson	Sweden
Mitsubishi Electric	Japan	Brown Boveri (BBC)	Switz.
NEC	Japan		
Sanyo	Japan		

Pharmaceuticals

Abbott Laboratories	American Home Products
Bristol-Meyers Company	Eli Lilly & Company
Johnson & Johnson	Glaxo — United Kingdom
Schering-Plough Corporation	Fujisawa — Japan
Smithkline Beckman Corporation	Shionogi — Japan
Sterling Drug, Inc.	Takeda — Japan
Squibb Corporation	Roche — Switz.
Merck & Company	Sandoz — Switz.
Pfizer, Inc.	Ciba-Geigy — Switz.
Upjohn Company	Boeringer Ingh. — Germany
Warner-Lambert Company	Schering A.G. — Germany

Chemicals

Allied Corporation	Hoechst — Germany
American Cyanamid Company	AKZO — Netherlands
Hoechst Celanese Corporation	Rhone-Poulenc — France
Dow Chemical Company	Solvay — Belgium
E.I. duPont de Nemours Company	Montedison — Italy
Monsanto Company	ICI — United Kingdom
Union Carbide Corporation	Asahi — Japan
W.R. Grace & Company	Mitsubishi — Japan
Olin Corporation	Showa Denko — Japan
Bayer — Germany	Sumitomo — Japan
BASF — Germany	Toray — Japan

Tires and Rubber

Michelin — France	B.F. Goodrich & Company
Bridgestone — Japan	General Tire Company (Gencorp)
Yokahama — Japan	Uniroyal, Inc.
Continental — Germany	Cooper Tire Company
Armstrong Rubber Company	Dunlop-Pirelli — United Kingdom
Goodyear Tire & Rubber Company	Italy
Firestone Tire & Rubber Company	

Notes

1. This paper is one in a series on *Global Corporate Competition: Who's Winning, Who's Losing and Why* based on the International Competitive Analysis Data base. Acknowledgment is gratefully made to the General Electric Foundation for its support of this work. Acknowledgment is also made to Robert Jan Davis and to Veronica de Jesus for their assistance in statistical tests and compilations, and in company research.

References

Alberts, W.W. 1966. The profitability of growth by merger. In *The Corporate Merger,* eds. W.W. Alberts and J.E. Segall. University of Chicago Press.

Amihud, Y., and Lev, B. 1981. Risk reduction as a managerial motive for conglomerate mergers. *Bell Journal of Economics* 12: 605–17.

Beman, L. 1981. Exxon's $600 million mistake. *Fortune,* 19 October.

Bernhard, A. *The Value Line investment survey, a subscriber's guide,* New York: Value Line, Inc., Undated.

Bettis, R.A., and Hall, W.K. 1982. Diversification strategy, accounting determined risk, and accounting determined return. *Academy of Management Journal* 25 (2): 254–64.

Biggadike, R. 1979. The risky business of diversification. *Harvard Business Review* 2 (May–June): 254–64.

Behind the revolving door at B.F. Goodrich. 1984. *Business Week.* 15 October, pp. 150–53.

Behind the ITT deal: Will Araskog's radical surgery work? 1986. *Business Week.* 14 July, pp. 62–64.

Byrne, A. 1983. A new act in Akron. *Forbes,* 21 November, pp. 78–80.

Can VW regain its magic touch? 1984. *Business Week.* 6 August, pp. 50–58.

Capon, N.; Hulbert, J.M.; Farley, J.U.; and Martin, L.E. 1988. Corporate diversity and economic performance: The impact of market specialization. *Strategic Management Journal* 9 (1): 61–74.

Carr, J. 1986. Triumph-Adler chief to step down. *Financial Times,* 17 September, pp. 19.

Cuff, D.F. 1985. Major refocusing at Goodrich. *New York Times,* 19 June.

Davis, M.S. 1985. Two plus two doesn't equal five. *Fortune,* 9 December, pp. 171–73.

De Saint Phalle, T. 1980. *U.S. productivity and competitiveness in international trade.* Washington, D.C.: Georgetown University, Center for Strategic and International Studies.

Fisher, A. 1987. Conti makes tracks into the US. *The Financial Times,* July 1.

Franko, L.G. 1983. *The threat of Japanese multinationals, and how the west can respond.* New York: John Wiley & Sons.

———. 1987. *International Competitive analysis working paper series manuscripts:* (*a*) Global corporate competition: Who's winning, who's losing and the R&D factor as one reason why; (*b*) Global corporate performance: The geographical dimension.

Hamermesch, R. 1986. Making planning strategic. *Harvard Business Review,* July–Aug. pp. 115–20.

Harris, M. 1986. A you-are-there history of Xerox's comeback: Review of Xerox: American samurai. *Business Week.* 30 June, pp. 13–17.

Hill, C.W.L. 1983. Conglomerate performance over the economic cycle. *Journal of Industrial Economics* 32 (2): 197–211.

Inside the troubled empire of Peter Grace. 1986. *Business Week,* 16 June, pp. 68–69.

ITT: groping for a new strategy. 1980. *Business Week.* 15 December, p. 66.

ITT: Sovereign State Humbled. 1984. *The Economist.* 14 July, pp. 69–70.

Jacobson, G. and Hillkirk, J. 1985. *Xerox: American samurai,* New York: Macmillan.

Kitching, J. 1973. *Acquisitions in Europe: Causes of corporate successes and failures.* Geneva: Business International.

Lauenstein, M.C. 1985. Diversification—the hidden explanation of success. *Sloan Management Review,* 27 (1): 49–55.

Levy, H., and Sarnat, M. 1970. Diversification, portfolio analysis, and the uneasy case for conglomerate mergers. *Journal of Finance,* 25 (4): 795–802.

Montgomery, C.A. 1979. Diversification, market structure, and firm performance: an extension of Rumelt's model. Ph.D. diss. Purdue University.

A note on the Boston consulting group concepts of competitive analysis and corporate strategy. 1974. *Harvard Business School,* no. 9-175-175. Rev. 6/76.

Palepu, K. 1985. Diversification strategy, profit performance, and the entropy measure. *Strategic Management Journal* 6: 239–55.

RCA trades a headache for $1.5 billion. 1983. *Business Week.* 10 October, p. 31.

RCA: will it ever be a top performer? 1984. *Business Week.* 2 April, p. 52.

Rumelt, R.P. 1974. *Strategy, structure, and economic performance, division of research.* Boston: Harvard Graduate School of Business Administration.

———. 1982. Diversification strategy and profitability, *Strategic Management Journal* 3: 359–69.

Sanger, D.E. 1986. Honeywell retreats from computers. *New York Times.* 25 September.

Stopford, J.M. and Turner, L. 1985. *Britain and the multinationals,* New York: John Wiley & Sons.

Taylor, P. 1984. The challenge facing ITT. *Financial Times,* 13 January, pp. 17.

Value Line Investment Survey. New York: Value Line, Inc. Weekly.

Vernon, R. 1980. Gone are the cash cows of yesteryear. *Harvard Business Review,* Nov.–Dec. pp. 150–55.

Wayne, L. 1986. ITT: the giant slumbers, *New York Times,* 2 July.

13
Technology Strategy for Global Competitiveness

Rolf Bühner

G lobal competitiveness increasingly becomes a central element in company strategy (Abernathy, Clark and Kantrow 1981). For most American and European firms this new focus is usually not self-induced but forced by new, strong foreign competitors. Notably, Asian countries have captured important world market shares and thus deteriorated American and European firms' revenue situation. To create—or at least to preserve—corporate value managers do have to reformulate product and market strategy. In this context technology orientation is often considered to be a powerful instrument to achieve comparative and competitive advantages.

In this chapter we evaluate technology strategy as a remedy to cope with global competition. To investigate the suitability of technology orientation for shareholders' wealth, we cast a close look at its accounting performance, market performance, and risk effects. Furthermore, we discuss emphasized product and international diversification as risk-moderating collateral strategies. Data has been taken from large West German corporations.

Technological Reorientation

As a reaction to the increased global competitive pressure many West German firms have decided to pursue a higher technological level (Bühner 1986a, 1987a). Within ten years the average degree of technology of the companies under study has risen from 1.76 to 1.86.[1] Technology orientation has been undertaken in two different manners: Either firms have entered high-technology markets and left their traditional businesses or they have upgraded their existing product lines by equipping them with new technological features. The first strategy can be used to quit mature markets in favor of new growth markets (Sommers, Nemec, and Harris 1987). Mannesmann, formerly a pure steelmaker, has consequently sold off most parts of its steel activities and in successive stages acquired firms in business such as machinery, plant construction, process engineering, and computers. The second strategy of add-on high tech aims at growing young again in stagnant businesses (Dowdy and Nikolchev 1986). Thus, the German machine-tool industry became rejuvenated by the use of numerical control and manufacturing integration. The audio market has benefited from the development of digital recording and broadcasting.

Several reasons might have caused this technological reorientation. Superior growth of high-technology markets is one of them. High market growth has often shown to raise company return (Scherer 1980). In our study of forty large West German corporations we found that high-technology firms did not grow faster than their low-technology counterparts.[2] One explanation might be that several areas of high technology like aerospace or aircraft are not growth markets; others like data processing, cameras, or audio equipment are growing in unit volume but not in sales revenue. Furthermore, certain new growth markets lack sufficiently high entry and mobility barriers (Caves and Porter 1977) to keep potential competitors out of the business. Thus, a great number of new entrants has raised competition in the personal computer market and widely prevented company growth in spite of overall market growth.

A second reason for technology orientation might be West German firms' intention to emphasize their country's specific advantages. These advantages, among others, consist of a functioning scientific and technical infrastructure in the form of universities and other technology-transfer centers. As the installation of such institutions can only be achieved on a very long-term basis, the resulting advantages are more durable than other comparative advantages such as exchange rate benefits. West German firms, like companies in other European countries, the United States, and Japan, therefore, possess a great amount of scientific and engineering know-how that is not available to firms operating in less developed countries.

Third, the West German traditional dual job education system fostering apprentices, journeymen and master craftsmen suggests concentration on high technology. On the one hand, it offers a hybrid work force qualification suitable for the manufacturing of sophisticated products. On the other hand, it forces companies into high value-added activities because labor costs are too high for low cost strategies. Table 13–1 compares employment and cost patterns for West Germany, the United States, and Japan (Romanosky 1985).

According to these considerations—and the overall redirection trend toward high technological industries—technology orientation should be expected to offer superior performance. But, as table 13–2 indicates, the results from our study cannot confirm these expectations.

Accounting determined performance is ambiguous. Although return on assets is higher for technology-oriented firms, return on equity is slightly lower. This finding indicates two things: First, it seems that technological engagements require superior investments that are not yet compensated by higher revenues. This seems in a sense logical as both spendings on research

Table 13–1
Comparison of Employment and Cost Patterns in Different Countries

	Germany	United States	Japan
High tech employees per 1,000 employees	56	39	49
Direct labor costs in percent of total costs	19%	13%	14%

Table 13–2
Return Features of High- and Low-Technology Firms

	High Techology	Low Technology	F-Value [a]
Return on assets	7.84	6.53	2.53
Return on equity	5.86	6.18	0.04
Market return	0.58	0.60	0.04
Jensen 'α'	0.44	0.51	0.12

[a] None significant at the 0.05 level.

and development and process amelioration can be interpreted as investments in the future. Second, high technology firms apparently have to pay more for debt than low technology firms. Obviously, financiers consider technological investments risky.

Capital market assessment, in general, agree with the results and interpretations given earlier. Market return of high-technology firms was below average. With respect to a risk adjusted market return measure, the performance of high-technology firms was poor. Jensen's risk-adjusted performance measure 'α' was 0.44 for high-tech firms compared to 0.51 for low-tech companies. Either investors might not be aware of future potentials of high technological engagements and thus are not willing to pay a price for technology orientation, or they may have the right perception of future technological developments but they anticipate that high investment requirements will not allow short-run dividend payments. In high-tech sectors research and development investments alone represent up to 15 percent of sales compared to 2 to 4 percent in low-tech industries.

At first glance technology firms seem to be less risky. Table 13–3 shows that high-technology strategy implies much lower total risk than low-technology strategy does. But at a closer look one finds that total market risk variance (of market returns) is only low because unsystematic, or company determined, risk is extremely low. Instead, systematic, or market determined, risk is high for technology firms.

High systematic risk indicates that technology sectors are very much influenced by general economic fluctuations. In times of declining economic

Table 13–3
Risk Features of High- and Low-Technology Firms

	High Technology	Low Technology	F-Value
β	1.09	1.04	0.44
r^{2} [a]	0.44	0.30	15.26 [c]
σ^{2}	34.41	42.49	3.02 [b]

[a] r^2 represents unsystematic risk inversely. A high value represents low risk.

[b] $p < 0.05$

[c] $p < 0.01$

activity technology firms are more affected than other companies. It seems that high-technology products are heavily in demand in times of prosperity but they are considered dispensable in times of recession. Apparently, this applies more to investment goods than to consumer goods. Advantages of new technological investment goods like plant automation or information systems help to create speed, flexibility, and quality improvements. They are difficult to assess and thus difficult to justify when it comes to investment decisions (Kaplan 1986). Technological consumer goods such as luxury cars, high-end audio and video equipment, or cameras evidently have a lower price elasticity that makes them less susceptible to economic turnarounds. Hence, Williams's (1983) hypothesis of low systematic risk for high-tech firms cannot be fully rejected. He expected low price elasticity for new technological products and markets and, thus, low systematic risk.

Finding that technology firms have low unsystematic risk is astonishing. The fact that firms in high technological environments are confronted with rapidly changing markets and technical requirements (Ansoff 1987) should rather make their activities risky, at least as far as company-determined, unsystematic risk is concerned. As far as low unsystematic risk is a proxy for good management, one could conclude that high-tech firms' management must be especially qualified and farsighted. Accordingly, management's decision to pursue technology could be expected to be correct in the long run.

Still, the present risk pattern reveals that technology strategy offers a mostly useless risk-reduction service to the investor. It contributes at lowering unsystematic risk which the investor could easily do by means of simple portfolio diversification.[3] But on the other hand, technology strategy does not reduce systematic risk which is the kind of risk that the investor cannot diversify away.

When referring to the capital asset pricing model (CAPM) technology strategy is not only useless to the investor, but it also does harm. According to the CAPM, market return is a positive function of market risk (Markowitz 1976; Modigliani and Pogue 1974).[4] But, in the case of technology firms, high risk was found to go along with low return. Either technology orientation is not a wealth creating strategy for investors, or its success depends on some additional strategic actions. In the next section, product and international diversification are tested as appropriate strategies for raising the performance of high-tech firms. Their pursuit as a collateral strategy might be the key for technology strategy success for global competitiveness.

Technology Strategy and Product Diversification

Product diversification is a widely practiced strategy among high-tech firms. The diversification index is 0.63 compared to 0.42 for low-tech firms.[5] Apparently, high-tech companies consider a technology transfer from one product line to another or from one business to another to incorporate synergies or scope advantages. But as previous studies have shown, product diversification is only partially successful. It turned out to be a suitable instrument to reduce risk but not to raise return (Bühner 1986b). Performance improvement, therefore, can be expected to be limited to the risk dimension. Table 13–4 summarizes the impact of product diversification on high-technology strategy. The dividing line between high and low product diversification has been the all firm average of 0.52.

Results strongly support our earlier expectations. Although risk has slightly reduced through product diversification, both market and accounting return have decreased. Apparently, potential synergies are often overestimated and hard to realize. Numerous analyses have proved that firms perform best

Table 13–4
Performance Features of High-Technology Firms with High and Low Product Diversification

	Product Diversification		
	Low	*High*	*F-Value*
Return on assets	10.90	6.56	6.28[c]
Return on equity	7.27	5.29	2.44[b]
Market return	0.59	0.57	0.06
Jensen 'α'	0.45	0.43	0.00
β	1.10	1.09	0.02
r^2 [a]	0.41	0.44	0.34
σ^2	38.42	32.94	0.63

[a] r^2 represents unsystematic risk inversely. A high value represents low risk.
[b] $p < 0.05$
[c] $p < 0.01$

when concentrating on activities close to the firm's core business (Rumelt 1974; Montgomery 1979; Peters and Waterman 1982; Dubofsky and Varadarajan 1987). With growing product variety, firms lose market and technical competence and it becomes more difficult for them to meet changing market requirements. This holds notably true for companies in high-tech industries with substantial competence and specialization requirements (Maidique and Hayes 1984).

In general, poor performance of high-tech firms, as it was pointed out in table 13–2, might be at least partially a result of excessive product diversification of those firms. Hence, product diversification strategy, seems to be an inadequate collateral strategy to technology orientation to improve international competitiveness.

Technology Strategy and International Diversification

International diversification is a strategy widely practiced in West German industry. It includes both exports as well as direct foreign investments. The importance of foreign business varies very much across industries. It is highest for automobiles and chemicals where it represents up to 75 percent of total sales. Although differences across industries are substantial, no divergence between low- and high-technological firms could be found. Both categories show an international diversification index of 0.59. This could mean that international diversification strategy does not offer any particular advantage for either high or low technology firms. Table 13–5 shows the effect of international diversification on both kinds of companies. The cut-off line between low and high international diversification has been the all firm average of 0.59.

Results show that international diversification tends to be positively related with technology strategy. High-tech firms going international seem to have improved their performance.

Compared to the general influence of internationalization on firms' performance (see Bühner 1987b) its distinctive effect on high-tech firms' performance is particularly strong. This fact might have several reasons.

First, high technological know-how and competence are well-suited for international diffusion (Flaherty 1986; Hitt and Ireland 1987). There are culture-free preferences for technological goods. Only marketing related product characteristics, such as design, have to be individualized for distribution in different regional markets.

Second, technology's suitability for global use enables firms to share high research and development expenditures on an international basis (Hout, Porter, and Rudden 1982). Without internationalization high-tech firms in small countries could not afford necessary investments (Dekker 1986).

Table 13–5
Performance Features of High-Technology Firms with High and Low
International Diversification

| | International Diversification | | |
	Low	High	F-Value
Return on assets	7.12	10.15	3.67[b]
Return on equity	4.17	7.97	4.11[b]
Market return	0.51	0.71	0.33
Jensen 'α'	0.37	0.54	0.40
β	1.15	0.99	4.45[b]
r^2 [a]	0.39	0.51	5.96[b]
σ^2	42.20	22.17	13.28[c]

[a] r^2 represents unsystematic risk inversely. A high value represents low risk.
[b] $p < 0.05$
[c] $p < 0.01$

Third, globalization in manufacturing and distribution leads to the realization of substantial economies of scale (Bartlett and Ghoshal 1987). In some industries, such as the aircraft business, economies of scale are an important factor for competitiveness (Hartley 1965).

Fourth, in high-tech industries close cooperation with foreign suppliers and customers is increasingly important when it comes to developing and producing competitive products (Caves 1982; Flaherty 1986). Firms that are operating from a multinational basis, therefore, might possess competitive advantages over their home-market-oriented counterparts.

Fifth, international diversification is a powerful instrument to reduce the high systematic, or market determined, risk of technology firms. On the one hand, globalization reduces systematic risk because the firm's share price evaluation is done on an international basis (Hughes, Sweeney, and Logue 1975). On the other hand, internationally different cost and demand developments reduce risk, even if country specific risks are perfectly correlated (De Meza and Van der Ploeg 1987). Therefore, international diversification seems to be a suitable complementary strategy to technology orientation. Although technology strategy tends to lower unsystematic risk, globalization tries to reduce systematic risk. Accordingly, globally oriented technology firms offer advantages in the form of low total risk.

Conclusions

In this chapter we have studied technology orientation and internationalization as a strategy for global competitiveness. Our results reveal that a high-technology orientation seems to be only partially successful. On the one hand, high technology contributes to reduced market risk, but on the other hand, high technology does not improve returns. Furthermore, our findings suggest that firms entering high technology markets perform better by simultaneously intensifying international diversification. Globalization of high-tech products enables firms to use their existing technological know-how together with economies of scale in production and R&D to achieve worldwide technological competitiveness.

Appendix I: Sample Firms

The study is based on a sample of forty large West German corporations, all publicly traded at the Frankfurt Stock Exchange. None of the firms was a subsidiary of another company so that strategic choice can be assumed. All information has been derived from publicly available company publications, notably their annual reports. The analysis covers the period from 1966 to 1981. Table 13–6 gives a list of the firms studied by industries.

Appendix 2: Technology Measure

Technology orientation has been captured by using a combined qualitative and quantitative measure that weights the proportions of a firm's different businesses with their individual degrees of technological complexity.

$$T = \sum_{k=1}^{k} p_k \cdot t_k,$$

where T = degree of technology of the firm,

K = number of technologically different businesses within a firm,

P_k = proportion of business k relative to the firm's sales in total, and

t_k = technology factor of business k.

Technology factors are ranging on an ordinal scale from 1 to 3. A value of 1 indicates low technology, a value of 2 describes medium technology, and a value of 3 stands for high technological complexity. The technological appraisal has been made by three experts using Delphi-method out of a 1987 technology perspective. The classification is highly congruent with the OECD classification of high, middle, and low technology (see table 13-7).

Table 13–6
Sample Firms

Classification Number	Industry	Corporations
200	Chemicals	9
201	Petroleum	1
21	Rubber	1
230–233	Metallurgy	6
242	Machinery	7
244	Automobile	3
25	Electrotechnics	4
26	Paper	1
28–29	Food	2
30	Construction	5
50	Transportation	1

Table 13–7
Estimation of Technological Complexity

Low	Medium	High
I ———————	I ———————	I
steel	machinery	electronics
building	chemicals	biotechnology
food	machine-tools	aerospace

Appendix 3: Diversification Measures

A quantitative measure developed by Berry (1971) on the basis of a Herfindahl type index (Hirschman 1964) has been used to separately determine product and international diversification (see also Bühner 1987b):

$$D = 1 - \sum_{i=1}^{n} p_i^2,$$

where p_i = sales proportion of a firm's i-th businesses and

n = number of different business.

$$D = 1 - \sum_{i=1}^{m} p_j^2,$$

where p_j = sales proportion of a firm's j-th geographical market and

m = number of regional markets.

Both indices incorporate the number of different product and/or regional markets as well as their relative importance. Theoretically, indices may vary between 0 and +1. A low value represents little diversification whereas a high value stands for high diversification.

Appendix 4: Performance Measures

Performance has been measured both on the basis of accounting data and on the basis of stock market data. Company growth has been measured by growth in sales.

Return on equity has been calculated as a fraction of net income to shareholders' equity. Return on assets has been computed as the relation of net income plus interest expenses to total assets.

Market performance has been computed by using the one-index market model. This model assumes that market return and the return on an individual share represent a linear functional relationship (Sharpe 1966). Parameters were computed by means of a regression analysis. The German Commerzbank-index was used as market index. Market return and share price return were computed on a monthly basis:

$$R_{it} = \alpha_i + \beta_i \cdot R_{Mt} + \epsilon_{it},$$

where R_{it} = return on share i during period t,

R_{Mt} = return on market index during period t,

α_i, β_i = regression parameters, and

ϵ_{it} = random error term.

Share price returns were calculated as follows:

$$R_{it} = \frac{P_{it} - P_{it-1} + D_{it}}{P_{it} - 1},$$

where P_{it} = price of share i at the end of period t,

P_{it-1} = price of share i at the end of period $t - 1$, and

D_{it} = dividend of share i during period t.

To capture risk aspects, additional one-parametric performance measures were examined. Because correlation among different measures (Treynor 1965; Sharpe 1966) was very high, Jensen's risk adjusted performance index 'α' was exclusively applied (Jensen 1968). This measure describes abnormal performance above a risk-free rate of return. The risk-free rate of return was represented by the interest rate of fixed deposits as officially published by the German Federal Reserve Bank. A high and positive value is an indicator for good company policy. Here, it can be taken as a sign of a promising global competitive strategy:

$$`\alpha_1' = R_{it} - R_f = \alpha_i + \beta_i \cdot (R_{Mt} - R_f) + \epsilon_{it},$$

where R_{it} = return on share i during period t,

R_f = risk-free rate of return,

R_{Mt} = return on the market index during period t,

α_i, β_i = regression parameters, and

ϵ_{it} = random error term.

Notes

1. A firm's degree of technology indicates the technological complexity of its activities. It ranges from 1, indicating low technology to 3, representing high technology. A closer description of the technology measure is given in appendix 2.

2. High technology firms have been classified as those companies that had above-average degrees of technology; low technology firms were consequently those with below-average degrees of technology. The sample is described in appendix 1.

3. Peavy (1984) shows that unsystematic risk in case of firm specific risk evaluation may still be of importance for the investor. Unsystematic risk together with systematic risk represents a firm's total risk from which the important systematic risk is directly derived. Thus, unsystematic risk exerts a certain influence on systematic risk.

4. Market risk here is limited to systematic risk as unsystematic risk can be diversified away by investors and is thus not compensated (Aaker and Jacobson 1987).

5. Product diversification has been measured by using a Herfindahl type measure. Detailed information on its calculation is given in appendix 3.

References

Aaker, D.A., and Jacobson, R. 1987. The role of risk in explaining differences in profitability. *Academy of Management Journal* 30: 277–96.

Abernathy, W.J.; Clark, K.B.; and Kantrow, A.M. 1981. The new industrial competition. *Harvard Business Review* 59 (Sept.–Oct.): 68–81.

Aggarwal, R. 1979. Multinationality and stock market valuation: An empirical study of U.S. markets and companies. *Management International Review* 19(2): 5–21.

Agmon, T., and Lessard, D.R. 1977. Investor recognition of corporate international diversification. *Journal of Finance* 32: 1049–55.

Ansoff, H.I. 1987. Strategic management of technology. *Journal of Business Strategy* 7 (Winter): 28–39.

Bartlett, C.A., and Ghoshal, S. 1987. Managing across borders: new strategic requirements. *Sloan Management Review* 28(4): 7–17.

Berry, C.H. 1971. Corporate growth and diversification. *Journal of Law and Economics* 14: 371–83.

Bühner, R. 1986a. Production technology and organization. *Human Systems Management* 6: 201–10.

———. 1986b. Market performance and managerial motives of diversification in West German corporations. *Strategic Management Research,* ed. J. Mc.Gee and H. Thomas, 123–38. Chichester: Wiley.

———. 1987a. Diversifikation, finanzkraft und wettbewerb. Report for the German Monopolies Commission. Passau.

———. 1987b. Assessing international diversification of West German corporations. *Strategic Management Journal* 8: 25–37.

Caves, R. 1982. *Multinational enterprise and economic analysis.* New York: Cambridge University Press.

——— and Porter, M.E. 1977. From entry barriers to mobility barriers: Conjectural decisions and contrived deterrence to new competition. *Quarterly Journal of Economics* 91: 241–61.

Dekker, W. 1986. Managing a global electronics company in tomorrow's world. *Long Range Planning* 19(2): 31–37.

De Meza, D., and Van der Ploeg, F. 1987. Production flexibility as a motive for multinationality. *Journal of Industrial Economics* 35(S): 343–51.

Dowdy, W.L., and Nikolchev, J. 1986. Can industries de-mature? Applying new technologies to mature industries. *Long Range Plannning* 19(2): 38–49.

Dubofsky, P., and Varadarajan, R.R. 1987. Diversification and measures of performance: Additional empirical evidence. *Academy of Management Journal* 30: 597–608.

Flaherty, M.T. 1986. Coordinating international manufacturing and technology. *Competition in Global Industries,* ed. M.E. Porter, 83–109. Boston: Harvard Business School.

Hamel, G., and Prahalad, C.K. 1985. Do you really have a global strategy? *Harvard Business Review* 63 (July–Aug.): 139–48.

Harrigan, K.R. 1982. Exit decisions in mature industries. *Academy of Management Journal* 25: 707–32.

———. 1985. Strategic flexibility: A management guide for changing times. Lexington, Mass.: Lexington Books.

Hartley, K. 1965. The learning curve and its application. *Journal of Industrial Economics* 13: 122–28.

Hirschman, A.O. 1964. The paternity of an index. *American Economic Review* 54: 761–62.

Hitt, M.A., and Ireland, R.D. 1987. Building competitive strength in international markets. *Long Range Planning* 20(1): 115–22.

Hout, T.; Porter, M.E.; and Rudden, E. 1982. How global companies win out. *Harvard Business Review* 60 (Sept.–Oct.): 98–108.

Hughes, J.S.; Logue, D.E.; and Sweeney, R.J. 1975. Corporate international diversification and market assigned measures of risk and diversification. *Journal of Financial and Quantitative Analysis* 10: 627–37.

Jensen, M.C. 1968. The performance of mutual funds in the period of 1945–1964. *Journal of Finance* 23: 389–416.

Kaplan, R.S. 1986. Must CIM be justified by faith alone? *Harvard Business Review* 64 (Mar.–Apr.): 87–95.

Levitt, T. 1983. The globalization of markets. *Harvard Business Review* 61 (May–June): 92–102.

Madura, J., and Rose, C. 1987. Are product specialization and international diversification strategies compatible? *Management International Review* 27(3): 38–44.

Maidique, M.A., and Hayes, R.H. 1984. The art of high-technology management. *Sloan Management Review* 25 (Winter): 17–31.

Markowitz, H.M. 1976. Portfolio selection: Efficient diversification of investment, 4th ed. New York: Yale University Press.

Modigliani, F., and Pogue, G.A. 1974. An introduction to risk and return. *Financial Analysts Journal* 29 (March–April): 68–80 and (May–June): 69–86.

Montgomery, C. 1979. Diversification, market structure and firm performance. An extension of Rumelt's model, Ph.D. diss., Purdue University.

Peavy III, J.W. 1984. Modern financial theory, corporate strategy, and public policy: Another perspective. *Academy of Management Review* 9: 152–57.

Peters, T.J., and Waterman, R.H. 1982. *In search of excellence.* New York: Harper & Row.

Porter, M.E., ed. 1986. Competition in global industries. Boston: Harvard Business School.

Romanosky, J. 1985. The 1983 global manufacturing futures study preliminary report synopsis. *The Management of Productivity and Technology in Manufacturing,* ed. Paul R. Kleindorfer, 259–72. New York: Plenum Press.

Rumelt, R.P. 1974. *Strategy, structure, and economic performance.* Boston: Harvard Graduate School of Business.

Scherer, F.M. 1980. *Industrial market structure and economic performance,* 2d ed. Chicago: Rand McNally.

Sharpe, W.F. 1966. Mutual funds performance. *Journal of Business* 39: 119–38.

Sommers, W.P.; Nemec, J. Jr.; Harris, J.M. 1987. Repositioning with technology: making it work. *Journal of Business Strategy* 7 (Winter): 16–27.

Treynor, J.L. 1965. How to rate management of investment funds. *Harvard Business Review* 43 (Jan.–Feb.): 63–75.

Williams, J.R. 1983. Technological evolution and competitive response. *Strategic Management Journal* 4: 55–65.

Index

About the Contributors

Syed Humayun Akhter, an assistant professor of marketing at Marquette University, earned his Ph.D. in business at the University of Oklahoma in Norman. He also taught at the University of Karachi and Western Illinois University. His primary research interests involve marketing, including international marketing, foreign direct investment, strategic marketing, and systems analysis. Dr. Akhter's articles have appeared in *Advances in International Marketing,* and *Journal of Consumer Marketing* and will appear in *Journal of Global Marketing.* Dr. Akhter has done consulting work for business firms.

Peter J. Buckley (B.A., M.A., Ph.D) is professor of managerial economics at the University of Bradford Management Centre and a visiting professor of economics at the University of Reading. He has published nine books in English and one in German as well as written many articles on the theory and strategy of multinational enterprises in British, American, European, and Japanese journals. He is the chairman of the United Kingdom Region of the Academy of International Business and in 1985 was elected a Fellow of the Academy of International Business. His current research interests include an ESRC-funded study of the foreign market servicing policies and competitiveness of British firms, the theory of international joint ventures, and European direct investment in Japan.

Rolf Bühner is a professor of business administration at the University of Passau, West Germany. He received his Ph.D. from the University of Augsburg. His teaching and research interests are in the fields of strategic management, technology-based firms, and organizational change. Currently he is involved with problems concerning international technology management. His latest books are titled *Diversification Strategy* and *Personnel Development in High-Tech Firms.*

Norman Coates is a professor of management, coordinator of international business, and director of the Institute for International Business at the College of Business Administration, University of Rhode Island. He received his B.A. from Sir George Williams University (1957), and M.S. (1959), and Ph.D. (1967) from Cornell University. Professor Coates has been a manager and consultant, as well as serving on the boards of ten companies. He headed up management development for Canadian National—an integrated, international transportation system—and, at the Ford Foundation's invitation, served as a consultant on management development in the Middle East, Africa, and Latin America. Recent research interests have focused on Japanese management, with current articles on the subject appearing in the *Academy of Management Executive* and the *Leadership and Organization Development Journal*.

William H. Davidson earned an A.B. in economics, an M.B.A. and a Ph.D. in international management from Harvard University. He is an associate professor of management and organization at the School of Business Administration, University of Southern California. Formerly, he was a faculty member of the University of Virginia and Dartmouth College. He has been a visiting professor at INSEAD (France), and the Dalian Institute (People's Republic of China). Davidson is heavily involved with United States–Japan and United States—China business relations and business development. He is particularly interested in the information industry, cooperative ventures, and the essential elements of achieving and maintaining global competitive superiority—the focus of his current research. Davidson has written a series of books on global business and management, including *U.S. Competitiveness, Revitalizing American Industry, The Amazing Race,* and *Global Strategic Management*. He is currently writing books on the emergence and evolution of information networks, and on new forms of business organization.

Hyun B. Eom is an assistant professor of management–information systems (MIS) at Auburn University. Professor Eom received a B.A. from Korea University, and M.B.A. in international business from Seoul National University in Korea, an M.Sc. in international business from the University of South Carolina at Columbia, and a Ph.D. in Business Administration from the University of Nebraska–Lincoln in 1985. Currently he is teaching an undergraduate course in MIS and several graduate courses in advanced MIS and decision support systems. He is continuing his research in the design and implementation of multiple criteria decision support systems and group decision support systems for global strategic financial planning of the multinational corporation. Dr. Eom has published articles in journals such as *Journal of Management Information Systems, Information & Management,* and

International Economic Review (Korea). In recognition of his scholarly accomplishments, Eom received a 1986–87 Research Scholar Award from the College of Business. He is a member of the DSI, TIMS, Academy of International Business, and Financial Management Association.

Lawrence G. Franko is professor of finance and business strategy at the University of Massachusetts, Boston. He received a D.B.A. from the Harvard Business School and has an M.A. and M.A.L.D. (International Economics) from The Fletcher School, Tufts University, and an A.B. (Economics) from Harvard College. Dr. Franko has taught at INSEAD, The European Institute of Business Administration, Fontainebleau, France; The International Management Institute, Geneva, Switzerland; The Fletcher School, Tufts University, Medford, Massachusetts; and Georgetown University, Washington, D.C. He has also served as head of international affairs in the U.S. Congressional Budget Office and has worked as a portfolio manager and currency specialist for a money management firm in Geneva. Dr. Franko is the author of numerous books, including *The European Multinationals; European Industrial Policy: Past, Present, and Future; The Threat of Japanese Multinationals: How the West Can Respond;* and *Joint Venture Survival in Multinational Corporations.* His published articles include works on global corporate competitiveness and strategy, international finance and international public policy issues. His current research focuses on the question: "Global Corporate Competition: Who's Winning, Who's Losing, and Why?"

Roberto Friedman (Ph.D. Kansas) is assistant professor of marketing, and coordinator of international business programs at the College of Business Administration, University of Georgia. Prior to entering academia, Dr. Friedmann worked in private industry in South America, an area in which he is still involved through his research and consulting work. His research areas of interest are both domestic and international marketing strategy, as well as the roles and effects of selected psychological variables on consumer behavior. Professor Friedmann's work has appeared in the *Journal of Product Innovation Management, Journal of Marketing, Journal of Consumer Marketing, Psychology and Marketing,* and *Columbia Journal of World Business.*

Laurent Jacque is an Associate Professor of International Management at the Carlson School of Management. A graduate from ecole des Hautes Etudes Commerciales (France), he received his MA, MBA, and Ph.D. degrees from the Wharton School (University of Pennsylvania) where he taught from 1976 to 1987. His research has appeared in various journals including the *Journal of International Business Studies, Journal of Operations Research Society, Insurance: Mathematics and Economics, Scandanavian Actuarial Journal* and the *Journal of Risk and Insurance.* His book *Management of Foreign*

Exchange Risk is now in its sixth printing. A frequent lecturer in executive seminars, Jacque also serves as a consultant to Wharton Econometrics Forecasting Associates.

Sang M. Lee is the University Eminent Scholar, Regents Distinguished Professor, chairman of the management department, and the executive director of the Nebraska Productivity Center at the University of Nebraska-Lincoln. Dr. Lee has published twenty-one books, including *Goal Programming for Decision Analysis, Management Science, Micro Management Science, Operations Management,* and *Japanese Management,* and two software packages. He has published over 150 research papers in various leading journals of management. He is on the editorial board of sixteen journals. He has been a distinguished visiting scholar at many leading universities in the United States, Japan, Korea, and China. He received the Outstanding Research Award and the AMOCO Distinguished Teaching Award at the University of Nebraska. Dr. Lee served as the president, program chair, and chairman of the executive committee for the Decision Science Institute, an organization of over 5,000 professors and practicing managers in the United States and 30 other nations. He is also president of the Pan-Pacific Business Association.

Peter Lorange is a professor of management at The Wharton School and director of Wharton's Center for International Management Studies. A specialist in strategic planning systems and processes, he has completed extensive surveys of United States-based and international corporations, studying how to design and revise planning systems. Dr. Lorange has written extensively on the subject of corporate planning and strategic management, including his books, *Strategic Planning Systems, Corporate Planning: An Executive Viewpoint, Implementation of Strategic Planning* and *Strategic Control.* A book, *The C.E.O.'s Perspective on Strategic Planning,* is scheduled to be published soon. He has also published more than fifty articles. Dr. Lorange is a strategic management consultant to major corporations in the United States, Europe, South America, and the Far East. He is a faculty principal of MAC, Inc., a consulting firm based in Cambridge, Massachusetts. Dr. Lorange is a director of Camp Dresser & McKee, Inc., a Boston-based environmental engineering firm.

Briance Mascarenhas is an associate professor of management and international business at New York University. He has a Ph.D. in international business from the University of California, Berkeley. His research interests include international business strategy, global competition, international innovation diffusion, and strategic groups. He has been a consultant to multinational companies and national governments.

Allen Morrison is a doctoral student in international business at the University of South Carolina. His research interests are in the areas of the strategic management of multinational corporations, strategy content in the MNC, and international business theory.

Howard V. Perlmutter has been a professor of social architecture and management at The Wharton School, University of Pennsylvania since 1969. He holds a B.S. in Mechanical Engineering from M.I.T., an Honorary Master's Degree from the University of Pennsylvania, and a Ph.D. from the University of Kansas in Social Psychology. Perlmutter has held professorial, lecturing, and research posts at Harvard; Yale; the Sorbonne; the Institut pour les Methodes de Direction des Enterprise (IMEDE) at the University of Lausanne and the Center for International Management, University of Geneva, in Switzerland; the Center for International Studies at M.I.T.; the Menninger School of Psychiatry; the Stockholm School of Economics; and the University of Hawaii. Currently he teaches comparative management, global strategic planning, and global strategy and policy in the management department at The Wharton School. His article, "The Tortuous Evolution of the Multinational Corporation," was voted the best article in the field of International Business Research by seventy-five international business scholars.

Carl A. Rodrigues, DPA is an assistant professor of management and international business at Montclair State College. His current research interests include leadership, decision making, and implementation. Dr. Rodrigues is an editor for *Issues in International Business.* He has published in *The Columbia Journal of World Business, Strategy and Executive Action, Central State Business Review, Northeast Decision Sciences Institute, World Marketing Congress, Association of Human Resources Management and Organizational Behavior,* and others.

Kendall Roth is an assistant professor of international business at the University of South Carolina. His primary research interests are in the areas of competitive analysis in global industries, strategic control of the multinational corporation, and international new venture management.

Uma Sekaran is chairperson and professor in the department of management at Southern Illinois University in Carbondale. She obtained her MBA from the University of Connecticut at Storrs and her Ph.D. from U.C.L.A. Her main research thrusts are in the areas of cross-cultural management research and the careers of professional women. Sekaran has published four books and several articles in such journals as the *Academy of Management, Administrative Science Quarterly, Journal of International Business Studies,* and the

Internal Review of Applied Psychology. Sekaran has received research awards from the Academy of Management and the American Biographical Society for her contributions to international management research.

Coral R. Snodgrass received a Ph.D. in business policy from the University of Pittsburgh in 1984. Snodgrass is an assistant professor whose primary area of expertise is business policy. She has presented papers and published articles in the areas of strategic management, strategic control, and international management. Her dissertation research studied strategic control systems in the United States and Japan. This study has been expanded to include a sample of firms from West Germany. Snodgrass is also involved in research on women in business and has been a featured speaker at conferences on women in business.

About the Authors

Professor Anant Negandhi is a professor of International Business at the University of Illinois. He received his Ph.D. from Michigan State University. Professor Negandhi's teaching and research interests are research methodology and design, organization theory, international business, and multinational corporations and the United Nations.

Professor Negandhi's institutional contributions include developing a curriculum in international and comparative management for the M.B.A. and Ph.D. degrees at the University of Illinois. He played a major role in the founding of the Comparative Administration Research Institute at Kent State University prior to coming to the U of I.

He has published over seventy articles in academic and professional journals and has authored, coauthored, or edited more than twenty-five books. His latest book is *International Management*, published in 1987.

Arun Savara expects to receive a Ph.D. in Strategic Management at Purdue University in December, 1988. He will then join a private firm in Hawaii as Director, Operations Planning.

He has twelve years of industrial experience—mostly involving international trade. During his last three years of industrial experience, he served as general manager of a company in Singapore that specialized in international distribution and software consultancy. He has traveled extensively on business in the Persian Gulf, the Indian subcontinent, and South East Asia.

He has assisted in the development of international management courses for undergraduate and graduate students at Purdue University. He has taught international management, business policy, and marketing management in the United States and Singapore.

His research interest lies in the international dimensions of strategic management. He is currently investigating the impact of certain strategic variables on the performance of firms participating in international industries. As an engineer, he is convinced the battle in global competition will be won or lost on the shop floor.